New
SAT 2019
MATH PRACTICE BOOK

AMERICAN MATH
ACADEMY

By H. TONG, M.Ed.
Math Instructional & Olympiad Coach
www.americanmathacademy.com

New SAT 2019 MATH PRACTICE BOOK

Writer: H.Tong
Copyright © 2019 The American Math Academy LLC.

Printed in United States of America.

ISBN: 9781798956885

SAT is registered trademark of the College Entrance Examination Board, which is not involved in the production of, and does not endorse, this product.

Although the writer has made every effort to ensure the accuracy and completeness of information contained this book, the writer assumes no responsibility for errors, inaccuracies, omissions or any inconsistency herein. Any slighting of people, places, or organizations unintentional.

Questions, suggestions or comments, please email: americanmathacademy@gmail.com

"The laws of Nature are written in the language of mathematics... the symbols are triangles, circles and other geometrical figures, without whose help it is impossible to comprehend a single word."
Galileo Galilei

Table of Contents

About the Author

Mr. Tong teaches at various private and public schools in both New York and New Jersey. In conjunction with his teaching, Mr. Tong developed his own private tutoring company. His company developed a unique way of ensuring their students' success on the math section of the SAT. His students, over the years, have been able to apply the knowledge and skills they learned during their tutoring sessions in college and beyond. Mr. Tong's academic accolades make him the best candidate to teach SAT Math. He received his master's degree in Math Education. He has won several national and state championships in various math competitions and has taken his team to victory in the Olympiads. He has trained students for Math Counts, American Math Competition (AMC), Harvard MIT Math Tournament, Princeton Math Contest, and the National Math League, and many other events. His teaching style ensures his students' success he personally invests energy and time into his students and sees what and what they're struggling with. His dedication towards his students is evident through his students' achievements.

Acknowledgements

I would like to take the time to acknowledge the help and support of my beloved wife, my colleagues, and my students {their feedback on my book was invaluable. I would like to say an additional thank you to my dear friend Robert for his assistance in making this book complete. Without everyone's help, this book would not be the same. I dedicate this book to my precious daughter Vera, my inspiration to take on this project.

"Mathematics reveals its secrets only to those who approach it with pure love, for its own beauty."
Archimedes

Linear Equations

Definiton of Linear Equation

In a linear equation with two variables, x is an equation that can be written in the form Ax+By+C=0

Example:

5x + 6y = 10

Standard Form

Ax + By = C

When A, B and C are real numbers and A and B are not equal to zero, A must be positive.

Example:

2x + 7y = 15

Slope

Suppose there are two points on a line, (x_1, y_1) and (x_2, y_2).

The Slope m of the line is:

$$m = \frac{\text{change in y (Rise)}}{\text{change in x (Run)}} = \frac{y_2 - y_1}{x_2 - x_1}$$

Example:

Find the equation of the line passing through the point (1, 2) and (3, 6)

Solution:

$$\text{Slope} = m = \frac{6 - 2}{3 - 1} = \frac{4}{2} = 2$$

Slope - Intercept Form

$y = mx + b$
$m = $ slope
$b = y$ - intercept $= (0, b)$

Point - Slope Form

$y - y_1 = m(x - x_1)$

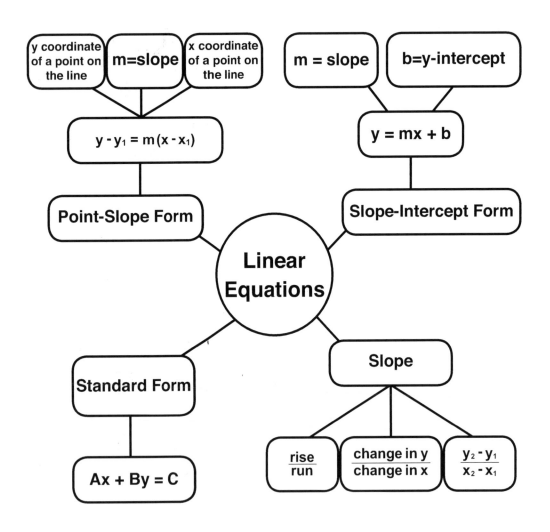

Linear Equations
Test 1

1. Which of the following equations have a slope of 6 and pass through the point (2,4)?

A) $y - 4 = 6(x-2)$
B) $y - 2 = 6(x-4)$
C) $y - 4 = 2(x-6)$
D) $y - 6 = 4(x-2)$

2. Which of the following equations passes through the coordinates (1,2) and (-3,-6)?

A) $y = 2x$

B) $y = 2x + 1$

C) $y = \frac{1}{2}x + 2$

D) $y = 2x + 2$

$\dfrac{2+6}{1+3}$

$\dfrac{8}{4}$

2

3. Which of the following equations have a slope of $\frac{2}{3}$?

A) $2x + 3y + 4 = 0$
B) $3x + 2y + 4 = 0$
C) $3x = 2y$
D) $-2x + 3y + 4 = 0$

4. If $3x-ay+12=0$ and the slope of the equations is $\frac{3}{4}$, then what is the value of a?

A) 4

B) $\frac{1}{4}$

C) 2

D) $\frac{1}{2}$

5. Which graph has an equation of y=2x+1?

A)
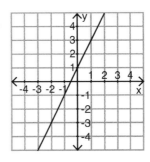

B)
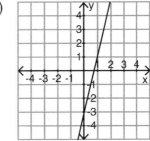

C)
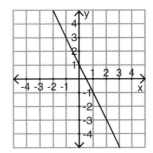

D)
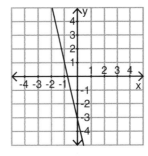

6. From the graph below, which two points have the same slope in reference to origin?

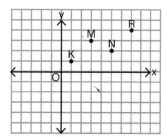

A) R and M
B) M and K
C) R and N
D) N and K

7. The line M is shown on the graph. Which equation represents the line M?

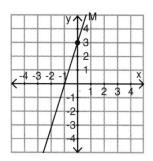

A) $y = 3x + 3$

B) $y = \dfrac{1}{3x + 3}$

C) $y = 3x$

D) $y = -3x + 3$

8. Of the following graphs, which have a negative slope?

A)
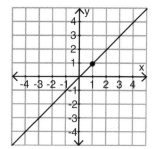

B)
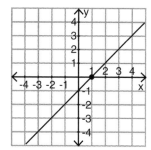

C)
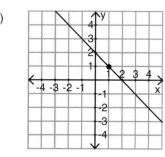

D)
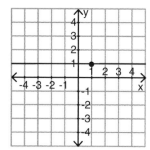

9. Which of the graphs have a slope of 2?

A)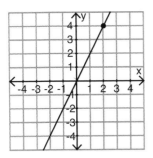

B)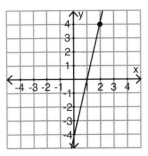

C)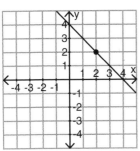

D)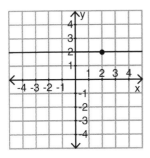

10. Which of the following is the slope of the graph?

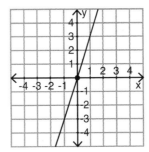

A) 3

B) -3

C) $\frac{1}{3}$

D) 0

11. The equation that represents the graph that is shown below is written in standard form. If Ax+By=C, and A=2, what is the value of B?

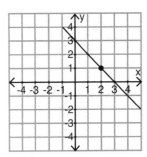

A) 3

B) -3

C) -2

D) 2

12. Which of the following graphs represents $y = \frac{2x}{3} + 4$?

A)
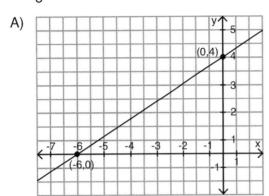

B)
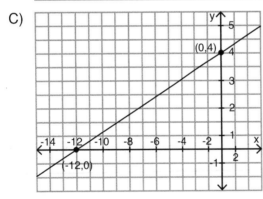

C)
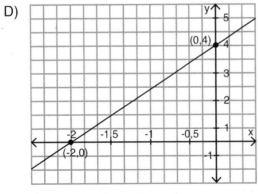

D)

13. Line M passes the coordinate points $(-2, \frac{1}{3})$ and $(1, \frac{-2}{6})$. What is the slope of line M?

A) $\frac{1}{9}$

B) $-\frac{2}{9}$

C) $-\frac{9}{2}$

D) -9

14. Which equation has an undefined slope?

A) $x = 4$

B) $y = 6$

C) $x = y$

D) $\frac{x}{y} = 6$

Grid Questions

15. Write the following equation in standard form: $15y = -12x + 20$

Answer:...

16. Write the equation of the line below in slope-intercept form.

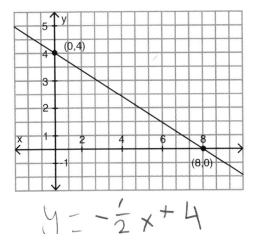

$$y = -\frac{1}{2}x + 4$$

Answer:...

17. Write the equation in slope-intercept form for the line that passes through the points (-2,4) and (6,-4).

Answer:...

18. Find the x-intercept for the graph accompanying the equation $\frac{2y}{3} = -\frac{x}{4} + 12$

Answer:...

19. Find the y-intercept for the graph accompanying the equation $\frac{3y}{3} = \frac{-6x}{3} + \frac{18}{3}$

$$y = -2x + 6$$

Answer:.........(0,6)......................

20. The points (-3,6) and (4,-8) are on line A. Write the equation accompanying line A in standard form.

Answer:...

Test 1
Answer Key

1)	A
2)	A
3)	D
4)	A
5)	A
6)	B
7)	A
8)	B
9)	A
10)	A
11)	D
12)	A
13)	B
14)	A
15)	$12x + 15y = 20$
16)	$y = -\frac{1}{2}x + 4$
17)	$y = -x + 2$
18)	x-intercept (48, 0)
19)	y-intercept (0, 6)
20)	$2x + y = 0$

1. Slope $m = 6$ and $(2, 4)$

$y - y_1 = m(x - x_1)$

$y - 4 = 6(x - 2)$

Correct Answer : A

2. The slope of points $(1, 2)$ and $(-3, -6)$

$m = \dfrac{\text{Rise}}{\text{Run}} = \dfrac{y_2 - y_1}{x_2 - x_1}$

$m = \dfrac{-6 - (2)}{-3 - (1)} = \dfrac{-8}{-4}$

$m = 2, \; y = mx + b, \; (1, 2)$

$2 = 2.(1) + b$

$0 = b$

$y = 2x$

Correct Answer : A

3. Only choice D has a slope of $\dfrac{2}{3}$

$-2x + 3y + 4 = 0$

$y = mx + b$

$3y = 2x - 4$

$y = \dfrac{2}{3}x - 4$

$m = \dfrac{2}{3}$

Correct Answer : D

4. $3x - ay + 12 = 0$ and $m = \dfrac{3}{4}$

slope equation : $m = \dfrac{3}{a}$

$\dfrac{3}{a} = \dfrac{3}{4}$, then $a = 4$

Correct Answer : A

5. Plot and label 2 points from the graph then find the slope of $(0, 1)$ and $(1, 3)$

$m = \dfrac{y_2 - y_1}{x_2 - x_1}$

$m = \dfrac{3 - 1}{1 - 0} = \dfrac{2}{1} = 2$

Correct Answer : A

6. From the graph, only Point K and Point M have the same slope.

Point M slope $= \dfrac{3}{3} = 1$

Point R slope $= \dfrac{5}{7}$

Point K slope $= \dfrac{1}{1} = 1$

Point N slope $= \dfrac{2}{5}$

Correct Answer : B

7. Find 2 exact points from the graph.

$(-1, 0)$ and $(0, 3)$

slope $= m = \dfrac{y_2 - y_1}{x_2 - x_1}$

$m = \dfrac{3 - 0}{0 - (-1)} = \dfrac{3}{1} = 3$

$y = mx + b$

$y = 3x + b, \quad y = 3x + 3$

Correct Answer : A

8. **Negative Slope:** A line with a negative slope is a line that is trending downward from left to right.
   Correct Answer : B

9. Plot and label 2 points from the graph, then find the slope.

$$(1, 2) \, (2, 4)$$

$$m = \frac{Rise}{Run} = \frac{y_2 - y_1}{x_2 - x_1}$$

$$m = \frac{4 - 2}{2 - 1} = \frac{2}{1}$$

$$m = 2$$

   Correct Answer : A

10. $$m = \frac{Rise}{Run} = \frac{y_2 - y_1}{x_2 - x_1}$$

$$(0, 0) \, (1, 3)$$

$$m = \frac{3 - 0}{1 - 0}$$

$$m = 3$$

   Correct Answer : A

11. $Ax + By = C$ and $A = 2$

   $2x + By = C$, from the graph plot 2 exact points $(2, 1)$ and $(0, 3)$

$$slope = m = \frac{3 - 1}{0 - 2} = \frac{2}{-2}$$

   graph slope $m = -1$

   equation slope $= m = -\frac{2}{B}$

   $\left.\begin{array}{c}\\ \\\end{array}\right\}$ $-\frac{2}{B} = -1$

   $B = 2$

   Correct Answer : D

12. $y = \frac{2x}{3} + 4$

$$m = \frac{2}{3} \, , \, (0, 4)$$

   Only graph A has the same slope and same y - intercept.

   Correct Answer : A

13. Coordinate Points

   $(-2, \frac{1}{3})$ and $(1, \frac{-2}{6})$

$$m = \frac{y_2 - y_1}{x_2 - x_1}$$

$$m = \frac{\frac{-2}{6} - \frac{1}{3}}{1 - (-2)} = \frac{\frac{-1}{3} - \frac{1}{3}}{3}$$

$$m = \frac{\frac{-2}{3}}{3}$$

$$m = \frac{-2}{3} \times \frac{1}{3} = \frac{-2}{9}$$

   Correct Answer : B

14. Choice A has an undefined slope

   A) $x = 4$,   slope = undefined

   B) $y = 6$,   slope = 0

   C) $x = y$,   slope = 1

   D) $\frac{x}{y} = 6$,   slope $= \frac{1}{6}$

   Correct Answer : A

15. $15y = -12x + 20$

   Standard form $Ax + By = C$

   $12x + 15y = 20$

   Correct Answer : 12x + 15y = 20

16. First, find 2 points from the graph, then use
$y = mx + b$ formula, then find the equation.

$(0, 4)$ $(8, 0)$

$m = \dfrac{y_2 - y_1}{x_2 - x_1} = \dfrac{0 - 4}{8 - 0}$

$m = \dfrac{-4}{8} = \dfrac{-1}{2}$

$y = mx + b$

$y = \dfrac{-1}{2}x + b \qquad (0, 4)$

$b = 4$

$y = \dfrac{-1}{2}x + 4$

Correct Answer : $y = \dfrac{-1}{2}x + 4$

17. First find 2 points from the
graph, then use the $y = mx + b$
formula, then find the equation.
Slope of two points:

$m = \dfrac{y_2 - y_1}{x_2 - x_1}$

$m = \dfrac{-4 - 4}{6 - (-2)} = \dfrac{-8}{8}$

$m = -1$

$y = mx + b$

use $(-2, 4)$ to find b

$y = mx + b$

$4 = -2(-1) + b$

$4 = 2 + b$

$2 = b$

Correct Answer : $y = -x + 2$

18. $\dfrac{2y}{3} = \dfrac{-x}{4} + 12$

To find the x - intercept, use $y = 0$ and find x.

$\dfrac{2 \times 0}{3} = \dfrac{-x}{4} + 12$

$0 = \dfrac{-x}{4} + 12$

$-12 = \dfrac{-x}{4}$

$x = 48$

Correct Answer : (48, 0)

19. $\qquad 3y = -6x + 18$

To find the y-intercept, use $x = 0$ and find y.

$3y = -6.0 + 18$

$3y = 0 + 18$

$3y = 18$

$y = 6$

Correct Answer : (0, 6)

20. $(-3, 6)$ and $(4, -8)$

$\text{slope} = m = \dfrac{y_2 - y_1}{x_2 - x_1}$

$m = \dfrac{-8 - 6}{4 - (-3)} = \dfrac{-14}{7}$

$m = -2$

$y - y_1 = m(x - x_1)$

$y - 6 = -2(x + 3)$

$y - 6 = -2x - 6$

$y = -2x$

$y + 2x = 0$

Correct Answer : $y + 2x = 0$

Positive Slope

Positive slope is the same as direct variation (m>0). When x increases, y increases as well. When x decreases, y decreases as well.

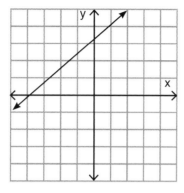

Negative Slope

A negative slope is the same as inverse variation (m<0). When x increases, y is decreasing. When x decreases, y increases.

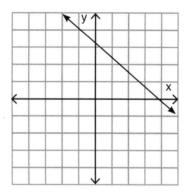

Zero Slope

Zero slopes are a horizontal line (y=0x+b). When the x axis is equal to zero, the y axis can be any number.

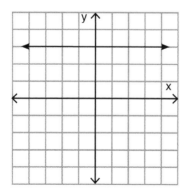

Undefined Slope

An undefined slope is the slope of the y-axis. The x-axis never changes no matter what the y-axis is.

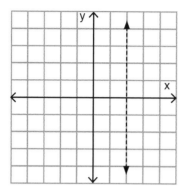

System of Linear Equations

One solution (intersecting lines)

The graphs intersect each other at a single point.

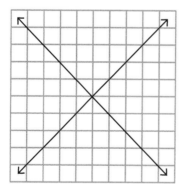

Example:

$$3x + 2y = 8$$
$$x - 2y = 12$$

13

No solution (parallel lines)

The equations have same slopes and different y-intercepts. The graphs are parallel.

$$d_1 : y = m_1 x + n_1$$
$$d_2 : y = m_2 x + n_2$$
$$\left. \right\} \ d_1 \ /\!/ \ d_2 \Longleftrightarrow m_1 = m_2$$

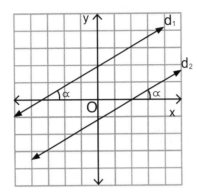

- Same slope($m_1 = m_2$)
- Different y-intercepts

Example:

2x + y = 3
6x + 3y = 12

Infinite solutions (coincident lines)

The two lines in this system have same slopes and same y-intercepts.

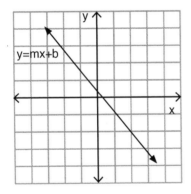

Example:

3x + 3y = 9
  x + y = 3

Perpendicular lines

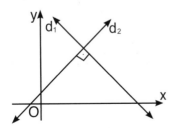

- Slopes are negative reciprocals of each other.
$$\left(d_1 \perp d_2 \ \text{then} \ m_1 = -\frac{1}{m_2} \right)$$

1. The following equation is a line in the xy plane and n is a constant. If the slope of the line is 6, what is the value of n?

3x - 12 = ny

  A) -1

  B) 1

  C) 2

  D) $\frac{1}{2}$

2. Which of the following is an equation of the line K in the xy plane below?

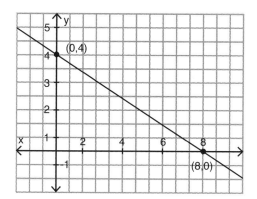

  A) y = -2x + 4

  B) y = $\frac{1}{2}$x + 2

  C) y = -$\frac{1}{2}$x + 4

  D) y = x + 4

3. Which of the following is the graph of the equation y=3x-6?

A)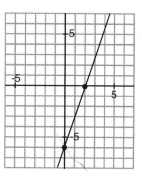

B)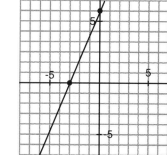

C)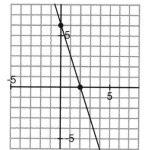

D)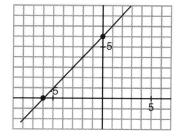

4. On the xy coordinate grid, a line M contains the points (2,3) and (-2,7). If the line N is perpendicular to M at (3,1), which of the following is the equation of the line N?

A) $y = x + 2$
B) $y = x - 2$
C) $y = -x$
D) $y = x + 1$

5. On the xy coordinate grid, a line K contains the points (2,3) and (-2,7). If the line L is **parallel** to line K at (3,1), which of following is the equation of the line L?

A) $y = x + 4$
B) $y = -x + 4$
C) $y = 2x + 4$
D) $y = 3x + 4$

6. Which of the following equations represents a line that is perpendicular to the line that passes through points A(3,6) and B(4,8)?

A) $y = 2x - 9$
B) $y = -\frac{1}{2}x + \frac{15}{2}$
C) $y = 2x + 3$
D) $y = x + 8$

7. Which of the following lines below is a perpendicular equation of 3x-4y=12?

A) $y = \frac{3x}{4} + 12$
B) $y = -\frac{4x}{3} + 12$
C) $y = \frac{2x}{3} + 12$
D) $y = \frac{x}{3} + 12$

8. If the sum of three consecutive integers is 96, which of the following is the smallest one?

A) 31
B) 32
C) 33
D) 34

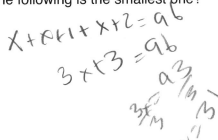

9. The perimeter of a rectangle is 48m. If the width of the rectangle is three times the length, what is the width?

A) 6
B) 9
C) 15
D) 18

10. Mr. Tong's family went to the movies and bought two adult tickets and one child ticket and paid $48. Mr. Robert's family went to the movies and bought 5 adult tickets and two child tickets and paid $120. What is the total amount Mr. Tong's family paid for adults?

    (A) $24
    B) $32
    C) $48
    D) $56

11. Mr. Robert bought 12 T-shirts and 6 hoodies for the SAT Camp and paid a total of $360. Mr. Tong bought 10 T-shirts and 4 hoodies for the Math Counts team and paid a total of $260. Find how much Mr. Robert pays for each T-shirt.

    A) $5
    B) $10
    C) $20
    D) $40

12. Mr. Tong plans to take his Math Counts Team A and Team B to dinner for their achievements. The cost of dinner is $240. The cost for each Team A member is $6 and for each Team B member it is $8. If the Team A members are twice the amount of Team B members, how much did he pay for Team B?

    A) $48
    B) $56
    C) $72
    D) $96

13. What is the solution to the equation below?

$$4\left(\frac{x-1}{8}\right) = \frac{4}{6} + 3x$$

    A) $\frac{6}{7}$
    B) $\frac{7}{6}$
    C) 1
    D) $-\frac{7}{15}$

14. Consider the system of equations:

    $3a + 4b = 12$
    $3(3a+1) = 2b + 18$
    What is a + b?

    A) 7
    B) $\frac{1}{7}$
    C) $\frac{7}{2}$
    D) $\frac{2}{7}$

15. In the system of equations below, D and E are both constant. If the system has many solutions, what is the value of D?

    $4x - 3Dy = 12$
    $8x + 6y = E$

    A) 0
    B) 1
    C) -1
    D) 2

16. How many solutions does the system of equations shown below have?

$2a = 3b + 6$
$4a - 5b = 20$

A) Zero

B) 1

C) 2

D) $\dfrac{Many}{Infinity}$

17. The graph of line L is shown in the xy plane below. Which of following is an equation of a line that is parallel to line L?

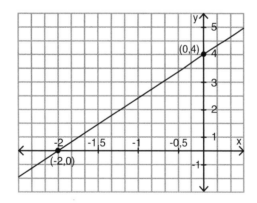

A) $y = 2x + 3$
B) $y = x + 2$
C) $y = 3x + 1$
D) $y = -2x + 4$

18. What is the solution to the equation below?

$-3(2y-5) = 6(3y-12.5)$

A) 3

B) 4

C) $\dfrac{4}{15}$

D) $\dfrac{15}{4}$

Grid Questions

19. Write the equation in slope-intercept form of the line that is **parallel** to the graph of each equation and passes through the given point.

$y = 4x + 12; (2, 3)$

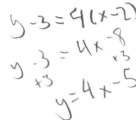

Answer:..

20. Graph the following linear equation:

$y = 3x + 4$

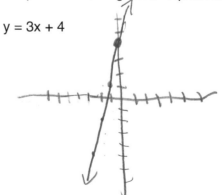

Answer:..

21. Jennifer went to a farm and bought tomatoes for $2 per pound and garlic for $3 per pound. If Jennifer spent $72 on tomatoes and garlic, how many pounds can she buy if she buys only garlic?

Answer:..

22. Are the lines of the following equations parallel, perpendicular or neither?

$2x - 3y = 12$

$y = \dfrac{3x}{12} + 12$

Answer:..

23. Decide is the following system of equations has a single solution, no solutions or infinite solutions.

$\dfrac{2x}{3} + y = 6$

$3x - 2y = 18$

Answer:..

Test 2
Answer Key

1)	D
2)	C
3)	A
4)	B
5)	B
6)	B
7)	B
8)	A
9)	D
10)	C
11)	B
12)	D
13)	D
14)	C
15)	C
16)	B
17)	A
18)	D
19)	$y = 4x - 5$
20)	
21)	24 pounds
22)	Neither
23)	$\left(\dfrac{90}{13}, \dfrac{18}{13}\right)$ One solution.

1. $m = 6$

$3x - 12 = ny$

$\frac{3}{n} = 6$, $n = \frac{3}{6} = \frac{1}{2}$

Correct Answer : D

2. From the graph extract 2 points $(0, 4)$ and $(8, 0)$

slope $= m = \frac{0 - 4}{8 - 0}$

$m = \frac{-1}{2}$

$y = mx + b$

$y = \frac{-1}{2}x + b$, $\quad (0, 4)$

$y = \frac{-1}{2}x + 4$

Correct Answer : C

3. $y = 3x - 6$

slope $= 3$

Only choice A has a slope of 3.

Correct Answer : A

4. Point M

$(2, 3)$ $\quad (-2, 7)$

$m_1 = \frac{7 - 3}{-2 - 2} = \frac{4}{-4} = -1$

$m_1 = -1$

$m_1 \perp m_2$, then $m_2 = 1$

$m_2 = 1$ and point $(3, 1)$

$y = mx + b$

$y = x + b$

$1 = 3 + b$

$-2 = b$

$y = x - 2$

Correct Answer : B

5. $(2, 3)$ and $(-2, 7)$

$m_1 = \frac{7 - 3}{-2 - 2} = \frac{4}{-4} = -1$

$m_1 = -1$

$m_1 \parallel m_2$

$m_2 = -1$, $(3, 1)$

$y = mx + b$

$y = -x + b$

$1 = -3 + b$

$4 = b$

$y = -x + 4$

Correct Answer : B

6. $A(3, 6)$ and $B(4, 8)$

$m = \frac{y_2 - y_1}{x_2 - x_1} = \frac{8 - 6}{4 - 3}$

$m = \frac{2}{1} = 2$

$y = mx + b$

$y = 2x + b$, $\quad (3, 6)$

$6 = 2.3 + b$

$6 = 6 + b$

$0 = b$

$y = 2x$

$m_1 = 2$

if m_1 is perpendicular to the m_2

$m_2 = -\frac{1}{2}$

Only Choice B has a slope of $-\frac{1}{2}$.

Correct Answer : B

7. $3x - 4y = 12$

$m_1 = \dfrac{3}{4}$

if m_1 is perpendicular to m_2

$m_2 = \dfrac{-4}{3}$

Correct Answer : B

8. The sum of three consecutive integers is 96.

$x + x + 1 + x + 2 = 96$

$3x + 3 = 96$

$3x = 93$

$x = 31$

Correct Answer : A

9. The perimeter of the rectangular is 48m.

$2L + 2W = 48$

$W = 3L$

$2L + 2(3L) = 48$

$2L + 6L = 48$

$8L = 48$

$L = 6m \qquad W = 18m$

Correct Answer : D

10. $2a + c = 48$

$5a + 2c = 120$

then,

$\quad -4a - 2c = -96$

$\underline{+\quad 5a + 2c = 120}$

$\qquad a = \$24, 2a = \$48$

$\qquad c = 0$

Correct Answer : C

11. $2 \Big/ 12t + 6h = 360, \quad 24t + 12h = 720$

$-3 \Big/ 10t + 4h = 260, \quad -30t - 12h = -780$

then,

$-6t = -60, t = 10$

$\qquad h = 40$

Correct Answer : B

12. $6A + 8B = 240$

$A = 2B$

$6.2B + 8B = 240$

$12B + 8B = 240$

$20B = 240$

$B = 12$

Team B $= 12 \times 8 = \$96$

Correct Answer : D

13. $4\left(\dfrac{x-1}{8}\right) = \dfrac{4}{6} + 3x$

$6\left(\dfrac{x-1}{2} = \dfrac{2}{3} + \dfrac{3x}{1}\right)$

$3(x - 1) = 2 \times 2 + 6(3x)$

$3x - 3 = 4 + 18x$

$-7 = 15x$

$\dfrac{-7}{15} = x$

Correct Answer : D

14. $3a + 4b = 12$

$3(3a + 1) = 2b + 18$

$3a + 4b = 12$

$9a + 3 = 2b + 18$

$3a + 4b = 12$

$2\Big/ 9a - 2b = 15$

$3a + 4b = 12$

$18a - 4b = 30$

$\underline{+\qquad\qquad\qquad}$

$21a = 42$

$a = 2$

$b = \dfrac{3}{2}$

$a + b = 2 + \dfrac{3}{2} = \dfrac{7}{2}$

Correct Answer : C

15. $4x - 3Dy = 12$
$8x + 6y = E$

$8x - 6Dy = 24$
$8x + 6y = E$

$-6D = 6$
$D = -1$
Correct Answer : C

16. $2a = 3b + 6, -2 / 2a - 3b = 6$
$4a - 5b = 20, 4a - 5b = 20$

$-4a + 6b = -12$
$+ 4a - 5b = 20$
$b = 8 \quad a = 15$
set solution (15, 8)
Correct Answer : B

17. From graph slope = 2
m_1 is parallel to m_2
$m_1 = m_2 = 2$
Only Choice A has the same slope.
Correct Answer : A

18. $-3(2y - 5) = 6(3y - 12.5)$
$-6y + 15 = 18y - 75$
$90 = 24y$
$\frac{90}{24} = y$
$\frac{15}{4} = y$
Correct Answer : D

19. $y = 4x + 12 ; (2, 3)$
$m_1 = 4$
if m_1 is parallel to m_2
$m_2 = 4$
$y = mx + b$
$y = 4x + b$
$3 = 4.2 + b$
$-5 = b$
$y = 4x - 5$
Correct Answer : y = 4x - 5

20. $y = 3x + 4$
when $x = 0 , y = 4$
when $y = 0 , x = \frac{-4}{3}$

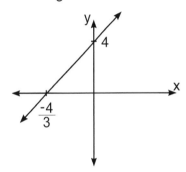

21. Jennifer spent a total of $72 and $3 per pound
for garlic.
$\frac{72}{3} = 24$ pounds.
Correct Answer : 24 pounds

22. $2x - 3y = 12$ $m_1 = \dfrac{2}{3}$

$y = \dfrac{3x}{12} + 12$ $m_2 = \dfrac{3}{12} = \dfrac{1}{4}$

Correct Answer : Neither

23. $\dfrac{2x}{3} + y = 6$

$3x - 2y = 18$

$\left.\begin{array}{l} \dfrac{4}{3}x + 2y = 12 \\[2mm] 3x - 2y = 18 \end{array}\right\} \quad \begin{array}{l} \dfrac{13}{3}x = 30 \\[2mm] x = \dfrac{90}{13} \end{array}$

$3x - 2y = 18$

$3 \cdot \dfrac{90}{13} - 2y = 18$

$y = \dfrac{18}{13}$

Correct Answer : One Solution

Systems of Equations

Solve Linear Equations: A set of two or more linear equations containing two or more variables.

Variable: Represents an unknown number. Any letter can be used as a variable.

Example: x, x+7, x-8 ... etc.

Coefficient: A number placed before a formula in an equation.

Example: 3x, 5(x+5)

Constant: A symbol which represents a specific number.

Example: 5, 3x+10

Equation: A sentence that states that two mathematical expressions are equal.

Example: 4x-6 = 10

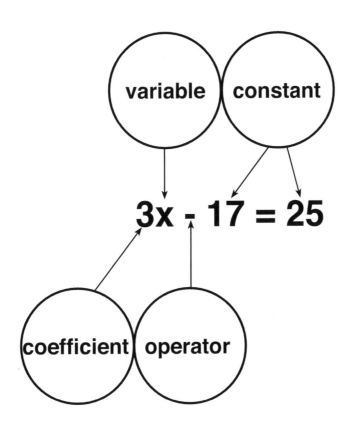

Solve linear equations by using the substitution method

Example: Solve the following system of equations with the **substitution method.**

x - 2y = 18
2x + 3y = 15

Solution:

Step 1: Solve for one variable of the equations (either y or x).

If x - 2y = 18 then x = 2y + 18

Step 2: Substitute this expression into the other equation.

2x + 3y = 15
2(2y+18) + 3y = 15

Step 3: Solve the equation for y.

2(2y+18) + 3y = 15

Then,

4y + 36 + 3y = 15
7y = 15 - 36
7y = -21
y = -3

Step 4: Substitute -3 for y in the equation.

x = 2y + 18
x = 2(-3) + 18
x = -6 + 18

x = 12
Solution (12, -3)

Solve linear equations by using the elimination method:

Example: Solve the following system of equations by using the **elimination method.**

$3x - 2y = 12$
$2x + y = -5$

Solution:

Step 1: Multiply the second equation by 2. Then take out y and keep the first one the same.

$3x - 2y = 24$
$2(2x+y) = -5(2)$ then...

$3x - 2y = 24$
$4x + 2y = -10$

Step 2: Add the revised equations and solve for x.

$3x - 2y = 24$
$4x + 2y = -10$
_____

$7x = 14$ then $x = 2$

Step 3: Substitute the value of x into one of the equations and then solve for y.

$3x - 2y = 24$ if x=2 then

$3(2) - 2y = 12$
$6 - 2y = 12$
$-6 \qquad -6$
_____

$-2y = 6$
$y = -3$ \qquad solution (2, -3).

Solving linear equations by using the graphing method

Example: Solve the following system of equations by using the **graphing method.**

Solution: To find the graph of the equations we will find the y-intercept and x-intercept for each equation.

To find the y-intercept substitute x=0

y = 2 x 0 + 4
y = 4   (0, 4)

Then to find x-intercept substitute y=0

0 = 2x + 4
-4 = 2x
-2 = x   (-2, 0)

Graph the first equation

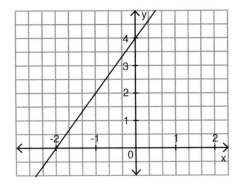

Lets do the same process for the second equation.

y = x-2 to find the y-intercept substitute x=0
y = 0-2 then y=-2   (0, -2)

Then to find the x-intercept substitute y=0
0 = x-2 then x=2   (2, 0)

Graph the second equation

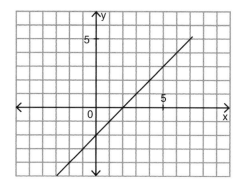

Both graphs together

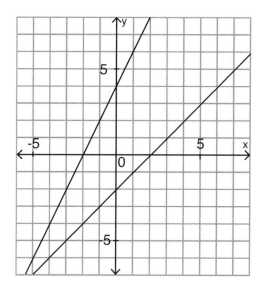

29

Systems of Equations

Test 3

1. What is the solution of the following system of equations?

   $2x + 3y = -12$
   $4x + 3y = 8$

   A) $(10, -\frac{32}{3})$
   B) (5,4)
   C) (10,0)
   D) (-5,6)

2. What is the value of k in the equation shown below?

   $3k - 5 + 4k = -4(k+4)$

   A) 0
   B) 1
   C) -1
   D) 2

3. What is the value of x in the equation shown below?

   $\frac{1}{3}(x - 12) + 6 = 2x - 8$

   A) 0
   B) 1
   C) 2
   D) 6

4. What is the solution of the following system of equations?

   $3y = 6 + 4x$
   $y = 8 - 2x$

   A) (1,4)
   B) (1.8,4.4)
   C) (2,4)
   D) (-1.8,4)

5. What is the value of x in the equation shown below?

   $\frac{5}{8}(8x + 24) = 4(x - 3)$

   A) 27
   B) -27
   C) 30
   D) -30

6. Mr. Robert charges $50 per hour for math tutoring and charges $40 per hour for language arts tutoring. How many hours of math tutoring must be mixed with 5 hours of ELA Tutoring to make $45 per hour?

   A) 5
   B) 10
   C) 15
   D) 20

7.
$$2x + y = 20$$
$$3x - 2y = 16$$

In the system of equations above, what is the value of x+y?

A) 6
B) 10
C) 12
D) 18

8. This week, Tony studied a total of 24 hours for his SAT test next month. This total was more than 6 times the amount of hours he studied last week. Find how many hours Tony studied last week.

A) 4
B) 5
C) 6
D) 7

$$\frac{24}{6}$$

9. The perimeter of a rectangular garden is 48 cm. The width of the garden is 3 cm longer than 2 times the length. What is the length of the garden?

A) 7 cm
B) 9 cm
C) 10 cm
D) 12 cm

10.
$$x + 2y = 15$$
$$3x - 4y = 10$$

In the system of equations above, solve for the x value.

A) 8
B) 16
C) -8
D) -16

11.
$$\frac{2x}{3} + \frac{2y}{6} = 15$$
$$x - y = 10$$

In the system of equations above, solve for the y value.

A) 3
B) $\frac{25}{3}$
C) $\frac{3}{25}$
D) 25

12. The total fare of 4 child movie tickets and 2 adults movie tickets cost $48. If each child's fare is one-third of each adult's ticket, what is the cost for 1 child ticket?

A) $4
B) $4.8
C) $5
D) $6

$$2x + 4y = 48$$
$$y = \frac{1}{3}x$$
$$2x + \frac{4}{3}x = 48$$
$$(3) \frac{10}{3}x = 48 \left(\frac{3}{10}\right)$$

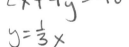

$$y = \frac{1}{3}(14.4)$$
$$x = 14.4$$

13. If $6x = 8y + 10$ and $x - 3y = -30$ than what is the value of $\frac{y}{2}$?

   A) $-\frac{17}{2}$

   B) -17

   C) $\frac{2}{19}$

   D) $\frac{19}{2}$

14.
$$3m + 2n = 10$$
$$2m - 4n = 4$$

In the system of equations above, what is the value of $m-n$?

   A) 2.5

   B) 6

   C) 9

   D) 12

15. Tony is 4 years younger than twice his sister's age. If Tony is 30 years old, then how old is Tony's sister?

   A) 15

   B) 16

   C) 17

   D) 18

$2x - 4 = 30$
$2x = 34$
$x = 17$

16.
$$x + 3ky = 12$$
$$5x - 12y = 18$$

In the system of equations above, k is a constant. For what value of k will the system of equations have no solutions?

   A) $-\frac{4}{5}$

   B) $\frac{4}{5}$

   C) $\frac{5}{4}$

   D) $-\frac{5}{4}$

Grid Questions

17. Find the solution of the system of equations by graphing.

$$-2x + 6y = 12$$
$$x + y = 14$$

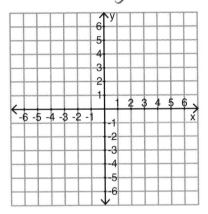

$y = -x + 14$

Answer :...

18. Solve the following system of equations.

3x - 4y = 12
x + 2y = 4

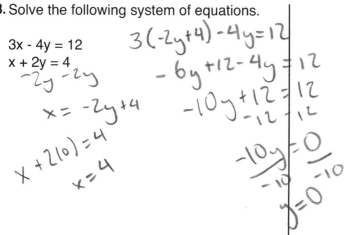

$3(-2y+4) - 4y = 12$

$-6y + 12 - 4y = 12$

$-10y + 12 = 12$
$\quad -12 \; -12$

$-2y \quad -2y$

$x = -2y + 4$

$\dfrac{-10y}{-10} = \dfrac{0}{-10}$

$x + 2(0) = 4$

$x = 4$

$y = 0$

$\left(4, 0\right)$

Answer :..

19. Solve the following system of equations.

3x - 4y = 10
2x + 3y = 30

Answer :..

Test 3
Answer Key

1)	A
2)	C
3)	D
4)	B
5)	B
6)	A
7)	C
8)	A
9)	A
10)	A
11)	B
12)	B
13)	D
14)	A
15)	C
16)	A
17)	
18)	$x = 4, y = 0$
19)	$x = \dfrac{150}{17}, y = \dfrac{70}{17}$

1.

$$2x + 3y = -12$$
$$-/ \quad 4x + 3y = 8$$

$$2x + 3y = -12$$
$$+ \quad -4x - 3y = -8$$
$$\overline{\qquad -2x = -20}$$
$$x = 10, \quad y = \frac{-32}{3}$$

Correct Answer : A

2.

$$3k - 5 + 4k = -4(k+4)$$
$$7k - 5 = -4k - 16$$
$$11k = -11$$
$$k = -1$$

Correct Answer : C

3.

$$\frac{1}{3}(x - 12) + 6 = 2x - 8$$
$$\frac{x}{3} - 4 + 6 = 2x - 8$$
$$10 = \frac{5}{3}x$$
$$x = 6$$

Correct Answer : D

4.

$$3y = 6 + 4x$$
$$y = 8 - 2x$$

$$3(8-2x) = 6 + 4x$$
$$24 - 6x = 6 + 4x$$
$$24 - 6 = 4x + 6x$$
$$18 = 10x$$
$$1.8 = x$$
$$4.4 = y$$

Correct Answer : B

5.

$$\frac{5}{8}(8x + 24) = 4(x - 3)$$
$$5x + 15 = 4x - 12$$
$$x = -27$$

Correct Answer : B

6.

$$50h + 200 = 45(h+5)$$
$$50h + 200 = 45h + 225$$
$$5h = 25$$
$$h = 5$$

Correct Answer : A

7.

$$2/ \quad 2x + y = 20$$
$$\quad \quad 3x - 2y = 16$$

$$4x + 2y = 40$$
$$3x - 2y = 16$$
$$+ \quad \overline{\qquad \qquad}$$
$$7x = 56$$

$$x = 8 \text{ then } y = 4$$
$$x + y = 8 + 4 = 12$$

Correct Answer : C

8.

$$\frac{24}{6} = 4$$

Correct Answer : A

9.

$$2L + 2W = 48$$
$$W = 2L + 3$$
$$2L + 2(2L+3) = 48$$
$$2L + 4L + 6 = 48$$
$$6L = 42$$
$$L = 7cm$$

Correct Answer : A

10.   2 / $x + 2y = 15$
            $3x - 4y = 10$

            $2x + 4y = 30$
            $3x - 4y = 10$
        + _____
            $5x = 40$
            $x = 8$

Correct Answer : A

11. $\dfrac{2x}{3} + \dfrac{2y}{6} = 15$

$x - y = 10$

$\dfrac{2x}{3} + \dfrac{y}{3} = 15,\quad 2x + y = 45$

$2x + y = 45,\qquad 2x + y = 45$

$x - y = 10,\qquad -2x + 2y = -20$
_____
$\qquad\qquad\qquad 3y = 25$

$\qquad\qquad\qquad y = \dfrac{25}{3}$

Correct Answer : B

12. $2a + 4c = 48$ and $c = \dfrac{1}{3}a$

$2a + \dfrac{4}{3}a = 48$

$\dfrac{10}{3}a = 48$

$a = 14.40$

$c = 4.8$

Correct Answer : B

13. $6x = 8y + 10$
            $x - 3y = -30$

            $6x - 8y = 10$
    -6 / $x - 3y = -30$

            $6x - 8y = 10$
            $-6x + 18y = 180$
        + _____
            $10y = 190$
            $y = 19$ $\dfrac{y}{2} = \dfrac{19}{2}$

Correct Answer : D

14. 2 / $3m + 2n = 10$
            $2m - 4n = 4$

            $6m + 4n = 20$
            $2m - 4n = 4$
    + _____
            $8m = 24\qquad m = 3$
            $2 \cdot (3) - 4n = 4$
            $6 - 4n = 4$
            $2 = 4n$
            $\dfrac{1}{2} = n$
$m - n = 3 - \dfrac{1}{2} = \dfrac{5}{2} = 2.5$

Correct Answer : A

15. $2s - 4 = t$
            $2s - 4 = 30$
            $2s = 34$
            $s = 17$

Correct Answer : C

16. $x + 3ky = 12$

$5x - 12y = 18$

$m_1 = \dfrac{-1}{3k}$, $m_2 = \dfrac{+5}{12}$

if a system has no solution

$m_1 = m_2$

$\dfrac{-1}{3k} = \dfrac{+5}{12}$, $k = \dfrac{-4}{5}$

Correct Answer : A

18.

$2 \;/\quad\begin{array}{l}3x - 4y = 12\\ x + 2y = 4\end{array}$

$\begin{array}{l}3x - 4y = 12\\ 2x + 4y = 8\end{array}$

$+$ ─────────

$5x = 20$

$x = 4$, $y = 0$

17. $-2x + 6y = 12$ ①

$\qquad\qquad x + y = 14$ ②

Start with the first equation

if $x = 0$, $y = 2$ $\qquad(0, 2)$

if $y = 0$, $x = -6$ $\qquad(-6, 0)$

Second equation

$x + y = 14$

if $x = 0$, $y = 14$

if $y = 0$, $x = 14$

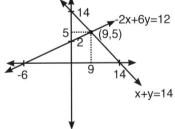

19.

$\begin{array}{l}3 \;/\\ 4 \;/\end{array}\quad\begin{array}{l}3x - 4y = 10\\ 2x + 3y = 30\end{array}$

$\begin{array}{l}9x - 12y = 30\\ 8x + 12y = 120\end{array}$

$+$ ─────────

$17x = 150$

$x = \dfrac{150}{17}$

$\dfrac{2 \cdot 150}{17} + 3y = 30$

$\dfrac{300}{17} + 3y = 30$

$3y = 30 - \dfrac{300}{17}$

$3y = \dfrac{510 - 300}{17}$

$3y = \dfrac{210}{17}$, $y = \dfrac{70}{17}$

Inequalities

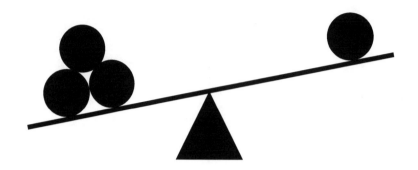

Inequality Symbols	Number Line Symbols
$\leq$	⬤————←
$\geq$	⬤————➤
$<$	○————←
$>$	○————➤

Study Tips:

1) If $a < x$ and $x < b$ then $a < x < b$

2) If $a \leq b$ then $a < b$ or $a = b$

3) If $a \geq b$ then $a > b$ or $a = b$

4) If $a < b$ and $c < d$ then $a + c < b + d$

5) If $\frac{1}{a} < \frac{1}{x} < \frac{1}{b}$ then $a > x > b$

Inequalities

1. x and y are integer numbers.

   $-10 < x < 8$
   $2 < y < 6$

   What is the maximum value of $x^2 + y^2 = ?$

   A) 72
   B) 86
   C) 106
   D) 120

2. $\dfrac{2x + 4}{6} - \dfrac{x}{4} = \dfrac{3}{2}$ find the value of x.

   A) 10
   B) 12
   C) 16
   D) 18

3. $\dfrac{3x}{2} - 4 < x + 3$ which of following is the solution for the inequality?

   A) $(18, -\infty)$
   B) $(-18, +\infty)$
   C) $(-12, -\infty)$
   D) $(14, -\infty)$ $(-\infty, 14)$ smaller bigger

4. Which of the following numbers is not a solution to the inequality?

   $4x - 12 < 8 < x + 8$

   A) 1
   B) 3
   C) 4
   D) 5

5. What is the one possible value of x+y?

   $\dfrac{6}{8} < \dfrac{x}{2} + \dfrac{2y}{4} < \dfrac{3}{2}$

   A) 1
   B) 2
   C) 3
   D) 4

6. What is the possible integer value of x?

   $\dfrac{7}{6} < \dfrac{2x - 3}{12} < \dfrac{3}{2}$

   A) 7
   B) 8
   C) 9
   D) 11

Inequalities

Test 4

7.

$$x < 2$$
$$y \geq -2$$

Which of following ordered pairs (x,y) satisfies the system of equations above?

A) (-3,2)
B) (2, 2)
C) (2,-2)
D) (3,-2)

$x < 2$
$y \geq -2$

8.

$$x = \$7 + 5k$$
$$y = \$5.5 + 10k$$

In the above equation, x represents the price in dollars of apple juice and y represents the price in dollars of orange juice at the farmers market and k is the same amount per week. What is the price of orange juice when it's the same as the price of apple juice?

A) $5
B) $6
C) $6.5
D) $8.5

9. Mr. Robert is planning a summer vacation with his family. The flights cost $1800, the hotel costs $110 per night and he has a budget of $4000 for hotel and flights. How many nights maximum can Mr. Robers afford in the hotel?

A) 10
B) 15
C) 20
D) 25

$1800 + 100 \times \leq 4000$
$110 x \leq 2200$
$x \leq 20$

10.

$$\left| \frac{2x}{3} - 4 \right| < 12$$

What is a possible value of x in the above inequality?

A) -12
B) -5
C) 24
D) 25

11. For the following inequality which of the following **MUST** be true?

$$\frac{x}{5} - 2 < 1$$

A) 10
B) 15
C) 20
D) 25

$\frac{x}{5} < 3$
$x < 15$

12. In Mr. Tong's math team, students are trying to solve an easy test and a hard test. For each of the correct question in the easy test students will earn 10 points. For each of the hard test questions, students will earn 15 points. Jennifer solved a total of 20 questions and earned 275 points in all. How many easy questions did Jennifer solve?

A) 5
B) 6
C) 8
D) 10

13.
$$(2x+4) - (4x-3) = 19$$

What is the value of x in the equation shown above?

A) -8
B) -6
C) 6
D) 5

14. Mr. Robert is planning to register at Star Fitness. If the center's monthly fee is $25 and $5 per hour, which of following functions gives Mr. Robert the cost, in dollars, for a month in which he spends x hours training?

A) $F(x) = 5x$
B) $F(x) = 25x$
C) $F(x) = 5 + 25x$
D) $F(x) = 25 + 5x$

15.
$$7x - 8 \geq 3(x - 6)$$

Which of the following numbers is NOT a solution of the above inequality?

A) -3
B) -2
C) -1
D) 0

16. For the following graph, which of the inequalities corresponds to it?

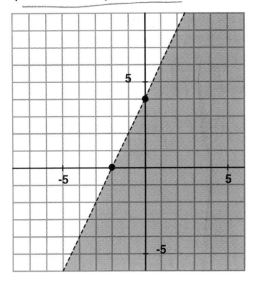

A) $y < x + 2$
B) $y < 2x + 4$
C) $y > 2x + 4$
D) $y < 2x - 4$

17. For the following inequalities graph which part of the graph could represent all of the solutions to the system?

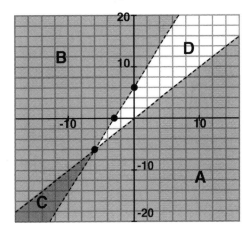

A) A
B) B
C) C
D) D

Grid Questions

18. Solve the following inequality.

$$36 + m \geq 2(-6 + 4m)$$

Answer:..

19. Solve the following inequality.

$$-3(1 + 2x) < 5(1 - 7x)$$

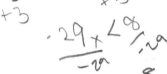

$$-3 - 6x < 5 - 35x$$
$$+35+ \qquad +35x$$
$$-3 + 29x < 5$$
$$+3 \qquad +3$$
$$\frac{.29x < 8}{-29} \; / \; {}_{29}$$

Answer:............$x < \dfrac{8}{29}$..............

20. Solve the following inequality.

$$3x - (x + 5) > -2(2 + x) + 7$$

Answer:..

Test 4
Answer Key

1)	C
2)	A
3)	D
4)	D
5)	B
6)	C
7)	A
8)	D
9)	C
10)	B
11)	A
12)	A
13)	B
14)	D
15)	A
16)	B
17)	C
18)	$m \le \frac{48}{7}$
19)	$x < \frac{8}{29}$
20)	$x > 2$

1. $-10 < x < 8$

$2 < y < 6$

$x = -9$

$y = 5$

max. value of $x^2 + y^2 = (-9)^2 + (5)^2$

$\qquad = 106$

Correct Answer : C

2. $\dfrac{2x+4}{6} - \dfrac{x}{4} = \dfrac{3}{2}$

$\dfrac{4x+8}{12} - \dfrac{3x}{12} = \dfrac{18}{12}$

$4x + 8 - 3x = 18$

$x + 8 = 18$

$x = 10$

Correct Answer : A

3. $\dfrac{3x}{2} - 4 < x + 3$

$x + 3 > \dfrac{3x}{2} - 4$

$7 > \dfrac{1}{2}x$

$x < 14, x = (-\infty, 14)$

Correct Answer : D

4. $4x - 12 < 8 < x + 8$

$\begin{array}{ll} 4x - 12 < 8 & 4x < 20 \\ \quad \text{or} & \quad \text{or} \\ 8 < x + 8 & \quad 0 < x \end{array}$

$0 < x < 5$

$x = 1, 2, 3, 4$

Correct Answer : D

5. $\dfrac{6}{8} < \dfrac{x}{2} + \dfrac{2y}{4} < \dfrac{3}{2}$

$6 < 4x + 4y < 12$

$\dfrac{3}{2} < x + y < 3$

Correct Answer : B

6. $\dfrac{7}{6} < \dfrac{2x-3}{12} < \dfrac{3}{2}$

$\dfrac{14 < 2x-3 < 18}{+3 \quad\ +3 \quad\ +3}$

$17 < 2x < 21$

$8.5 < x < 10.5$

$x = 9$

Correct Answer : C

7. if, $x < 2$

$\qquad y \geq -2$

Correct Answer : A

8. $7 + 5k = 5.5 + 10k$

$\qquad k = 0.3$

Price of orange juice

$\qquad y = 5.5 + 10k$

$\qquad y = 5.5 + 10 \cdot (0.3)$

$\qquad y = 5.5 + 3$

$\qquad y = 8.5$

Correct Answer : D

9. $1800 + 110x \leq 4000$

$110x \leq 2200$

$x \leq 20$

Correct Answer : C

10. $\left| \dfrac{2x}{3} - 4 \right| < 12$

$\dfrac{2x}{3} - 4 < 12$

or

$\dfrac{2x}{3} - 4 > -12$

$\dfrac{2x}{3} < 16$ or $\dfrac{2x}{3} > -8$

$x < 24$ or $x > -12$

$-12 < x < 24$

Correct Answer : B

11. $\dfrac{x}{5} - 2 < 1$

$\dfrac{x}{5} < 3$

$x < 15$

Correct Answer : A

12. $e + h = 20$

$10e + 15h = 275$

$5e = 25$

$e = 5$

Correct Answer : A

13. $(2x + 4) - (4x - 3) = 19$

$2x + 4 - 4x + 3 = 19$

$-2x + 7 = 19$

$-2x = 12$

$x = -6$

Correct Answer : B

14. Monthly Fee = $25

$5 Per Hour

Monthly Spending x Hours

$F(x) = 25 + 5x$

Correct Answer : D

15. $7x - 8 \geq 3(x - 6)$

$7x - 8 \geq 3x - 18$

$4x \geq -10$

$x \geq -2.5$

Correct Answer : A

16. From the graph when $x = 0$, $y < 4$

Only Choice B will give you the correct answer.

Correct Answer : B

17. Graph C can be the only answer .

Correct Answer : C

18. $36 + m \geq 2(-6 + 4m)$

$36 + m \geq -12 + 8m$

$48 \geq 7m$

$m \leq \dfrac{48}{7}$

19. $-3(1 + 2x) < 5(1 - 7x)$

$-3 - 6x < 5 - 35x$

$29x < 8$

$x < \dfrac{8}{29}$

20. $3x - (x + 5) > -2(2 + x) + 7$

$3x - x - 5 > -4 - 2x + 7$

$2x - 5 > -2x + 3$

$4x > 8$

$x > 2$

Rates, Ratios, Proportions, Variations, Percentages, and Integers

Distance = rate x time
   d   = r x t

Distance = mile/miles
Rate = miles per hours (mph)
Time = hour/hours

Proportions: A proportion is an equation that is equivalent to two ratios. $\frac{a}{b} = \frac{c}{d}$ then, use cross multiplication ad = bc.

Direct variation: A direct variation is a relationship between two quantities of x and y that can be written as the following form:

y = kx then k $\neq$ 0 (k is a constant of variation and must be different than zero)

Inverse variation: An inverse variation is a relationship between two quantities of x and y that can be written as the following form:

xy = k then k $\neq$ 0 (k is a constant of variation and must be different than zero)

Percent: A fraction that is a partition of 100.

$$\text{Percent change} = \frac{\text{amount of change}}{\text{original amount}}$$

Example: $20\% = \frac{20}{100}$

3 types of percent questions

Example:

1) What is 20% of 40?

   Solution: $P = \frac{20 \times 40}{100} = 8$

2) What percent of 30 is 120?

   Solution: $\frac{n \times 30}{100} = 120$ then, $n = 400$

3) 15 is 25% of what number?

   Solution: $15 = \frac{25 \times m}{100}$ then, $m = 60$

Example: If Vera's car goes 30 miles per gallon of gas, how far can it go on 12 gallons of gas?

Solution:

   30 miles takes 1 gallon

   x miles takes 12 gallons

   x = 30x12 = 360

Integers and Rational Numbers

Key Note:

Integers: Integers - represented as Z - are the set of all numbers that can be written without a fractional component. To be more specific, numbers in the form of....,-5,-4,-3,-2,-1,0,1,2,3,4,5,....are all integers.

Positive Integers: Integers that are greater than 0.

Negative Integers: Integers that are less than 0.

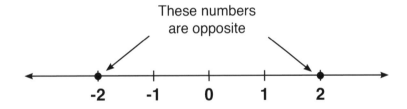

I = {...-5, -4, -3, -2, -1, 0, 1, 2, 3, 4, 5...}

| Negative Integers | 0 is neither positive nor negative | Positive Integers |

Opposites: The same distance from zero but on different sides of zero.

These numbers are opposite

-2 -1 0 1 2

Rational numbers: Represented as Q, a rational number is a number that can be written in the form of $\frac{a}{b}$ where a; b are integers.

Example:

$0, 1, -1, 0.25, \frac{3}{4}$ .....etc.

Irrational Numbers: A real number that cannot be written in the form of $\frac{a}{b}$ where a, b are integers. Numbers such as $\pi, \sqrt{2}$, and etc. are all irrational numbers.

Examples:

$\pi, e, \sqrt{2}, \sqrt{3}, \ldots \ldots$ etc.

Absolute value: The distance of integers from zero on the number line.

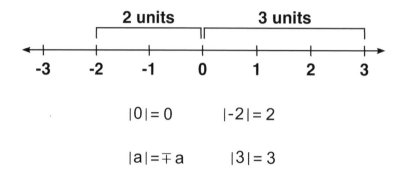

$$|0| = 0 \qquad |-2| = 2$$

$$|a| = \mp a \qquad |3| = 3$$

if $a > 0$ then $|a| = a$

if $a < 0$ then $|a| = -a$

Numerical Expression
A mathematical phrase that contains numbers or operations.

Example: +, -, *, 1, 2, ... etc

Algebraic Expression
A mathematical phrase that can contain a variable.

Example: z, y, z, a, b, c, ... etc

Key for problem solving questions

Addition	Subtraction	Multiplication	Division
Add	Subtract from	Times	Divided by
Altogether	Change	Double	As much
Both	Difference	Each group	Cut up
How many	Fewer	Of	Quotient
Total	Take away	Product	How many in each part
Sum	Less than		Separated
More than	How much more		Share something equally
Increased by	Decreased by		

1. Star Cleaning company charges $400 to clean 20 classrooms. What is the company's price for cleaning a single classroom?

   A) $10
   B) $15
   C) $20
   D) $25

2. Robert can solve 96 questions in 6 days. How many questions can Robert do in 12 days?

   A) 72
   B) 96
   C) 192
   D) 48

3. There are 28 students in Mr. Tong's math class and they are completing their classwork and then turn to their group to discuss their work. The ratio of complete work to incomplete work was 3 to 4. How many students did not complete their classwork?

   A) 3
   B) 7
   C) 8
   D) 16

4. What is the value of $\frac{m}{n}$?

$$\frac{18}{m} = \frac{12}{n}$$

   A) $\frac{3}{2}$
   B) $\frac{2}{3}$
   C) 2
   D) 3

5. Find the ratio of 3.5 to 4.5 .

   A) 9 to 7
   B) 7 to 9
   C) 3 to 7
   D) 2 to 3

6. $\frac{m-4}{3} = \frac{k}{7}$ Find m in terms of k.

   A) $\frac{3k-4}{7} = m$
   B) $\frac{3k+28}{7} = m$
   C) $\frac{4k-7}{3} = m$
   D) $\frac{3k-7}{4} = m$

7. 30% of 70 equals what percent of 84?

    A) 15%
    B) 25%
    C) 35%
    D) 40%

8. What percent of 25 is 20?

    A) 40%
    B) 50%
    C) 60%
    D) 80%

9. There are 8 students on Mr.Tong's math team. If 75% of the team members are girls, how many students on the math team are boys?

    A) 1
    B) 2
    C) 3
    D) 4

10. In Star Middle School, 40% of students are attending Science Olympiad, 25% of students who are attending Science Olympiad were also attending Robotics Club. What percent of students in the Star School attend Robotics Club?

    A) 10%
    B) 35%
    C) 40%
    D) 45%

11. A house in the New Jersey real estate market sold last year for $400,000. The same property sold one year later for $560,000. At what percent did the house price increase?

    A) 40%
    B) 45%
    C) 50%
    D) 50%

12. A microwave originally priced at $40 is decreased by 25%. What is the sale price?

    A) $40
    B) $35
    C) $30
    D) $25

13. The price of a book has been discounted 20%. The sale price is $45. What is the original price?

A) $45.5
B) $51.5
C) $51.75
D) $56.25

14. Tony bought a new car for $12,800 plus 8% state tax. Find the total cost Tony needs to pay.

A) $13,000
B) $13,800
C) $13,824
D) $13,500

15. In Star School, 180 students favorite subjects are math out of 480 students. Find out what percent of students favorite subject is math?

A) 37%
B) 37.5%
C) 40%
D) 45%

16.
$$1\frac{1}{8}$$
Write the above fraction as a percent.

A) 12%
B) 125%
C) 112.5%
D) 175%

17. At Star College, next year's tuition will increase by 8% per credit. If this year tuition at Star College was $675, what will it be next year?

A) $720
B) $725
C) $729
D) $730

18. At a Star dealership, a car sale price is $18,000 plus 7.5% sales tax. If the dealer applies a discount of 25% off from the sales price, find the price after including the discount and sales tax.

A) $14,512.5
B) $14,450
C) $14,520
D) $14,530

19. If x and y are positive integers and 3x+4y=3 then find $27^x \times 81^y$.

A) 3
B) 6
C) 9
D) 27

Test 5
Answer Key

1)	C
2)	C
3)	D
4)	A
5)	B
6)	B
7)	B
8)	D
9)	B
10)	A
11)	A
12)	C
13)	D
14)	C
15)	B
16)	C
17)	C
18)	A
19)	D

1. $\dfrac{\$400}{20} = \$20$

   Correct Answer : C

2. $\dfrac{96}{x} = \dfrac{6}{12}$

   $x = 192$

   Correct Answer : C

3. Ratio of complete to incomplete is 3 to 4.

   $3x + 4x = 28$
   $7x = 28$
   $x = 4$

   Complete = $3x$ = 12
   Incomplete = $4x$ = 16

   Correct Answer : D

4. $\dfrac{18}{m} = \dfrac{12}{n}$

   $18n = 12m$
   $3n = 2m$
   $\dfrac{3}{2} = \dfrac{m}{n}$

   Correct Answer : A

5. Ratio of 3.5 to 4.5

   35 to 45

   7 to 9 or $\dfrac{7}{9}$

   Correct Answer : B

6. $\dfrac{m - 4}{3} = \dfrac{k}{7}$

   $7m - 28 = 3k$
   $m = \dfrac{3k + 28}{7}$

   Correct Answer : B

7. 30% of 70 $= \dfrac{30}{100} \times 70$

   $= \dfrac{2100}{100} = 21$

   $x = \dfrac{21 \div 7}{84 \div 7} = \dfrac{3}{12} = \dfrac{1}{4}$

   $x = 25\%$

   Correct Answer : B

8. $25x = 20$

   $x = \dfrac{20}{25} = \dfrac{80}{100} = 80\%$

   Correct Answer : D

9. From 8 students, if 75% are girls

   # of girls $= \dfrac{75 \times 8}{100}$

   # girls = 6

   # boys = 2

   Correct Answer : B

10. Suppose the school has a total of 100 students. If 40% of students are attending Science Olympiad

    $\dfrac{40 \times 100}{100} = 40$ students.

    From 40 students if 25% are attending Robotics Club.

    $\dfrac{40 \times 25}{100} = 10$ student

    Percent of students attending Robotics Club $= \dfrac{10}{100} = 10\%$

    Correct Answer : A

11. $560,000 - 400,000 = 160,000$

Percent of increase $= \dfrac{160,000}{400,000}$

$= \dfrac{4}{10} = \dfrac{40}{100}$

Correct Answer : A

12. Original price = $40 decrease by 25%

$40 \times \dfrac{25}{100} = \dfrac{40 \times 25}{100}$

$= \$10$

Sale price $= \$40 - \$10$

$= \$30$

Correct Answer : C

13. Discount 20%

Original Price $= 100x$

Discount 20% $= 20x$

Sale Price = Original Price - Discount

$\$45 = 100x - 20x$

$45 = 80x$

$\dfrac{45}{80} = x$

$x = 56.25\$$

Correct Answer : D

14. Car price $= \$12,800 + $ Tax

Tax $= \dfrac{8 \times \$12,800}{100} = \$1,024$

Total cost : $\$12,800 + \$1,024 = \$13,824$

Correct Answer : C

15. $\dfrac{180}{480} = \dfrac{18}{48} = \dfrac{3 \times 12.5}{8 \times 12.5} = \dfrac{37.5}{100} = 37.5\%$

Correct Answer : B

16. $1\dfrac{1}{8} = 1.125 \times 100$

$= 112.5\%$

Correct Answer : C

17. Next years tuition

$675 \times \dfrac{8}{100} = \$54$

Total $= \$675 + \$54$

$= \$729$

Correct Answer : C

18. Discount 25%

$\dfrac{25}{100} \times \$18,000 = \$4,500$

New price $= \$18,000 - \$4,500$

$= \$13,500$

Sale Tax 7.5% $= \dfrac{7.5}{100} \times \$13,500$

Sale Tax $= \$1,012.5$

Final Price $= \$13,500 + \$1,012.5$

$= \$14,512.5$

Correct Answer : A

19. $3x + 4y = 3$

$27^x \cdot 81^y$

$= 3^{3x} \cdot 3^{4y}$

$= 3^{3x+4y}$

$= 3^3$

$= 27$

Correct Answer : D

1. $\frac{2m+4}{3m-2} = \frac{6}{7}$ solve for m.

A) 5
B) 10
C) 15
D) 20

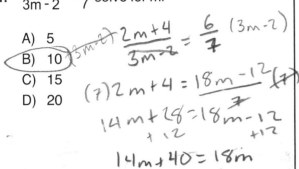

$(3m-2) \cdot \frac{2m+4}{3m-2} = \frac{6}{7} (3m-2)$

$(7) 2m+4 = 18m - 12 (7)$

$14m + 28 = 18m - 12$
$\quad +12 \qquad\qquad +12$

$14m + 40 = 18m$
$\qquad 40 = 4m$

2. If Tony's car can drive 480 miles on a full tank of 16 gallons, what is the miles per gallon?

A) 20mpg
B) 12mpg
C) 25mpg
D) 30mpg

3. Tony went to a restaurant with his family. He paid the bill of $160 plus $24 in tips. Find the percentage of the tip, based on the bill.

A) 5%
B) 10%
C) 15%
D) 20%

4. Convert 15 kilograms to grams. (1kg=1000gr)

A) 15
B) 150
C) 1500
D) 15000

5. The population of a country increased from 320,000 to 340,000 from 2010 to 2018. Find the percentage of the increase.

A) 6.25%
B) 7.5%
C) 10%
D) 12.5%

6. Convert 1 meter to millimeters. (1meter=100cm, 1cm=10mm)

$1 \; 000$

A) 10
B) 100
C) 1000
D) 10000

7. Convert 1 milliliter to liters. (1liter=1000milliliters)

A) 0.1
B) 0.001
C) 0.0001
D) 0.00001

8. If y varies inversely as x and x=12 when y=60, find y when x=18.

A) 20
B) 30
C) 40
D) 50

9. Chocolate milk costs $12 per gallon and milk costs $3 per gallon. How many gallons of chocolate should you mix with 2 gallons of milk to make chocolate syrup that costs $8 per gallon?

A) 1 gallon
B) 1.5 gallons
C) 2 gallons
D) 2.5 gallons

10. Tony purchases a combined total of 30 black and white pens for $155. The black pens cost $6 each, the white pens cost $5 each. How many black pens did Tony purchase?

A) 5
B) 10
C) 15
D) 20

11. Find y when x=3, if y varies directly as x and y=20 when x=5.

A) 6
B) 9
C) 12
D) 15

12. Which of the following graph shows direct variation?

A)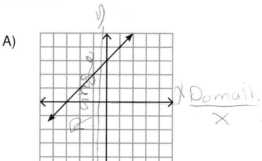

B)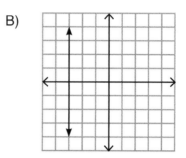

C)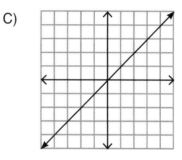

D)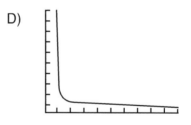

13. It takes 4 painters 9 hours to paint an entire apartment. How long would it take 6 painters to paint the same apartment?

    A) 2

    B) 4

    C) 6

    D) 8

14. Which of following equations is an example of inverse variation?

    A) $y = kx$

    B) $y = \dfrac{k}{x}$

    C) $y = \dfrac{x}{k}$

    D) $y = x$

15. $$3x + 5y = 12$$
Find the inverse of the above equation.

    A) $y = \dfrac{12 - 3x}{5}$

    B) $y = \dfrac{3x + 12}{5}$

    C) $y = \dfrac{-5x + 12}{3}$

    D) $y = 3x$

$$\frac{3x}{3} = \frac{12 - 5y}{3}$$

$$x = \frac{12 - 5y}{3}$$

$$y = \frac{-5x + 12}{3}$$

Test 6
Answer Key

1)	B
2)	D
3)	C
4)	D
5)	A
6)	C
7)	B
8)	C
9)	D
10)	A
11)	C
12)	C
13)	C
14)	B
15)	C

1. $\dfrac{2m+4}{3m-2} = \dfrac{6}{7}$, then m = ?

   14m + 28 = 18m - 12

   m = 10

   Correct Answer : B

2. $\dfrac{480\,\text{miles}}{x\,\text{miles}} = \dfrac{16\,\text{mpg}}{1\,\text{mpg}}$

   $x = \dfrac{480}{16} = 30\,\text{mpg}$

   Correct Answer : D

3. Percentage of tip = $\dfrac{24}{160}$

   = 15%

   Correct Aswer : C

4. 1kg = 1000gr

   15kg = 15000gr

   Correct Answer : D

5. Percent of change = 340 - 320

   = 20,000

   Percent of increase = $\dfrac{20}{320}$

   $= \dfrac{1}{16}$

   = 6.25%

   Correct Answer : A

6. 1meter = 100 cm

   1cm = 10 mm

   1meter = 1000 mm

   Correct Answer : C

7. 1liter = 1000 ml

   1millitter = 0.001 liter

   Correct Answer : B

8. $y = \dfrac{k}{x}$ (inverse)

   $60 = \dfrac{k}{12}$ k = 720

   when x = 18, yx = k

   y.18 = 720

   y = 40

   Correct Answer : C

9. 3.2 + 12x = 8 (x + 2)

   6 + 12x = 8x + 16

   4x = 10

   x = 2.5 gallons

   Correct Answer : D

10. Black pens = x

    White pens = 30 - x

    Total Cost = $155

    6x + 5(30 - x) = 155

    6x + 150 - 5x = 155

    x + 150 = 155

    x = 5

    Black Pens = x = 5

    Correct Answer : A

11. $y = kx$

$20 = k.5$

$\underline{k = 4}$

$y = kx$

$y = 4.3$

$y = 12$

Correct Answer : C

12. Only Choice C

can be Direct Variation

$y = kx$

Correct Answer : C

13. 4 Painters → 9 hours

6 Painters → x hours

Inverse Variation

$6x = 4.9$

$6x = 36$

$x = 6$ hours

Correct Answer : C

14. Inverse Variation

$y = \dfrac{k}{x}$

Correct Answer : B

15. $3x + 5y = 12$

$3x = 12 - 5y$

$x = \dfrac{12 - 5y}{3}$

Change x to y

$y = \dfrac{12 - 5x}{3}$

Correct Answer : C

Exponents, Radicals, Polynomials, and Rational Expressions

Laws of Exponents

1) Product (Multiplication) Rule:

$a^m * a^n = a^{m+n}$

When multiplying the same bases, always add the powers and keep the base the same.

Example:

$2^4 * 2^6 = 2^{10}$

2) Quotient (Dividing) Rule:

$\dfrac{a^m}{a^n} = a^{m-n}$

When dividing the same bases, always subtract the powers and keep the base the same.

Example:

$\dfrac{a^{28}}{a^6} = a^{22}$

3) Power to Power Rule:

$(a^m)^n = a^{m \times n}$

When you have one base but more than one power, keep the base and multiply all powers together.

Example:

$(a^6)^3 = a^{18}$

4) Inverse:

$(a^{-1})^3 = a^{-3} = \dfrac{1}{a^3}$

When you have a negative power always take the reciprocal of the base.

Example:

$(2^{-1})^3 = 2^{-3} = \dfrac{1}{2^3} = \dfrac{1}{8}$

5) Zero Exponents:

Any number to the zero power is always 1.

$$a^0 = 1$$

Example:

$$2^0 = 1$$

Laws of Radicals

1) $\quad (\sqrt[n]{m})^n = m$

Example:

$$(\sqrt[3]{4})^3 = 4$$

2) $\quad (\sqrt[k]{m \times n}) = \sqrt[k]{m} \times \sqrt[k]{n}$

Example:

$$(\sqrt[3]{4 \times 6}) = \sqrt[3]{4} \times \sqrt[3]{6}$$

3) $\quad \sqrt[k]{\dfrac{m}{n}} = \dfrac{\sqrt[k]{m}}{\sqrt[k]{n}}$

Example:

$$\sqrt[3]{\dfrac{4}{7}} = \dfrac{\sqrt[3]{4}}{\sqrt[3]{7}}$$

4) $\quad \sqrt[b]{(\sqrt[a]{n})} = \sqrt[a \times b]{n}$

Example:

$$\sqrt[3]{(\sqrt[4]{5})} = \sqrt[3 \times 4]{5}$$

Polynomials

1) $a^2 - b^2 = (a-b)(a+b)$

2) $a^2 + b^2 = (a+b)^2 - 2ab$

3) $a^2 + b^2 = (a-b)^2 + 2ab$

4) $a^3 - b^3 = (a-b)(a^2 + ab + b^2)$

5) $a^3 + b^3 = (a+b)(a^2 - ab + b^2)$

6) $a^3 - b^3 = (a-b)^3 + 3ab(a-b)$

7) $a^3 + b^3 = (a+b)^3 - 3ab(a+b)$

$$\frac{P(x)\ \big|\ Q(x)}{\big|\ B(x)}$$

$$K(x)$$

P(x)=Q(x).B(x)+K(x)

Monomial: 2x, 3x, ...etc.
Binomial: 2x+4y, ...etc.
Trinomial: 2x+3y+5.

Not Polynomials

Example:

$3x + \dfrac{1}{x}$

$\sqrt{x} - 7x^2 + 6$

Foil Method:

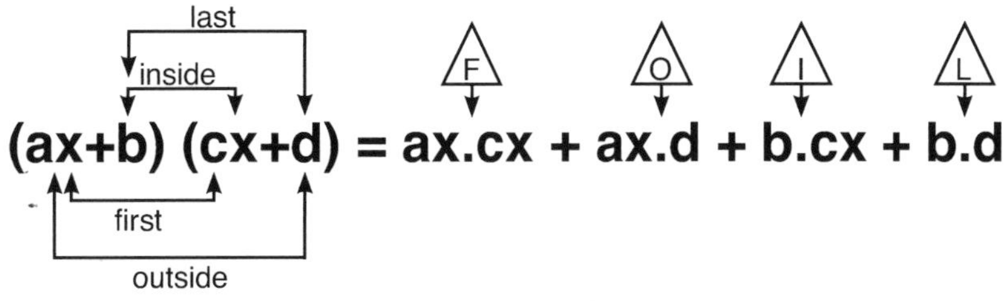

$$(ax+b)\,(cx+d) = ax.cx + ax.d + b.cx + b.d$$

last
inside
first
outside

F O I L

Handwritten notes:

$a-(-ab)$
$-a^2b$

Please Work on this

$a^3 - a^2b + ab^2 + a^2b - ab^2 + b^3$

$a^3 + b^3$

$a \cdot a \cdot a + b \cdot b \cdot b$

$(a+b)(a \cdot a, b \cdot b)$

$(a+b)(a^2 + b^2)$

$-ab$

65

1. If a and b are positive integers and $a^2 - b^2 = 7$, find $\dfrac{a}{b}$?

A) $\dfrac{4}{3}$

B) $-\dfrac{4}{3}$

C) $\dfrac{3}{4}$

D) $-\dfrac{3}{4}$

2. Find $\dfrac{2018^{2018}}{2018}$?

A) 2018

B) 2018^0

C) 2018^{2017}

D) 2018^{2018}

3. If $a^{\frac{b}{3}} = 8$ and $a \times b = 18$, then find a?

A) 1

B) 2

C) 4

D) 6

4. If a, b, c are positive integers and $ab = \dfrac{1}{4}$, $bc = \dfrac{1}{3}$ and $ac = \dfrac{1}{3}$, then find $a \cdot b \cdot c$?

A) $\dfrac{1}{6}$

B) 6

C) -6

D) -1

5. If $\dfrac{a^2}{b^2} + \dfrac{b^2}{a^2} = 7$, then find $\dfrac{a}{b} + \dfrac{b}{a}$?

A) 1

B) 3

C) 2

D) -1

6. Evaluate $4 + (2 + 3) \times 5 - 8 + (5 + 3)^0$?

A) 15

B) 16

C) 17

D) 22

7. If $x = 3^3$, then find x^x?

    A) 3^{27}

    B) 3^0

    C) 3^6

    D) 3^{81}

8. Solve $\dfrac{\frac{1}{2}}{2^3 - 2}$?

    A) 1

    B) $\dfrac{1}{12}$

    C) $\dfrac{1}{6}$

    D) 6

9. Find $101^2 - 99^2$?

    A) 100

    B) 200

    C) 300

    D) 400

10. If $\dfrac{x}{2^{12}} = \dfrac{8}{2^8}$ Solve for x.

    A) 2^7

    B) 2^{-7}

    C) 2^0

    D) 2^9

11. Simplify $\sqrt[3]{2^{3x+3}}$.

    A) 2^{2x+1}

    B) 2^{x+1}

    C) 2^1

    D) 2^2

12. Solve $\sqrt[3]{16}$.

    A) $2\sqrt[3]{2}$

    B) $4\sqrt[3]{2}$

    C) $\sqrt[3]{2}$

    D) 4

13. Evaluate $3^5 \times 3^{10} = 3^n \times 3^m \times 3^1$ then find m + n.

A) 10

B) 12

C) 14

D) 16

14. Evaluate $3^5 \times 3^{10} \times 3^6 \times 3^4 \times 3^1$.

A) 3^{10}

B) 3^{15}

C) 3^{16}

D) 3^{26}

Important

15. $\sqrt[2]{x + 32} - \sqrt[2]{x} = 4$; x can be which of following?

A) 2

B) -1

C) 4

D) 8

Test 7
Answer Key

1)	A
2)	C
3)	B
4)	A
5)	B
6)	D
7)	D
8)	B
9)	D
10)	A
11)	B
12)	A
13)	C
14)	D
15)	C

1. If $a > 0$ and $b > 0$

$a^2 - b^2 = 7$

$(a - b) \cdot (a + b) = 7$

$a - b = 1$

$a + b = 7$

$2a = 8 \qquad a = 4$

$\qquad\qquad b = 3$

Correct Answer : A

2. $\dfrac{2018^{2018}}{2018^1}$

$= 2018^{2018-1}$

$= 2018^{2017}$

Correct Answer : C

3. $a^{\frac{b}{3}} = 8$

$a^{\frac{b}{3}} = 2^3$ and $a \times b = 18$

a must be 2

b must be 9

Correct Answer : B

4. $ab = \dfrac{1}{4}$

$bc = \dfrac{1}{3} \qquad a^2 b^2 c^2 = \dfrac{1}{36}$

$ac = \dfrac{1}{3} \qquad a \cdot b \cdot c = \dfrac{1}{6}$

Correct Answer : A

5. $\dfrac{a^2}{b^2} + \dfrac{b^2}{a^2} = 7$, then

$\dfrac{a}{b} + \dfrac{b}{a} = ?$

$(\dfrac{a}{b} + \dfrac{b}{a})^2 - 2 = 7$

$(\dfrac{a}{b} + \dfrac{b}{a})^2 = 9$

$\dfrac{a}{b} + \dfrac{b}{a} = 3$

Correct Answer : B

6. $4 + (2 + 3) \times 5 - 8 + (5 + 3)^0$

$= 4 + 5 \times 5 - 8 + 1$

$= 4 + 25 - 8 + 1$

$= 29 - 8 + 1$

$= 21 + 1$

$= 22$

Correct Answer : D

7. If $x = 3^3$, then

$x^x = (3^3)^{(3^3)}$

$= (3^3)^{27}$

$= 3^{81}$

Correct Answer : D

8. $\dfrac{\frac{1}{2}}{2^3 - 2} = \dfrac{\frac{1}{2}}{8 - 2}$

$= \dfrac{\frac{1}{2}}{6} = \dfrac{1}{2} \cdot \dfrac{1}{6} = \dfrac{1}{12}$

Correct Answer : B

9. $101^2 - 99^2 = a^2 - b^2$

$= (a - b).(a + b)$

$= (101 + 99).(101 - 99)$

$= (200).2$

$= 400$

Correct Answer : D

10. $x \cdot \dfrac{1}{2^{12}} = \dfrac{8}{2^8}$

$x \cdot \dfrac{1}{2^{12}} = \dfrac{2^3}{2^8}$

$x \cdot \dfrac{1}{2^{12}} = 2^{-5}$

$x = 2^{12-5}$

$x = 2^7$

Correct Answer : A

11. $\sqrt[3]{2^{3x+3}}$

$= \sqrt[3]{2^{3(x+1)}}$

$= 2^{x+1}$

Correct Answer : B

12. $\sqrt[3]{16}$

$\sqrt[3]{16} = \sqrt[3]{2^3 . 2^1} = 2\sqrt[3]{2}$

Correct Answer : A

13. $3^5 \times 3^{10} = 3^n \times 3^m \times 3^1$

$3^{15} = 3^{n+m+1}$

$n + m + 1 = 15$

$n + m = 14$

Correct Answer : C

14. $3^5 x 3^{10} x 3^6 x 3^4 x 3^1$

$= 3^{5+10+6+4+1}$

$= 3^{26}$

Correct Answer : D

15. From all the choices only C works for the equation.

Correct Answer : C

1. If A,B,C are real numbers then what is A+C?

$$\frac{3x-2}{x^3-1} = \frac{A}{x-1} + \frac{Bx+C}{x^2+x+1}$$

A) $\frac{1}{3}$ B) $\frac{2}{3}$ C) $\frac{4}{3}$ D) $\frac{8}{3}$

2. If A and B are real numbers then what is A+B?

$$\frac{2x+6}{x^2-1} = \frac{A}{x-1} + \frac{B}{x+1}$$

A) 2
B) 4
C) -2
D) -4

3. If P(x+1)=3x+1, then what is P(x+3)?

A) $2x+7$
B) $3x+7$
C) $-3x+5$
D) $2x+1$

4. Which of the following is one of factors of $9x^2-49$?

A) $2x+7$
B) $3x+7$
C) $-3x+5$
D) $2x+1$

$ax^2 - 49$

$(3x-7)(3x+7)$

5. If $P(x+2) = x^2 + 3x + 1$, then find $P(x-1)$?

A) x^2+3x+1
B) x^2-3x+1
C) $x-2$
D) $x-3$

6. What is the solution of x^2-5x+6?

A) $(x-3)(x-2)$
B) $(x+3)(x-2)$
C) $(x+3)(x+2)$
D) $(x-3)(x-1)$

7. If $(2x - 1)^2 = (2z + 1)^2$ then x equals what?

A) z
B) z + 1
C) z - 1
D) 2z

8. If $x > 0$ and $x - 3 = \sqrt{x - 3}$ then which of following can be x?

A) 0
B) 1
C) 2
D) 4

9. In the polynomial below, a is the constant. If the polynomial is divisible by P(x+2) then find the value of a.

$$P(x) = 2x^3 + ax^2 - x + 2$$

A) 2
B) 3
C) 5
D) 7

10. If the following polynomial is divisible by P(x+1) then find the reminder.

$$x^{2015} + x^{2016} + x^{2017} + x^{2018}$$

A) 0
B) 1
C) -1
D) 2

11. If 2x-3y=3 then find $\dfrac{16^x}{64^y}$

A) 4
B) 8
C) 16
D) 64

12. $P(x) = 3x^3 - 7x^2 + 2$ and $Q(x) = 2x^3 + 2x^2 + 5$, then find $P(x) - Q(x)$?

A) $x^3 - 9x^2 - 3$
B) $x^3 + 9x^2 - 3$
C) $x^3 - 9x^2 + 7$
D) $x^3 - 2x^2 - 7$

13. What is the solution of the following equation?

$$\frac{3}{x+1} - \frac{2}{x} = \frac{1}{x-1}$$

A) $\frac{1}{2}$

B) $-\frac{1}{2}$

C) $\frac{1}{4}$

D) 2

14. Which of following equations is equivalent to the expression below?

$$(64x^{12})^{\frac{1}{6}}$$

A) $2x^3$

B) $2x^2$

C) $2x$

D) $3x$

15. Which of the following is equivalent to $x^{\frac{2}{3}}$?

A) $\sqrt{x}$

B) $\sqrt[3]{x^2}$

C) $\sqrt[2]{x^3}$

D) x

16. Which of the following has the same value of $\sqrt{0.16} \times \sqrt{144}$?

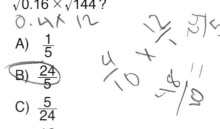

A) $\frac{1}{5}$

B) $\frac{24}{5}$

C) $\frac{5}{24}$

D) $\frac{12}{5}$

17. What value of x satisfies the equation below?

$$-9 - \frac{\sqrt{x}}{4} = -12$$

A) 12

B) 144

C) -12

D) -144

18. If $x = \frac{4^3}{\sqrt{64}}$ then find x.

A) 2

B) 4

C) 8

D) 16

Test 8
Answer Key

1)	D
2)	A
3)	B
4)	B
5)	B
6)	A
7)	B
8)	D
9)	B
10)	A
11)	D
12)	A
13)	A
14)	B
15)	B
16)	B
17)	B
18)	C

Exponents, Radicals, Polynomials, and Rational Expressions
Test 8 Solutions

1. $\dfrac{3x-2}{x^3-1} = \dfrac{A}{x-1} + \dfrac{Bx+C}{x^2+x+1}$

 $3x - 2 = A(x^2 + x + 1) + (Bx + C)(x - 1)$

 $3x - 2 = Ax^2 + Ax + A + Bx^2 - Bx + Cx - C$

 $3x - 2 = x^2(A + B) + x(A - B + C) + A - C$

 $A - C = -2$

 $A + B = 0, \quad B = -A$

 $A - B + C = 3$

 $A - C = -2 \qquad\qquad A - C = -2$

 $A - (-A) + C = 3 \qquad 2A + C = 3$

 $A = \dfrac{1}{3}, \quad C = \dfrac{7}{3}$

 $A + C = \dfrac{8}{3}$

 Correct Answer : D

2. $\dfrac{2x+6}{x^2-1} = \dfrac{A}{x-1} + \dfrac{B}{x+1}$

 $2x + 6 = A(x + 1) + B(x - 1)$

 $2x + 6 = Ax + A + Bx - B$

 $2x + 6 = x(A + B) + A - B$

 $2x = x(A + B)$

 $2 = A + B \qquad 2A = 8, \ A = 4$

 $6 = A - B \qquad\qquad B = -2$

 $A + B = 4 - 2 = 2$

 Correct Answer : A

3. $P(x+1) = 3x + 1$

 $P(x+2+1) = 3(x+2) + 1$

 $P(x+3) = 3x + 6 + 1 = 3x + 7$

 Correct Answer : B

4. $9x^2 - 49$

 $(3x - 7).(3x + 7)$

 Correct Answer : B

5. $P(x + 2) = x^2 + 3x + 1$

 $P(x - 3 + 2) = (x - 3)^2 + 3(x - 3) + 1$

 $P(x - 1) = x^2 - 6x + 9 + 3x - 9 + 1$

 $P(x - 1) = x^2 - 3x + 1$

 Correct Answer : B

6. $x^2 - 5x + 6$

 $x \quad x \qquad -2 \quad -3$

 $(x - 2).(x - 3)$

 Correct Answer : A

7. $(2x - 1)^2 = (2z + 1)^2$

 $2x - 1 = 2z + 1$

 $2x = 2z + 2$

 $x = z + 1$

 Correct Answer : B

8. $x - 3 = \sqrt{x - 3}$

 $(x - 3)^2 = x - 3$

 $x^2 - 6x + 9 = x - 3$

 $x^2 - 7x + 12 = 0$

 $x \quad x \qquad -4 \quad -3$

 $(x-3) . (x-4) = 0$

 $x = 3 \text{ or } x = 4$

 Correct Answer : D

9. $P(x + 2) = 0, \quad x + 2 = 0, \quad x = -2$

 $P(-2) = 2(-2)^3 + a(-2)^2 - (-2) + 2$

 $P(-2) = -16 + 4a + 2 + 2$

 $0 = -16 + 4a + 4$

 $0 = -12 + 4a$

 $12 = 4a$

 $3 = a$

 Correct Answer : B

10. $P(x + 1) = 0$

 $x + 1 = 0$

 $x = -1$

 $P(-1) = (-1)^{2015} + (-1)^{2016} + (-1)^{2017} + (-1)^{2018}$

 $P(-1) = -1 + (1) + (-1) + (1)$

 $P(-1) = -1 + 1 - 1 + 1$

 $P(-1) = 0$

 Correct Answer : A

11. If $2x - 3y = 3$, then

$$\frac{16^x}{64^y} = \frac{4^{2x}}{4^{3y}} = 4^{2x-3y}$$

$$= 4^3 = 64$$

Correct Answer : D

12. $P(x) = 3x^3 - 7x^2 + 2$

$Q(x) = 2x^3 + 2x^2 + 5$

$P(x) - Q(x)$

$= 3x^3 - 7x^2 + 2 - 2x^3 - 2x^2 - 5$

$= x^3 - 9x^2 - 3$

Correct Answer : A

13. $\dfrac{3}{x+1} - \dfrac{2}{x} = \dfrac{1}{x-1}$

$3(x-1) \cdot x - 2(x+1) \cdot (x-1) = x(x+1)$

$3(x^2 - x) - 2(x^2 - 1) = x^2 + x$

$3x^2 - 3x - 2x^2 + 2 = x^2 + x$

$x^2 - 3x + 2 = x^2 + x$

$-3x + 2 = x$

$2 = 4x$

$\dfrac{1}{2} = x$

Correct Answer : A

14. $(64x^{12})^{\frac{1}{6}}$

$= (2^6 x^{12})^{\frac{1}{6}}$

$= 2^{\frac{6}{6}} \cdot x^{\frac{12}{6}}$

$= 2^1 x^2$

$= 2x^2$

Correct Answer : B

15. $x^{\frac{2}{3}} = \sqrt[3]{x^2}$

Correct Answer : B

16. $\sqrt{0.16} \times \sqrt{144}$

$= \dfrac{4}{10} \times 12 = \dfrac{48}{10} = \dfrac{24}{5}$

Correct Answer : B

17. $-9 - \dfrac{\sqrt{x}}{4} = -12$

$-9 + 12 = \dfrac{\sqrt{x}}{4}$

$3 = \dfrac{\sqrt{x}}{4}$

$12 = \sqrt{x}$

$144 = x$

Correct Answer : B

18. If $x = \dfrac{4^3}{\sqrt{64}}$

$x = \dfrac{64}{8}$

$x = 8$

Correct Answer : C

Exponents, Radicals, Polynomials, and Rational Expressions
Test 9

1. $P(x) = 3x^3 - 7x^2 + 6$ and $Q(x) = 2x^3 + 2x^2 - 3$, find $P(x) + Q(x)$.

   A) $3x^3 - 5x^2 + 3$

   B) $5x^3 + 9x^2 - 3$

   C) $5x^3 - 9x^2 + 7$

   D) $5x^3 - 5x^2 + 3$

2. $P(x) = 2x - 1$ and $Q(x) = 2x^3 + 2x^2 - 1$, then find $P(x) \times Q(x)$.

   A) $4x^4 - 2x^3 - 2x^2 - 2x + 1$

   B) $4x^4 + 2x^3 + 2x^2 - 2x + 1$

   C) $4x^4 + 2x^3 - 2x^2 - 2x + 1$

   D) $4x^4 - 2x^3 - 2x^2 + 2x - 1$

$P(x-1) + P(x+1) = ax^2 + bx + c$

3. $P(x - 1) + P(x + 1) = 2x^2 - 2x + 12$. Find $P(x)$.

   A) $x^2 - 2x + 5$

   B) $x^2 - x + 12$

   C) $x^2 - 2x + 10$

   D) $x^2 - x + 5$

4. Simplify the following equation.

$$\frac{x^2 - 16}{x + 4} = ?$$

   A) $\frac{x - 4}{x + 4}$

   B) $\frac{x - 2}{x + 2}$

   C) $x - 4$

   D) $x + 4$

5. In the polynomial below, if the polynomial is divisible by $Q(x-2)$ then find the remainder.
$$Q(3x) = 12x + 2$$

   A) 1

   B) 5

   C) 10

   D) 15

6. If $x^2 + ax - 10 = (x - 1)(bx + c)$, then find $b + c$?

   A) 50

   B) 10

   C) 11

   D) 12

7. If $P(-3)=P(-2)=P(6)=0$ and $P(0)=36$ then $P(1)$?

A) 12

B) 16

C) 24

D) 60

8. If $P(x-1) = x^2 - 2x + 3$ then find $P(3)$?

A) 6

B) 11

C) 23

D) 15

9. Simplify $\sqrt[3]{0.064}$?

A) $\frac{2}{5}$

B) 5

C) $\frac{5}{2}$

D) 2

10. Simplify $\sqrt{75} - \sqrt{125}$?

A) $5\sqrt{3} + 5\sqrt{5}$

B) $5\sqrt{3} - 5\sqrt{5}$

C) $3\sqrt{5} - 5\sqrt{5}$

D) $3\sqrt{5} + 5\sqrt{5}$

11. What is a possible solution for x in the following equation?

$$\frac{\sqrt{4^{3x+1}}}{\sqrt{4^{2x+1}}} = 2$$

A) 1

B) 2

C) 3

D) 4

12. Solve $\dfrac{2}{2-\sqrt{2}}$.

A) 4

B) $-\sqrt{2}$

C) $2 + \sqrt{2}$

D) $2 - \sqrt{2}$

13. Solve $\sqrt{(-25)^2} + \sqrt{4^2} - (-2)^3$?

A) 5

B) -5

C) 37

D) -37

16. Solve $\dfrac{\sqrt{50}}{\sqrt{150}} \times \sqrt{48}$

A) 4

B) $\sqrt{2}$

C) 8

D) $\sqrt{3}$

14. If $x\sqrt{0.25} = 1$, then find x?

A) 1

B) 2

C) 3

D) 4

15. If $a = \sqrt{3} + 1$ and $b = \sqrt{3} - 1$, then find $\dfrac{a}{b} - \dfrac{b}{a}$?

A) 2

B) $\sqrt{3}$

C) $2\sqrt{3}$

D) $4\sqrt{3}$

Test 9
Answer Key

1)	D
2)	C
3)	D
4)	C
5)	C
6)	C
7)	D
8)	B
9)	A
10)	B
11)	A
12)	C
13)	C
14)	B
15)	C
16)	A

Exponents, Radicals, Polynomials, and Rational Expressions

Test 9 Solutions

1. $P(x) + Q(x)$

$= 3x^3 - 7x^2 + 6 + 2x^3 + 2x^2 - 3$

$= 5x^3 - 5x^2 + 3$

Correct Answer : D

2. $P(x) . Q(x)$

$(2x - 1) . (2x^3 + 2x^2 - 1)$

$= 4x^4 + 4x^3 - 2x - 2x^3 - 2x^2 + 1$

$= 4x^4 + 2x^3 - 2x^2 - 2x + 1$

Correct Answer : C

3. $P(x - 1) + P(x + 1) = 2x^2 - 2x + 12$

$P(x) = ax^2 + bx + c$

$P(x - 1) = a(x - 1)^2 + b(x - 1) + c$

$P(x + 1) = a(x + 1)^2 + b(x + 1) + c$

$P(x - 1) + P(x + 1) = 2ax^2 + 2bx + 2(a + c)$

$2x^2 - 2x + 12 = 2ax^2 + 2bx + 2(a + c)$

$2ax^2 = 2x^2$, $a = 1$

$-2x = 2bx$, $b = -1$

$2(a + c) = 12$ $a + c = 6$, $c = 5$

$x^2 - x + 5$

Correct Answer : D

4. $\dfrac{x^2 - 16}{x + 4} = \dfrac{(x - 4) . (x + 4)}{(x + 4)}$

$= x - 4$

Correct Answer : C

5. $Q(x - 2) = 0$

$x - 2 = 0$

$x = 2$

$Q(3x) = 12x + 2$

$Q(3 . \frac{2}{3}) = 12 . \frac{2}{3} + 2$

$Q(2) = \frac{24}{3} + 2$

$Q(2) = 8 + 2 = 10$

Correct Answer : C

6. $x^2 + ax - 10 = (x - 1)(bx + c)$

$x^2 + ax - 10 = bx^2 + cx - bx - c$

$bx^2 = x^2$, $b = 1$

$-10 = -c$, $c = 10$

$b + c = 11$

Correct Answer : C

7. $P(-3) = P(-2) = P(6) = 0$

and $P(0) = 36$

$y = a(x + 3)(x + 2) . (x - 6)$

$P(0) = 36$

$36 = a(3) . (2)(-6)$

$36 = -36a$

$-1 = a$

$P(x) = -1(x + 3)(x + 2) . (x - 6)$

$P(1) = -1(1 + 3) . (1 + 2) . (1 - 6)$

$= -1 . (4) . (3)(-5)$

$P(1) = 60$

Correct Answer : D

8. $P(x - 1) = x^2 - 2x + 3$

   $P(4 - 1) = 4^2 - 2.4 + 3$

   $P(3) = 16 - 8 + 3$

   $ = 8 + 3$

   $ = 11$

   Correct Answer : B

9. Simplify $\sqrt[3]{0.064}$

   $= \sqrt[3]{\dfrac{64}{1000}}$

   $= \sqrt[3]{\left(\dfrac{4}{10}\right)^3}$

   $= \dfrac{4}{10} = \dfrac{2}{5}$

   Correct Answer : A

10. $\sqrt{75} - \sqrt{125}$

    $= 5\sqrt{3} - 5\sqrt{5}$

    Correct Answer : B

11. $\sqrt{\dfrac{4^{3x+1}}{4^{2x+1}}} = 2$

    $\sqrt{4^{3x+1-2x-1}} = 2$

    $\sqrt{4^x} = 2$

    $4^x = 4^1$

    $x = 1$

    Correct Answer : A

12. Solve $\dfrac{2}{2 - \sqrt{2}}$

    $= \dfrac{2(2 + \sqrt{2})}{(2 - \sqrt{2})(2 + \sqrt{2})}$

    $\pm \dfrac{4 + 2\sqrt{2}}{4 - 2} = \dfrac{4 + 2\sqrt{2}}{2} = 2 + \sqrt{2}$

    Correct Answer : C

13. $\sqrt{(-25)^2} + \sqrt{4^2} - (-2)^3$

    $= +25 + 4 - (-8)$

    $= +25 + 4 + 8$

    $= 25 + 12$

    $= 37$

    Correct Answer : C

14. $x\sqrt{0.25} = 1$

    $x\sqrt{\dfrac{25}{100}} = 1$

    $x.\dfrac{5}{10} = 1$

    $x.\dfrac{1}{2} = 1$

    $x = 2$

    Correct Answer : B

15. $a = \sqrt{3} + 1$

    $b = \sqrt{3} - 1$

    $\dfrac{\sqrt{3} + 1}{\sqrt{3} - 1} - \dfrac{\sqrt{3} - 1}{\sqrt{3} + 1}$

    $= \dfrac{(\sqrt{3} + 1).(\sqrt{3} + 1) - (\sqrt{3} - 1)(\sqrt{3} - 1)}{(\sqrt{3} - 1).(\sqrt{3} + 1)}$

    $= \dfrac{3 + 2\sqrt{3} + 1 - (3 - 2\sqrt{3} + 1)}{3 - 1}$

    $= \dfrac{\cancel{3} + 2\sqrt{3} + \cancel{1} - \cancel{3} + 2\sqrt{3} - \cancel{1}}{2}$

    $= \dfrac{4\sqrt{3}}{2} = 2\sqrt{3}$

    Correct Answer : C

16. $\dfrac{\sqrt{50}}{\sqrt{150}}.\sqrt{48}$

    $= \sqrt{\dfrac{50}{150}}.\sqrt{48}$

    $= \dfrac{1}{\sqrt{3}}.4\sqrt{3}$

    $= 4$

    Correct Answer : A

1. If x is a positive real number and $x - 2\sqrt{x} - 3 = 0$ then find $\dfrac{x}{x-1}$

    A) $\dfrac{1}{2}$

    B) $\dfrac{1}{4}$

    C) $\dfrac{9}{8}$

    D) $\dfrac{5}{3}$

2. If $x^2 + xy = 30$ and $y^2 + xy = 19$, then find $x + y$?

    A) 2

    B) 3

    C) 7

    D) 9

3. If $2x^2 - 3x + 2 = 0$, then find $x^2 + \dfrac{1}{x^2}$?

    A) 2

    B) 4

    C) $\dfrac{1}{2}$

    D) $\dfrac{1}{4}$

4. If $a - b = b - c = 6$, then find $a^2 + c^2 - 2b^2$?

    A) 72

    B) 48

    C) 24

    D) 12

5. If $x + y = 6$ and $x^2 + y^2 = 8$, then find $x^3 + y^3$?

    A) -6

    B) 12

    C) 36

    D) -36

6. If $x + \dfrac{1}{x} = 6$ then find $x^3 + \dfrac{1}{x^3}$?

    A) 72

    B) 108

    C) 198

    D) 216

7. Simplify $\dfrac{x^2y + xy^2 - xy}{x^2 + xy - x}$.

   A) x

   B) y

   C) 2xy

   D) -x

8. Simplify $\dfrac{x^2 - 6x - 16}{x^2 - 9x + 8}$.

   A) x - 2

   B) $\dfrac{x - 2}{x + 1}$

   C) x - 1

   D) $\dfrac{x + 2}{x - 1}$

9. Simplify $\dfrac{x^2 - 8x + 15}{x^2 - 9} \div \dfrac{x^2 - 4x - 5}{x^2 + 3x}$.

   A) x - 1

   B) $\dfrac{x}{x + 1}$

   C) x + 1

   D) $\dfrac{x + 1}{x - 1}$

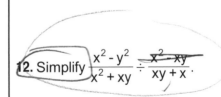

$\dfrac{(x-3)(x-5)}{(x+3)(x+3)} \cdot \dfrac{x(x+3)}{(x+1)(x-5)}$

$\dfrac{x}{x+1}$

10. If a+b=10 and axb=9 then which of following could be a-b?

   A) 4

   B) 8

   C) 12

   D) 16

11. Simplify $\dfrac{1}{x - 1} + \dfrac{1}{x + 1}$.

   A) x - 1

   B) x + 1

   C) 1

   D) $\dfrac{2x}{x^2 - 1}$

12. Simplify $\dfrac{x^2 - y^2}{x^2 + xy} \div \dfrac{x^2 - xy}{xy + x}$.

   A) x + 1

   B) y + 1

   C) $\dfrac{x + 1}{y}$

   D) $\dfrac{x + y}{x}$

13. If $x = 1 + \sqrt{3}$ and $y = 1 - \sqrt{3}$ then $x \times y$?

$\sqrt{3} + 1 \cdot 1 - \sqrt{3}$

$1 - 3$

A) -2

B) $\sqrt{3}$

C) $2\sqrt{3}$

D) 2

14. Which of the following is equal to $\dfrac{81^2 \times 9^3}{3^{10}}$?

A) 3^7

B) 3^4

C) 3^3

D) 3^0

15. For all values of x, which of the following is equal to $x^{\frac{6}{7}}$?

A) x^1

B) $\sqrt[6]{x^7}$

C) $\sqrt[7]{x^6}$

D) 1

16. Which of the following is equal to $3(x-4)(2x+1)$?

A) $6x^2 - 21x + 12$

B) $6x^2 + 21x + 12$

C) $6x^2 - 21x - 12$

D) $-6x^2 + 21x + 12$

17. Which of the following is equal to $ab\left(\dfrac{a}{b} - 2ab\right)$?

A) $a - 2b$

B) $b - 2a$

C) $a^2 + 2(ab)^2$

D) $a^2 - 2(ab)^2$

Test 10
Answer Key

1)	C
2)	C
3)	D
4)	A
5)	D
6)	C
7)	B
8)	D
9)	B
10)	B
11)	D
12)	D
13)	A
14)	B
15)	C
16)	C
17)	D

1. $x - 2\sqrt{x} - 3 = 0$
    $(x - 3)^2 = (2\sqrt{x})^2$
    $(x - 3)^2 = (\sqrt{4x})^2$
    $(x - 3)^2 = 4x$
    $x^2 - 6x + 9 = 4x$
    $x^2 - 6x - 4x + 9 = 0$
    $x^2 - 10x + 9 = 0$
    $x \quad x \qquad -9 \quad -1$
    $(x - 9) \cdot (x - 1) = 0$
    $x = 9 \quad$ or $\quad x = 1 (x \neq 1)$
    $\dfrac{x}{x - 1} = \dfrac{9}{8}$
    Correct Answer : C

2. $x^2 + xy = 30$
    $y^2 + xy = 19$

    $x^2 + 2xy + y^2 = 49$
    $(x + y)^2 = 49$
    $x + y = 7$
    Correct Answer : C

3. $2x^2 - 3x + 2 = 0$
    $\dfrac{2x^2}{2x} + \dfrac{2}{2x} = \dfrac{3x}{2x}$
    $x + \dfrac{1}{x} = \dfrac{3}{2}$
    $(x + \dfrac{1}{x})^2 = (\dfrac{3}{2})^2$
    $x^2 + \dfrac{1}{x^2} + 2 = \dfrac{9}{4}$
    $x^2 + \dfrac{1}{x^2} = \dfrac{9}{4} - 2 = \dfrac{1}{4}$
    Correct Answer : D

4. $a - b = b - c = 6$
    $a^2 + c^2 - 2b^2 = a^2 - b^2 + c^2 - b^2$
    $= (a - b) \cdot (a + b) + (c - b) \cdot (c + b)$
    $= 6(a + b) - 6(c + b)$
    $= 6a + 6b - 6c - 6b$
    $= 6a - 6c$
    $= 6(a - c)$
    $= 6 \times 12$
    $= 72$
    Correct Answer : A

5. $x + y = 6$
    $x^2 + y^2 = 8, \quad (x + y)^2 - 2xy = 8,$
    $36 - 2xy = 8, \quad xy = 14$
    $(x + y)^3 = 6^3$
    $x^3 + y^3 + 3xy(x + y) = 216$
    $x^3 + y^3 + 3(14) \cdot (6) = 216$
    $x^3 + y^3 + 252 = 216$
    $x^3 + y^3 = -36$
    Correct Answer : D

6. If $x + \dfrac{1}{x} = 6$, then
    $x^3 + \dfrac{1}{x^3} + 3(x + \dfrac{1}{x}) = 216$
    $x^3 + \dfrac{1}{x^3} + 3(6) = 216$
    $x^3 + \dfrac{1}{x^3} + 18 = 216$
    $x^3 + \dfrac{1}{x^3} = 198$
    Correct Answer : C

7. $\dfrac{x^2 y + xy^2 - xy}{x^2 + xy - x}$
    $= \dfrac{xy(x + y - 1)}{x(x + y - 1)}$
    $= \dfrac{xy}{x} = y$
    Correct Answer : B

8. $\dfrac{x^2 - 6x - 16}{x^2 - 9x + 8}$

   $= \dfrac{(x-8)(x+2)}{(x-8)(x-1)} = \dfrac{x+2}{x-1}$

   Correct Answer : D

9. $\dfrac{x^2 - 8x + 15}{x^2 - 9} \div \dfrac{x^2 - 4x - 5}{x^2 + 3x}$

   $\dfrac{(x-5)(x-3)}{(x-3)(x+3)} \times \dfrac{x(x+3)}{(x-5)(x+1)}$

   $= \dfrac{x}{x+1}$

   Correct Answer : B

10. $a + b = 10$

    $a \times b = 9$

    $a = 9 \quad b = 1$

    or

    $a = 1 \quad b = 9$

    $a - b = 9 - 1 = 8$

    Correct Answer : B

11. $\dfrac{1}{x-1} + \dfrac{1}{x+1} = \dfrac{x+1+x-1}{(x-1)(x+1)}$

    $= \dfrac{2x}{(x-1)(x+1)}$

    $= \dfrac{2x}{x^2 - 1}$

    Correct Answer : D

12. $\dfrac{x^2 - y^2}{x^2 + xy} \div \dfrac{x^2 - xy}{xy + x}$

    $\dfrac{(x-y)(x+y)}{x(x+y)} \times \dfrac{x(x+y)}{x(x-y)}$

    $\dfrac{x+y}{x}$

    Correct Answer : D

13. $x = 1 + \sqrt{3}$

    $y = 1 - \sqrt{3}$

    $x.y = (1 + \sqrt{3})(1 - \sqrt{3})$

    $\quad = 1 - 3$

    $\quad = -2$

    Correct Answer : A

14. $\dfrac{81^2 \cdot 9^3}{3^{10}} = \dfrac{(3^4)^2 \cdot (3^2)^3}{3^{10}}$

    $= \dfrac{3^8 \cdot 3^6}{3^{10}} = \dfrac{3^{14}}{3^{10}} = 3^4$

    Correct Answer : B

15. $x^{\frac{6}{7}} = \sqrt[7]{x^6}$

    Correct Answer : C

16. $3(x-4)(2x+1)$

    $3(2x^2 + x - 8x - 4)$

    $3(2x^2 - 7x - 4)$

    $6x^2 - 21x - 12$

    Correct Answer : C

17. $ab\left(\dfrac{a}{b} - 2ab\right)$

    $= \dfrac{a^2 b}{b} - 2a^2 b^2$

    $= a^2 - 2a^2 b^2$

    $= a^2 - 2(ab)^2$

    Correct Answer : D

1. Which of the following equations has a slope of $-\frac{1}{3}$?

A) $x+3y+4=0$

B) $3x+y+4=0$

C) $3x=y$

D) $x-3y+4=0$

2. Given $6x-ay+12=0$ if the slope of equation is $\frac{1}{3}$ then what is the value of a?

A) 9

B) $\frac{1}{9}$

C) 3

D) 18

3. How many solutions does the system of equations shown below have?

$2a = 3b + 6$
$4a - 6b = 12$

A) Zero

B) 1

C) 2

D) Many / Infinity

4. What is the value of k in the equation shown below?
$k - 10 + 4k = -4(k-2)$

A) 0

B) 1

C) -1

D) 2

5. If x>0 what is the value of x in $|2x-3|=7$?

A) -1

B) 1

C) 2

D) 5

6. If $x^2 + ax - 10 = (x - 1)(bx + c)$ then find a + c.

A) 9

B) 19

C) 18

D) 21

7. In the polynomial below, a is the constant. If the polynomial is the divisible by P(x+3) then find the value of a.

$$P(x) = x^3 + ax^2 - x - 6$$

A) 2

B) $\frac{10}{3}$

C) $\frac{3}{10}$

D) 5

8. Find y when x=6, if y varies directly as x and y=18 when x=3.

A) 6

B) 12

C) 24

D) 36

9. Which of the following is equal to $81x^2 - 4y^2 =$?

A) (9x-2y)(9x+2y)

B) 9x + 4y

C) 9x - 4y

D) (9x-2y)(9x-2y)

10. In ABC School 120 students favorite subjects is science out of 480 students. Find the percent of students whose favorite subject is not science?

A) 25%

B) 45%

C) 75%

D) 85%

11. If the equation $\frac{20a^2}{2a-1}$ is written in the form $m + \frac{5}{2a-1}$ which of the following gives M in terms of a?

A) 10a - 5

B) 10a + 5

C) 5a + 10

D) 5a - 10

12. If (x-3)(x+3)=m then in terms of m, what is the value of $x^2 + 9$?

A) 9 + m

B) 18 + m

C) m - 18

D) m - 9

13. If 4a - 3b = 22 and a = 7, then find b?

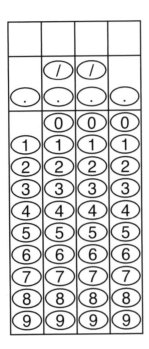

14. If $x^5 = -32$, then find x^3?

    A) 4

    B) -4

    C) 8

    D) -8

15. Last night, Tony spent $1\frac{1}{8}$ hours studying his math homework. John studied his math homework for $\frac{1}{4}$ as many hours as Tony did. How many hours did John spend doing his homework?

    A) $\frac{9}{32}$

    B) $4\frac{1}{2}$

    C) $\frac{3}{8}$

    D) $\frac{3}{16}$

16. If a ratio of $\frac{1}{3} : \frac{1}{b}$ is equal to $\frac{1}{18} : \frac{1}{12}$ what is the value of b?

    A) 9

    B) $\frac{9}{2}$

    C) $\frac{2}{9}$

    D) 2

17. If x is a positive integer (x > 1) and $x^2 - 3x + 2 = 0$, what is the value of x?

    A) 1

    B) 2

    C) 3

    D) 5

18. Leyla has $358.60 in her checking account. How much does she have in her checking account after she makes a deposit of $140.20 and a withdrawal of $178.60?

A) $320.20

B) $358.60

C) $140.20

D) $240.60

19. If the sum of three consecutive integers is 78 then what is the smallest number?

A) 15

B) 18

C) 21

D) 25 ✓

20. If $3^{2x-16} = 27^{x-6}$, then what is the value of x?

A) 1

B) -1

C) -2

D) 2 ✓

21. If $\frac{3x-1}{2x+1} = \frac{5}{3}$, then what is the value of x?

A) 2

B) -4

C) -8

D) 8

Mixed Review
Test 1
Answer Key

1)	A
2)	D
3)	D
4)	D
5)	D
6)	B
7)	B
8)	D
9)	A
10)	C
11)	B
12)	B
13)	2
14)	D
15)	A
16)	D
17)	B
18)	A
19)	D
20)	D
21)	C

1. $m = \dfrac{-1}{3}$ Only Choice A has same slope

Correct Answer : A

2. Slope of equation : $\dfrac{6}{a}$

$\dfrac{6}{a} = \dfrac{1}{3}$, then $a = 18$

Correct Answer : D

3. $2a = 3b + 6$
$4a - 6b = 12$

$\left. \begin{array}{l} 2a = 3b + 6 \\ 4a = 6b + 12 \end{array} \right\}$ $\quad \begin{array}{l} 2a = 3b + 6 \\ 2a = 3b + 6 \end{array}$

$3b + 6 = 3b + 6$
$\qquad 6 = 6$
$\qquad 0 = 0$

Correct Answer : D

4. $k - 10 + 4k = -4(k - 2)$
$\quad 5k - 10 = -4k + 8$
$\qquad\quad 9k = 18$
$\qquad\quad\, k = 2$

Correct Answer : D

5. If $x > 0$, then $|2x - 3| = 7$
$\quad 2x - 3 = 7$
$\qquad 2x = 10$
$\qquad\; x = 5$

Correct Answer : D

6. $x^2 + ax - 10 = (x - 1) . (bx + c)$

$x^2 + ax - 10 = bx^2 + cx - bx - c$

$x^2 = bx^2$, $b = 1$

$ax = x(c - b)$, $a = c - b$

$-10 = -c$, $c = 10$

$a = c - b$

$a = 10 - 1 = 9$

$a + c = 9 + 10 = 19$

Correct Answer : B

7. $P(x + 3) = 0 \qquad x + 3 = 0, x = -3$

$P(-3) = (-3)^3 + a(-3)^2 - (-3) - 6$

$0 = -27 + 9a + 3 - 6$

$0 = -30 + 9a, \qquad 9a = 30$

$a = \dfrac{30}{9} = \dfrac{10}{3}$

Correct Answer : B

8. Direct varies $y = kx$

$18 = 3.k$, $\quad k = 6$

$y = k.x$

$y = 6.6$

$y = 36$

Correct Answer : D

9. $81x^2 - 4y^2$

$= (9x - 2y) . (9x + 2y)$

Correct Answer : A

10. 480 - 120 = 360 students favorite subjects are not science.

$$\frac{360}{480} = \frac{36}{48} = \frac{6}{8} = \frac{3}{4}$$

= 75%

Correct Answer : C

11.

$$\begin{array}{r} 10a + 5 \\ 2a - 1 \overline{)20a^2} \\ -(20a^2 - 10a) \\ \hline 10a \\ -(10a - 5) \\ \hline 5 \end{array}$$

$$m + \frac{5}{2a-1} = 10a + 5 + \frac{5}{2a-1}$$

$$m = 10a + 5$$

Correct Answer : B

12. $(x - 3)(x + 3) = m$

$x^2 - 9 = m$

$x^2 - 9 + 18 = m + 18$

$x^2 + 9 = m + 18$

Correct Answer : B

13. $4a - 3b = 22$

$a = 7$

$4.7 - 3b = 22$

$28 - 3b = 22$

$28 - 22 = 3b$

$6 = 3b$

$2 = b$

Correct Answer : 2

14. $x^5 = -32$

$x^5 = -2^5$

$x = -2$

$x^3 = (-2)^3 = -8$

Correct Answer : D

15. Tony $= 1\frac{1}{8} = \frac{9}{8}$ hours

John $= \frac{9}{8} \times \frac{1}{4} = \frac{9}{32}$ hours

Correct Answer : A

16. $\frac{1}{3} : \frac{1}{b}$ and $\frac{1}{18} : \frac{1}{12}$

$$\frac{\frac{1}{3}}{\frac{1}{b}} = \frac{\frac{1}{18}}{\frac{1}{12}}$$

$$\frac{1}{3} \times \frac{b}{1} = \frac{1}{18} \times \frac{12}{1}$$

$$\frac{b}{3} = \frac{12}{18} \qquad 18b = 36, \quad b = 2$$

Correct Answer : D

17. If $x > 1$ $x^2 - 3x + 2 = 0$

$$\overset{x \quad x}{\wedge} \qquad \overset{-2 \quad -1}{\wedge}$$

$(x - 2) \cdot (x - 1) = 0$

$x = 2$ or $x = 1$

since $x > 1$ $x = 2$

Correct Answer : B

18. Checking Account

= $358.60 + $140.20 - $178.60

= $320.20

Correct Answer : A

19. The sum of three consecutive integers.

$$x + x + 1 + x + 2 = 78$$
$$3x + 3 = 78$$
$$3x = 75$$
$$x = 25$$

Correct Answer : D

20. $3^{2x-16} = 27^{x-6}$

$3^{2x-16} = 3^{3(x-6)}$

$3^{2x-16} = 3^{3x-18}$

$2x - 16 = 3x - 18$

$2 = x$

Correct Answer : D

21. $\dfrac{3x-1}{2x+1} = \dfrac{5}{3}$

$9x - 3 = 10x + 5$

$-8 = x$

Correct Answer : C

1. What is the solution to the equation below?

$$4\left(\frac{2}{x-3}\right) = \frac{x-3}{2}$$

A) $(7, -1)$

B) $(1, 7)$

C) $(1, -7)$

D) $(-1, -7)$

2. If $x = \dfrac{3^3}{\sqrt{81}}$, then find x?

A) 2

B) 3

C) $\dfrac{1}{3}$

D) 9

3. If $x^2 + xy = 63$ and $y^2 + xy = 1$, then find $x + y$?

A) 8

B) 12

C) 16

D) 20

4. Simplify $\dfrac{x^2 - 7x + 12}{x^2 - 9x + 20}$.

A) $\dfrac{x-3}{x-4}$

B) $\dfrac{x-3}{x-5}$

C) $\dfrac{x-4}{x-3}$

D) $\dfrac{x-5}{x-3}$

5. Which of the following is equal to $\dfrac{8^6 \times 32^3}{2^{10}}$?

A) 2^7

B) 2^{23}

C) 2^{15}

D) 2^{17}

6. A grocery store bought 45 pounds of tomatoes and sold $\dfrac{5}{9}$ on the same day. At the end of the day, how many pounds of tomatoes were left?

A) 25 pounds

B) 20 pounds

C) 45 pounds

D) 81 pounds

7. If y-4x=10 then, which of the following is equal to 4x?

A) y - 3

B) y - 6

C) y - 4

D) y - 10

8. If $-3x - 3 \leq -2(3x - 6)$ then which of the following is correct?

A) $x \geq 5$

B) $x \leq 5$

C) $x \geq -5$

D) $x \leq -5$

9. -7a + 3b = 18
   b - 3a = 4
   What is the value of a-2b?

A) 3

B) 13

C) 26

D) -23

10. If $x > 0$ and $2(3x - 6)^2 = 162$ then what is the value of x?

A) 3

B) 5

C) 10

D) 15

11. Which of the following is equal to $\left(x - \frac{1}{5}\right)\left(x + \frac{1}{5}\right)$?

A) $x^2 - 25$

B) $x^2 - \frac{1}{25}$

C) $x^2 - 2x - \frac{1}{25}$

D) $x^2 + 25$

12. If a, b, c are positive integers and $\frac{1}{ab} = \frac{1}{5}$, $\frac{1}{bc} = \frac{1}{4}$, and $\frac{1}{ac} = \frac{1}{20}$, then find $a \cdot b \cdot c$?

A) $\frac{1}{10}$

B) 10

C) -10

D) 20

13. If $-3x + 2y = -3$, then find $\dfrac{9^y}{27^x}$?

    A) -9

    B) $\dfrac{1}{9}$

    C) -27

    D) $\dfrac{1}{27}$

14. Which of following pairs of factors have the product $\dfrac{8}{56}$ in simplest form?

    A) $\dfrac{1}{4} \times \dfrac{8}{9}$

    B) $\dfrac{1}{8} \times \dfrac{1}{7}$

    C) $1 \times \dfrac{1}{7}$

    D) $\dfrac{4}{6} \times \dfrac{2}{9}$

15. The population of a city is increased from 112,000 to 168,000. Find the percentage of the increase.

    A) 20%

    B) 25%

    C) 50%

    D) 37.5%

Mixed Review
Test 2
Answer Key

1)	A
2)	B
3)	A
4)	B
5)	B
6)	B
7)	D
8)	B
9)	D
10)	B
11)	B
12)	D
13)	D
14)	C
15)	C

Mixed Review

Test 2 Solutions

1. $4\left(\dfrac{2}{x-3}\right) = \dfrac{x-3}{2}$

$\dfrac{8}{x-3} = \dfrac{x-3}{2}$

$x^2 - 6x + 9 = 16$

$x^2 - 6x - 7 = 0$

$(x-7)(x+1) = 0$

$x = 7 \quad \text{or} \quad x = -1$

Correct Answer : A

2. $x = \dfrac{3^3}{\sqrt{81}} = \dfrac{27}{9}$

$x = 3$

Correct Answer : B

3. $\quad x^2 + xy = 63$

$\underline{+\ y^2 + xy = 1}$

$\quad x^2 + 2xy + y^2 = 64$

$\quad (x+y)^2 = 64$

$\quad x + y = 8$

Correct Answer : A

4. $\dfrac{x^2 - 7x + 12}{x^2 - 9x + 20} = \dfrac{(x-3).(x-4)}{(x-4).(x-5)}$

$= \dfrac{x-3}{x-5}$

Correct Answer : B

5. $\dfrac{8^6 \times 32^3}{2^{10}} = \dfrac{(2^3)^6 \times (2^5)^3}{2^{10}}$

$= \dfrac{2^{18} \times 2^{15}}{2^{10}} = \dfrac{2^{33}}{2^{10}}$

$= 2^{23}$

Correct Answer : B

6. $45 \times \dfrac{5}{9} = 25$ Pounds sold

$45 - 25 = 20$ Pounds left

Correct Answer : B

7. $y = 4x + 10$

$y - 10 = 4x$

Correct Answer : D

8. $-3x - 3 \le -2(3x-6)$

$-3x - 3 \le -6x + 12$

$3x \le 15$

$x \le 5$

Correct Answer : B

9. $\quad -7a + 3b = 18$

$-3\big/\ b - 3a = 4$

$\quad -7a + 3b = 18$

$\underline{+\ -3b + 9a = -12}$

$\qquad 2a = 6$

$a = 3, \quad b = 13$

$a - 2b = 3 - 26 = -23$

Correct Answer : D

10. If $x > 0$, $2(3x-6)^2 = 162$

$(3x-6)^2 = 81$

$3x - 6 = 9$

$3x = 15$

$x = 5$

Correct Answer : B

11. $(x - \frac{1}{5})(x + \frac{1}{5}) = x^2 - \frac{1}{25}$

Correct Answer : B

12. $\frac{1}{ab} = \frac{1}{5}$, $\frac{1}{bc} = \frac{1}{4}$, $\frac{1}{ac} = \frac{1}{20}$

$\frac{1}{a^2b^2c^2} = \frac{1}{400}$

a.b.c = 20

Correct Answer : D

13. $-3x + 2y = -3$

$\frac{9^y}{27^x} = \frac{3^{2y}}{3^{3x}} = 3^{2y-3x}$

$= 3^{-3x+2y} = 3^{-3} = \frac{1}{27}$

Correct Answer : D

14. $\frac{8}{56} = \frac{1}{7}$

Correct Answer : C

15. 168 - 112 = 56 increase

$\frac{56}{112} = \frac{1}{2} = 50\%$

Correct Answer : C

1. 48 miles of road is paved $\frac{1}{3}$, and of the remaining road $\frac{1}{4}$ is paved. How much of the road is unfinished?

   A) 12
   B) 24
   C) 32
   D) 36

2. There are 24 students in Math class. If $\frac{2}{3}$ of the students in this class are male students, find the number of female students.

   A) 6
   B) 8
   C) 12
   D) 16

3. $P(x) = 5x^3 - 6x^2 + 3$ and $Q(x) = x^3 + 2x^2 + 7$ Then find $P(x) + Q(x) = ?$

   A) $6x^3 - 4x^2 + 10$
   B) $5x^3 - 4x^2 + 5$
   C) $6x^3 - 4x^2 - 10$
   D) $6x^3 - 8x^2 + 10$

4. Given x+ay-6=0 if the slope of equation is $\frac{1}{3}$, what is the value of a=?

   A) -3
   B) $\frac{1}{3}$
   C) 3
   D) $\frac{1}{6}$

5. Tony has 12 pencils and wants to give $\frac{3}{4}$ of them to a friend and keep the rest for himself. How many pencils would his friend get?

   A) 3
   B) 6
   C) 8
   D) 9

6. If $25 = 5(\frac{1}{x} - 10)$ then what is the value of x?

   A) 15
   B) $\frac{1}{15}$
   C) -15
   D) 20

7. If you have $3\frac{1}{4}$ cookies and you give each of your friends $\frac{1}{4}$ cookies, how many friends will get cookies?

A) $\frac{1}{13}$

B) $\frac{4}{13}$

C) 4

D) 13

8. $\frac{a-1}{6} = \frac{8}{a+1}$ Find the possible value of a.

A) 7

B) 6

C) 8

D) 5

9. $0.3\overline{)0.72}$ Find the quotient.

A) 0.24

B) 2.4

C) 24

D) 42

10. Vera visits a market to buy cucumbers and tomatoes to make a salad. Cucumbers cost $1.25 per pound and tomatoes cost $1.99 per pound .She has $15.92 to spend. If Vera buys only tomatoes, how many pounds of tomatoes will she buy?

A) 4

B) 6

C) 8

D) 12

11. If $a - b = 10$ and $a^2 - b^2 = 25$, what is the value of a?

A) -3.75

B) 3.75

C) 6.25

D) -6.25

12. If a and b are positive integers and $\sqrt{a} = b^2 = 4$, then which of following is the value of a-b?

A) 0

B) 1

C) 12

D) 14

13. If ab<0 and b>0 then which of following must be true?

    A) $a < 0$

    B) $b < 0$

    C) $a > 0$

    D) $a = 0$

14. If 2x+4y=7 then find y in term of x.

    A) $y = 2x - 7$

    B) $y = \dfrac{2x - 7}{4}$

    C) $y = \dfrac{7 - 2x}{4}$

    D) $y = 7 - 2x$

15. According to the formula $F = \dfrac{9}{5}C + 32$, it gives the temperature in degrees F for a given temperature in degrees Celsius C. Find the F when C=60 .

    A) $40°F$

    B) $80°F$

    C) $120°F$

    D) $140°F$

Mixed Review
Test 3
Answer Key

1)	B
2)	B
3)	A
4)	A
5)	D
6)	B
7)	D
8)	A
9)	B
10)	C
11)	C
12)	D
13)	A
14)	C
15)	D

1. $48 \times \dfrac{1}{3} = 16$ paved

48 - 16 = 32 left

$32 \times \dfrac{1}{4} = 8$ paved

32 - 8 = 24 left

Correct Answer : B

2. male $\longrightarrow$ 2x

female $\longrightarrow$ x

$3x = 24 \quad x = 8$

male $\longrightarrow$ 16

female $\longrightarrow$ 8

Correct Answer : B

3. $P(x) + Q(x)$

$= 5x^3 - 6x^2 + 3 + (x^3 + 2x^2 + 7)$

$= 6x^3 - 4x^2 + 10$

Correct Answer : A

4. Slope of equation : $\dfrac{-1}{a}$

$\dfrac{-1}{a} = \dfrac{1}{3}$, then a = - 3

Correct Answer : A

5. $12 \times \dfrac{3}{4} = 9$

Correct Answer : D

6. $25 = 5\left(\dfrac{1}{x} - 10\right)$

$5 = \dfrac{1}{x} - 10$

$\dfrac{1}{15} = x$

Correct Answer : B

7. $\dfrac{13}{4} \div \dfrac{1}{4}$

$\dfrac{13}{4} \times \dfrac{4}{1} = 13$

Correct Answer : D

8. $\dfrac{a - 1}{6} = \dfrac{8}{a + 1}$

$a^2 - 1 = 48$, $a^2 = 49$

$a = 7$ or $a = -7$

Correct Answer : A

9.

$$\begin{array}{r} 2.4 \\ 30\overline{)72} \\ \underline{60} \\ 120 \\ \underline{120} \\ 0 \end{array}$$

Correct Answer : B

10. $\dfrac{\$15.92}{\$1.99} = 8$ pounds

Correct Answer : C

11. $a - b = 10$

$a^2 - b^2 = 25$

$(a - b)(a + b) = 25$

$a + b = 2.5$

$a - b = 10$

$2a = 12.5, a = 6.25$

Correct Answer : C

12. $b = 2$

$a = 16$

$a - b = 16 - 2 = 14$

Correct Answer : D

13. if $ab < 0$ and $b > 0$

a must be negative

Correct Answer : A

14. $2x + 4y = 7$

$4y = 7 - 2x$

$y = \dfrac{7 - 2x}{4}$

Correct Answer : C

15. $F = \dfrac{9}{5}C + 32$

$F = \dfrac{9}{5} \times 60 + 32$

$F = 9 \times 12 + 32$

$F = 108 + 32$

$F = 140°F$

Correct Answer : D

FUNCTIONS

Function: If every element of A is paired with the elements of B at least once and A $\neq \emptyset$ and B $\neq \emptyset$, this correlation is called a function.

Function Notation

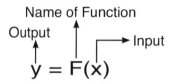

Example:

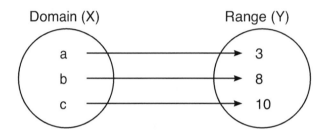

Not a Function: If the domain (x) is repeating, it's not a function. You do not need to check the range (y). It does not matter if range repeats.

Not a Function

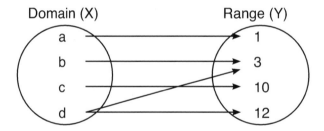

This is not a function because the domain (x) repeats.

Example:

Function

Domain (x)	Range (y)
1	3
2	5
3	12
4	15
5	20

Not a Function

Domain (x)	Range (y)
1	0
2	2
1	4
3	3
5	2

Example:

(a,1), (b,3), (c,5) is a function because the domains do not repeat.

(a,1), (b,3), (c,5), (a,10) is not a function because the domains repeat.

Types of graphs which are functions

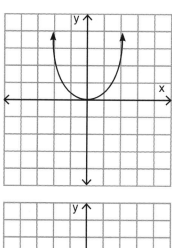
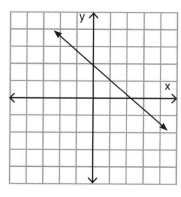
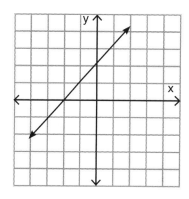

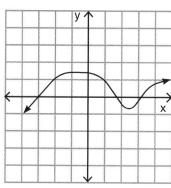
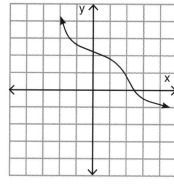

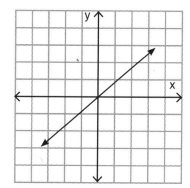
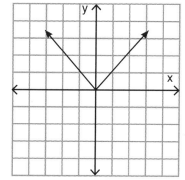
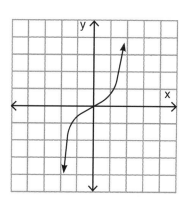

Types of graphs which cannot be functions

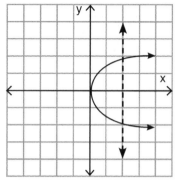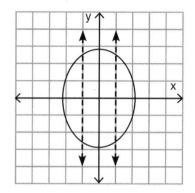

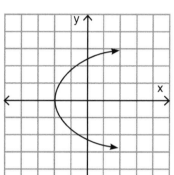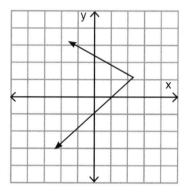

Function Operations

1) Addition: $(f+g)(x) = f(x) + g(x)$

Example: $f(x) = 4x-2$ and $g(x) = 2x-1$ then $(4x-2)+(2x-1) = 6x-3$

2) Subtraction: $(f-g)(x) = f(x) - g(x)$

Example: $f(x) = 4x-2$ and $g(x) = 2x-1$ then $(4x-2)-(2x-1) = 2x-1$

3) Multiplication: $(f \times g)(x) = f(x) \times g(x)$

Example: $f(x) = 4x - 2$ and $g(x) = 2x - 1$ then $(4x - 2) \times (2x - 1) = 8x^2 - 8x + 2$

4) Division: $(f \div g)(x) = f(x) \div g(x)$

Example: $f(x) = 4x - 2$ and $g(x) = 2x - 1$ then $(4x - 2) \div (2x - 1) = \dfrac{4x - 2}{2x - 1} = \dfrac{2(2x - 1)}{2x - 1} = 2$

Exponential Function

If $y = a^x$ and $\neq 0$ then y intercepts $(0, a)$

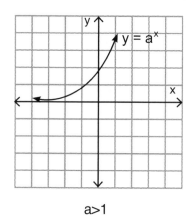

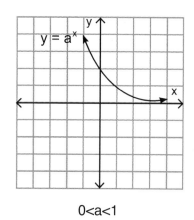

a>1   0<a<1

Absolute Value Function

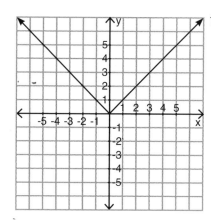

Quadratic Function

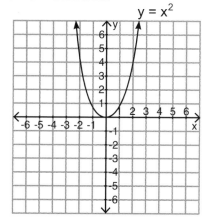

$$f(x) = ax^2 + bx + c$$

The roots of a quadratic function are:

$$x = \frac{-b \pm \sqrt{b^2 - 4ac}}{2a}$$

The term of $b^2 - 4ac$ is called the **discriminant.**

A) If $b^2 - 4ac < 0$ There are no real roots.
B) If $b^2 - 4ac = 0$ There is 1 real root.
C) If $b^2 - 4ac > 0$ There are 2 real roots.

Parabola Function

$f(x) = ax^2 + bx + c$

a) When a>0, parabola opens upward.

b) When a<0, the parabola opens downward.

Vertex form: $y = a(x - h)^2 + k$. The vertex of the parabola point is (h, k)

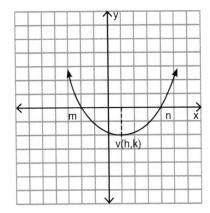

$$V(x) = a(x - h)^2 + k$$
$$h = \frac{m + n}{2} \text{ and } h = \frac{-b}{2a}$$

The Axis of Symmetry

$x = -\frac{b}{2a}$ This is also the x coordinate of the vertex of the parabola

Example: $f(x) = 2x^2 + 12x + 5$ solve and graph the quadratic equation.

Solution: $x = -\frac{b}{2a}$, then $x = \frac{-12}{4} = -3$, then $f(-3) = 2(-3)^2 + 12(-3) + 5 = -13$

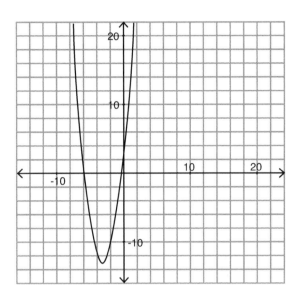

1. For the function below, m is a constant and f(3)=48. What is the value of f(6)?

$$f(x) = mx^2 + 18$$

A) 38
B) 120
C) 138
D) 150

(handwritten work):
$48 = m(3)^2 + 18$
$48 = m9 + 18$
$30 = m9$
$\frac{30}{9} = \frac{m9}{9}$
$\frac{10}{3} = m$

2. The linear function g(x) is shown in the table below. Which of following defines g(x)?

x	g(x)
1	15
2	17
3	19

A) 2x + 10
B) 2x + 13
C) 2x - 13
D) 2x + 5

3. What is the value of g(f(1)), when $f(x) = 2x^2 + 1$ and $g(x) = 3x^2 - 1$?

A) 6
B) 8
C) 26
D) 28

4. Suppose the function g(x), is defined by g(x)=2x-3m, where m is a constant. If g(3)+g(6)=48, what is the value of m?

A) 1
B) -1
C) 5
D) -5

(handwritten work):
$g(x) = 2x - 3m$
$2(3) - 3m + 2(6) - 3m = 48$
$6 - 3m + 12 - 3m = 48$
$18 - 6m = 48$
$-6m = 30$
$\frac{-6m}{-6} = \frac{30}{-6}$
$m = -5$

5. Suppose the function f(3)=8 and f(4)=12 and function g satisfies g(3)=6 and g(8)=16. What is the value of g(f(3))?

A) 3
B) 8
C) 12
D) 16

(handwritten): $f(3) = 8$ $g(8) = 16$

6. Which of the following could be the equation of the graph below?

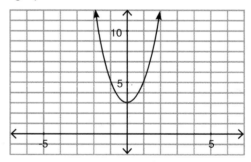

A) $y = x^2 + 3$
B) $y = 2x^2 + 3$
C) $y = -x^2 + 3$
D) $y = -2x^2 + 3$

-8+5 -3

7. If g(x)=4x+5, then what is the value of g(1)+g(-2)?

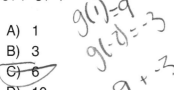

g(1)=9
g(-0)=-3
9 + -3

- A) 1
- B) 3
- C) 6
- D) 10

8. If g(x)=2x+7 and g(m)=17, then what is the value of m?

2m+7=17
2m=10
m=5

- A) -1
- B) 5
- C) 10
- D) 17

9. Let g(x)=6x+1. If g(m)=25 and g(n)=19, then what is m - n^2?

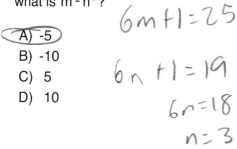

- A) -5
- B) -10
- C) 5
- D) 10

6m+1=25
6n+1=19
6n=18
n=3
4-9
6m=24
m=4

10. If g(x) = x^2 + 6 and g(2m) = 38, then what could be the value of m?

(2m)^2+6=38
2m(2m)+6=38
4m^2+6=38
4m^2=32
m^2=8
m=2√2

- A) 2
- B) 2√2
- C) √2
- D) - √2

11. If g(x + 1) = $\frac{2x-3}{3x+4}$, then find g(2)?

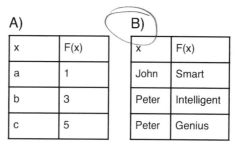

g(1+1) = $\frac{2-3}{3+4}$
g(1)= $-\frac{1}{7}$

- A) 7
- B) -$\frac{1}{7}$
- C) $\frac{1}{7}$
- D) -3

12. Which of the following tables does not represent a function?

A)

x	F(x)
a	1
b	3
c	5

B)

x	F(x)
John	Smart
Peter	Intelligent
Peter	Genius

C)

x	F(x)
e	1
l	3
m	1

D)

x	F(x)
m	4
n	5
k	4

13. Which of the following graphs represent a function?

A)

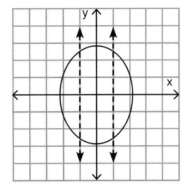

B)

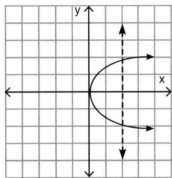

C)

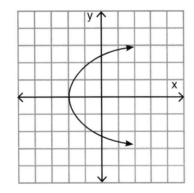

D)

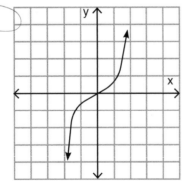

14. Determine which of the relations below are functions.

    A) (1,2),(3,4),(4,6),(3,7)
    B) (a,2),(b,4),(c,6),(b,7)
    C) (m,2),(n,4),(k,6),(m,7)
    D) (1,2),(3,4),(7,8),(10,4)

15. Find the domain of the inverse in the relation below.

$$\{(2,3),(4,6),(7,9),(10,12)\}$$

    A) (2,4,7,10)
    B) (3,6,9,12)
    C) No inverse of relation
    D) (2,3,4,6)

16. What is the range of the function $y = x^2 + 6$?

    A) $y \geq 6$
    B) $y \leq 6$
    C) All real numbers
    D) 0

17. If g(x)=2x-3, then find $g^{-1}(x)$?

A) $g^{-1}(x) = \dfrac{x+2}{3}$

B) $g^{-1}(x) = \dfrac{x-1}{3}$

C) $g^{-1}(x) = \dfrac{x+1}{3}$

D) $g^{-1}(x) = \dfrac{x+3}{2}$

18. $g(x) = \dfrac{x-1}{2}$, which of the following is equal to $g^{-1}(x)$?

A) $g^{-1}(x) = 2x + 1$

B) $g^{-1}(x) = 2x - 1$

C) $g^{-1}(x) = 2x$

D) $g^{-1}(x) = 3$

19. $f(x)=\begin{cases} -2x + 3, & x < 0 \\ x^2 + 5, & x \geq 0 \end{cases}$

From the above function find f(0)+f(-2).

A) 6
B) 12
C) -6
D) -12

Test 11
Answer Key

1)	C
2)	B
3)	C
4)	D
5)	D
6)	B
7)	C
8)	B
9)	A
10)	B
11)	B
12)	B
13)	D
14)	D
15)	B
16)	A
17)	D
18)	A
19)	B

1. $f(3) = 48$

$f(3) = m \cdot 3^2 + 18$

$48 = 9m + 18$

$\dfrac{10}{3} = m$

$f(x) = \dfrac{10}{3}x^2 + 18$

$f(6) = \dfrac{10}{3} \times 36 + 18 = 138$

Correct Answer : C

2. From table

$\text{slope} = \dfrac{17 - 15}{2 - 1} = 2$

$y = mx + b$

$y = 2x + b, \quad (1, 15)$

$15 = 2 \cdot 1 + b$

$13 = b$

$y = 2x + 13$

Correct Answer : B

3. $f(x) = 2x^2 + 1$

$g(x) = 3x^2 - 1$

$f(1) = 2 \cdot 1^2 + 1 = 3$

$g(3) = 3 \cdot 3^2 - 1 = 27 - 1 = 26$

Correct Answer : C

4. $g(3) = 2.3 - 3m$

$\quad\ = 6 - 3m$

$g(6) = 2 \cdot 6 - 3m = 12 - 3m$

$g(3) + g(6) = 48$

$6 - 3m + 12 - 3m = 48$

$18 - 6m = 48$

$-6m = 30$

$m = -5$

Correct Answer : D

5. $f(3) = 8$

$g(8) = 16$

Correct Answer : D

6. $y = a(x - h)^2 + k$

$V(h, k) = (0, 3)$

$y = a(x - 0)^2 + 3$

$y = ax^2 + 3$

use $(1, 5)$ from graph

$5 = a + 3$

$2 = a$

$f(x) = 2x^2 + 3$

Correct Answer : B

7. $g(1) = 4 \cdot 1 + 5 = 9$

$g(-2) = 4 \cdot (-2) + 5 = -8 + 5 = -3$

$g(1) + g(-2) = 9 - 3 = 6$

Correct Answer : C

8. $g(x) = 2x + 7$

$g(m) = 17$

$2m + 7 = 17$

$2m = 10$

$m = 5$

Correct Answer : B

9. $g(x) = 6x + 1$

$g(m) = 25$

$g(n) = 19$

$6m + 1 = 25, \quad m = 4$

$6n + 1 = 19, \quad n = 3$

$m - n^2 = 4 - 9 = -5$

Correct Answer : A

10. $g(x) = x^2 + 6$

$g(2m) = 38$

$(2m)^2 + 6 = 38$

$(2m)^2 = 32$

$4m^2 = 32$

$m^2 = 8$

$m = \pm 2\sqrt{2}$

Correct Answer : B

11. $g(x + 1) = \dfrac{2x - 3}{3x + 4}$

$g(1 + 1) = \dfrac{2 \cdot 1 - 3}{3 \cdot 1 + 4}$

$g(2) = \dfrac{2 - 3}{3 + 4} = \dfrac{-1}{7}$

Correct Answer : B

12. Choice B is not a fuction because domain is repeating.

Correct Answer : B

13. Choice D is only a function because in all other graphs x (domain) is repeating.

Correct Answer : D

14. Choice D is a function. The others are not functions because domian is repeating.

Corrnect Answer : D

15. $(2,3)(4,6),(7,9)(10,12)$

Domain = $(2,4,7,10)$

Range = $(3,6,9,12)$

Inverse of Domain = $(3,6,9,12)$

Correct Answer : B

16. $y = x^2 + 6$

$y - 6 = x^2$

$\sqrt{y - 6} = x$

change x to y

$y = \sqrt{x - 6}$

domain is all real numbers.

Range is $y \geq 6$

Correct Answer : A

17. $g(x) = 2x - 3$

$g^{-1}(x) = ?$

$y = 2x - 3$

$y + 3 = 2x$

$\dfrac{y + 3}{2} = x$

change x to y

$\dfrac{x + 3}{2} = y \qquad \dfrac{x + 3}{2} = g^{-1}(x)$

Correct Answer : D

18. $g(x) = \dfrac{x - 1}{2}, \qquad y = \dfrac{x - 1}{2}$

$2y = x - 1$

$2y + 1 = x$

change x to y

$2x + 1 = g^{-1}(x)$

Correct Answer : A

19. $f(0) = 0^2 + 5 = 5$

$f(-2) = -2 \cdot (-2) + 3 = 7$

$f(0) + f(-2) = 5 + 7 = 12$

Correct Amswer : B

2 - 4
-2
1-34+2
3 - 0
-3.0

1. Which of the following graphs is not a function?

A)

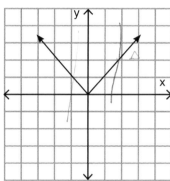

B)

C)

D)

2. f(x)=|x-3|-|2x| then, find f(-1)+f(0)+f(1).

A) 0
B) 3
C) 5
D) 7

6+3+(-2)
9 - 2
7

3. If $f(x) = 2^{x+1}$ then find $f(a + b - 2)$.

A) $\dfrac{2^a \times 2^b}{2}$

B) $2^a \times 2^b$

C) 2

D) 4

4. If $f(x) = x^3$ and $g(x) = 3x - 2$ then find $g(f(3))$.

A) 69
B) 79
C) 89
D) 99

5. If $f\left(\dfrac{a-1}{a+1}\right) = a^2 + 2a + 3$, then find $f(2)$.

A) 3
B) -3
C) 6
D) -6

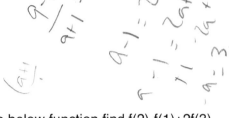

6. For the below function find $f(2)-f(1)+2f(3)$.

x	f(x)
1	7
2	8
3	9
4	10
5	11
6	12

A) 19
B) 26
C) -19
D) -26

7. If $g(4) = 7$ and $g(x+3) = x \times g(x) - 6$ then find $g(10)$.

A) 48
B) 138
C) 148
D) 158

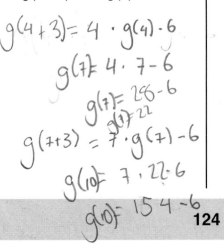

8. Below is the function $y=f(x)$. Find $f(-6)+f(4)$.

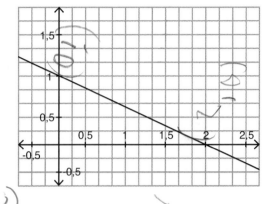

A) 2
B) 3
C) -3
D) -2

9. If $f(2x + 1) = \sqrt{x^3 + 8}$, then find $f(5)$.

A) 2
B) 4
C) 8
D) 16

10. $f(x)=\begin{cases} -2x + 3, & x < 0 \\ x^2 + 5, & x \geq 0 \end{cases}$

From the above function find $f(4)+f(-3)$.

A) 15
B) 30
C) -15
D) -30

11. If $f(x + 1) = \dfrac{2x - 3}{4}$, then find $f^{-1}(x)$?

   A) $\dfrac{x - 1}{5}$

   B) $\dfrac{3x - 5}{2}$

   C) $\dfrac{2x - 5}{3}$

   D) $\dfrac{4x + 5}{2}$

12. If $f(x)$ is a linear function and $f(3)=12$ and $f(-2)=2$, then find $f(-4)$.

   A) 2

   B) 4

   C) -2

   D) -4

(handwritten work:)
$f(x) = 2x + 6$
$f(x) = mx + b$
$12 = 3m + b$
$2 = -2m + b$
$10 = 5m$ → $\dfrac{10}{5} = \dfrac{5m}{5}$
$2 = m$
$12 = 3(-2) + b$
$6 = b$
$f(4) = 2(-4) + 6$
$-8 + 6 = -2$

13. $f(x) = \{(1, -2), (3, 2), (3, 5), (6, 4)\}$,
Find $f^{-1}(2) + f(1) + f^{-1}(4)$.

   A) 3

   B) -3

   C) -2

   D) 7

14. Which of the following graphs show $f(x) = x^2$?

A)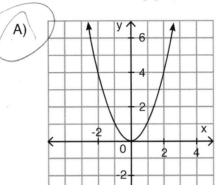

B)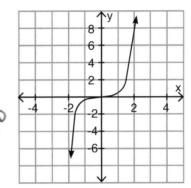

C)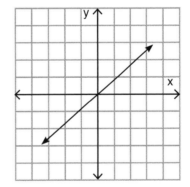

D)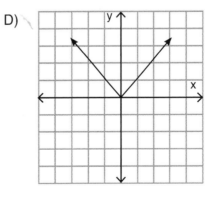

15. Which of the following graphs show f(x)=6?

A)

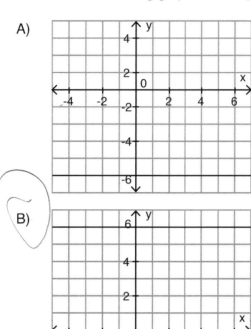

B)

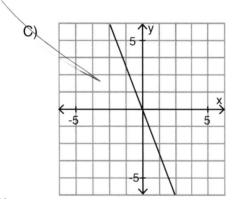

C)

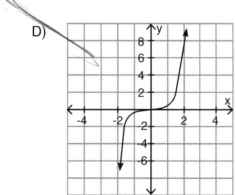

D)

16. If $g(x) = \dfrac{x+3}{2}$ and $f(x) = g(x) + 6$, then what is $f(9)$?

A) 6

B) 12

C) -6

D) -3

$f(a) = \dfrac{9+3}{2}$

$\dfrac{12}{2}$

$g(x) = 6$

$g(x) + 6 = 6 + 6$

Test 12
Answer Key

1)	D
2)	C
3)	A
4)	B
5)	C
6)	A
7)	C
8)	B
9)	B
10)	B
11)	D
12)	C
13)	D
14)	A
15)	B
16)	B

Functions

1. Choice D is not a function because domain is repeating.

   Correct Answer : D

2. $f(-1) = |-1 - 3| - |2(-1)|$

   $\quad\quad = |-4| - |-2|$

   $\quad\quad = 4 - 2$

   $\quad\quad = 2$

   $f(0) = |0 - 3| - |2.0|$

   $\quad\quad = 3 - 0 = 3$

   $f(1) = |1 - 3| - |2.1|$

   $\quad\quad = 2 - 2 = 0$

   $f(-1) + f(0) + f(1) = 2 + 3 + 0$

   $\quad\quad\quad\quad\quad\quad = 5$

   Correct Answer : C

3. $f(x) = 2^{x+1}$

   $f(a + b - 2) = 2^{a+b-2+1}$

   $\quad\quad\quad\quad = 2^{a+b-1}$

   $\quad\quad\quad\quad = \dfrac{2^{a+b}}{2} = \dfrac{2^a \times 2^b}{2}$

   Correct Answer : A

4. $f(x) = x^3$

   $g(x) = 3x - 2$

   $f(3) = 3^3 = 27$

   $g(27) = 3.27 - 2 = 81 - 2$

   $\quad\quad\quad = 79$

   Correct Answer : B

5. $f\left(\dfrac{a-1}{a+1}\right) = a^2 + 2a + 3$

   $a = -3$

   $f\left(\dfrac{-3-1}{-3+1}\right) = (-3)^2 + 2(-3) + 3$

   $f\left(\dfrac{-4}{-2}\right) = 9 - 6 + 3$

   $f(2) = 6$

   Correct Answer : C

6. From table

   $f(2) = 8$

   $f(1) = 7$

   $f(3) = 9$

   $= f(2) - f(1) + 2f(3)$

   $= 8 - 7 + 2.9$

   $= 8 - 7 + 18$

   $= 19$

   Correct Answer : A

7. $g(4) = 7$

   $g(x + 3) = x.g(x) - 6$

   when $x = 4$

   $g(4 + 3) = 4.g(4) - 6$

   $g(7) = 4.7 - 6$

   $g(7) = 28 - 6$

   $g(7) = 22$

   when $x = 7$

   $g(7 + 3) = 7.g(7) - 6$

   $g(10) = 7.22. - 6$

   $g(10) = 154 - 6$

   $g(10) = 148$

   Correct Answer : C

Functions

8. From graph 2

exact points $(0, 1)$ and $(2, 0)$

$m = \dfrac{y_2 - y_1}{x_2 - x_1} = \dfrac{-1}{2}$

$y = mx + b$

$y = \dfrac{-1}{2}x + 1$

$f(-6) = \dfrac{-1}{2} \cdot (-6) + 1 = 4$

$f(4) = \dfrac{-1}{2} \cdot (4) + 1 = -1$

Correct Answer : B

9. $f(2x + 1) = \sqrt{x^3 + 8}$

$x = 2, \qquad f(5) = ?$

$f(2 \cdot 2 + 1) = \sqrt{2^3 + 8}$

$f(5) = \sqrt{16}$

$f(5) = 4$

Correct Answer : B

10. $f(4) = 4^2 + 5 = 16 + 5$

$\qquad\qquad = 21$

$f(-3) = -2 \cdot (-3) + 3 = +6 + 3 = 9$

$f(4) + f(-3) = 21 + 9$

$\qquad\qquad = 30$

Correct Answer : B

11. $f(x + 1) = \dfrac{2x - 3}{4}$

$f(x - 1 + 1) = \dfrac{2(x - 1) - 3}{4}$

$f(x) = \dfrac{2x - 2 - 3}{4} = \dfrac{2x - 5}{4}$

$y = \dfrac{2x - 5}{4}, \qquad 2x - 5 = 4y$

$\qquad\qquad\qquad 2x = 4y + 5$

$x = \dfrac{4y + 5}{2} \qquad$ change x to y

$y = f^{-1}(x) = \dfrac{4x + 5}{2}$

Correct Answer : D

12. $3m + b = 12$

$-2m + b = 2$

$m = 2, \ b = 6$

$y = mx + b$

$f(x) = 2x + 6$

$f(-4) = 2 \cdot (-4) + 6 = -8 + 6 = -2$

Correct Answer : C

13. $f^{-1}(2) = 3$

$f^{-1}(4) = 6$

$f(1) = -2$

$= f^{-1}(2) + f^{-1}(4) + f(1)$

$= 3 + 6 - 2 = 7$

Correct Answer : D

14. Choice A is an exponential function. Choice C and D are linear functions.

Correct Answer : A

15. $f(x) = 6$

From the graph only choice B can be connect.

Correct Answer : B

16. $g(x) = \dfrac{x + 3}{2}$

$f(x) = g(x) + 6$

$f(9) = g(9) + 6$

$g(9) = \dfrac{9 + 3}{2} = \dfrac{12}{2} = 6$

$f(9) = g(9) + 6$

$\qquad = 6 + 6$

$f(9) = 12$

Correct Answer : B

Functions

1. If $f(x) = mx^2 - 6x - n + 6$ and the vertex point V is $(-3, 4)$ find m + n?

   A) 10
   B) 20
   C) 38
   D) 40

2. If $f(x) = x^2 - 2mx + n$ and the vertex point V is $(3, 2)$ find m + n?

   A) 6
   B) 9
   C) 11
   D) 14

3. Which equation could be the answer to the graphed parabola?

   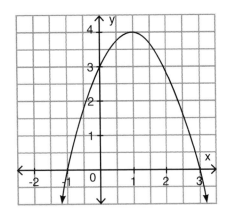

   A) $f(x) = -x^2 + 2x + 3$

   B) $f(x) = x^2 + 2x + 3$

   C) $f(x) = -x^2 - 2x - 3$

   D) $f(x) = -2x^2 + 2x - 5$

4. What is the vertex of the parabola $y = -2x^2 + 4x - 6$?

   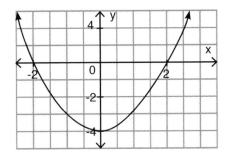

   A) $f(x) = -2(x-1)^2 - 4$

   B) $f(x) = 2(x-2)^2 - 3$

   C) $f(x) = -2(x-2)^2 + 4$

   D) $f(x) = 3(x-1)^2 - 6$

5. From the following parabola functions, what is the vertex point of V (h,k)?

   A) (0,2)
   B) (0,-4)
   C) (0,4)
   D) (0,-2)

6. If $f(x) = x^2 - 6x + 4$, what is the vertex point V(h,k)?

   A) (3,5)
   B) (3,-5)
   C) (4,-3)
   D) (-4,3)

7. If $y = x^{\frac{1}{3}}$, $y > 0$ and $x > 0$, which of the following equations gives x in terms of y?

A) $x = y$

B) $x = y^2$

C) $x = y^3$

D) $x = \dfrac{1}{y^3}$

8. The line shown could be the graph of which equation?

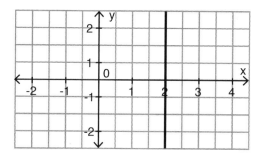

A) $x + y - 2 = 0$
B) $x = y$
C) $x + y - 2 = x$
D) $x + y - 2 = y$

9. Which of the following equations is the solution to the quadratic equation $x^2 + 6x - 16 = 0$?

A) $x = 2$, $x = -8$
B) $x = 3$, $x = -8$
C) $x = 8$, $x = -2$
D) $x = 0$, $x = -8$

10. Which of the following tables does not represent linear relations?

 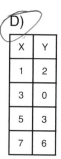

A)		B)		C)		D)	
X	Y	X	Y	X	Y	X	Y
-1	0	-1	-3	2	6	1	2
2	2	-2	-6	4	12	3	0
3	4	-3	-9	6	18	5	3
4	6	-4	-12	8	24	7	6

11. Which of the following parabola functions could represent the graph in the picture?

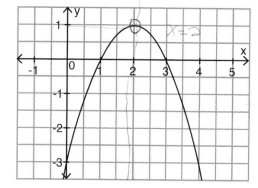

A) $f(x) = -x^2 + 4x + 3$

B) $f(x) = -x^2 - 4x + 3$

C) $f(x) = x^2 + 4x - 3$

D) $f(x) = -x^2 + 4x - 3$

12. If $x^2 + 12x - 45 = 0$ and $x > 0$, what is the value of x?

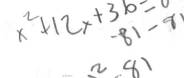
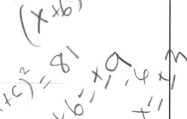

A) 3

B) -15

C) 9

D) 12

13. Solve for x in the equation below:

$x^2 + 4x - 12 = 0$

A) x = 2, x = -6

B) x = 3, x = -6

C) x = -2, x = -6

D) x = 2, x = 6

14. Solve for x in the equation below:

$x^2 + 4x - 8 = 0$

A) $x = -2 \pm 2\sqrt{3}$

B) $x = 2 \pm 2\sqrt{3}$

C) $x = 2 + \sqrt{3}$

D) $x = 2 - \sqrt{3}$

15. The difference between a number and its cube is 0. What is the number?

A) 1

B) 2

C) 3

D) 4

16. If $x^2 - 8x + 16 = 0$ and $x \cdot m = \dfrac{4}{3}$. Find the value of m.

A) $\dfrac{1}{4}$

B) 3

C) $\dfrac{1}{3}$

D) $\dfrac{3}{4}$

17. Which of the following is a root of the function

$f(x) = x^2 - 3x - \dfrac{27}{4} = 0$?

A) $\dfrac{2}{3}$

B) $-\dfrac{3}{2}$

C) 3

D) -2

Grid Questions

18. Complete the table of values to graph each function.

$f(x) = x^2 + 4x - 12$

x	0	1	2	3	4
f(x)	−12	−7			

Answer :...

19. If 4 is one of the solutions of the equation $x^2 - 4ax - 12 = 0$, what is the value of a?

Answer :...

20. If $x^2 + 12x - 13 = 0$ and $x < 0$, what is the value of $x + 10$?

Answer :...

Test 13
Answer Key

1)	A
2)	D
3)	A
4)	A
5)	B
6)	B
7)	C
8)	D
9)	A
10)	D
11)	D
12)	A
13)	A
14)	A
15)	A
16)	C
17)	B

18)

x	0	1	2	3	4
f(x)	-12	-7	0	9	20

19)	a = 0.25
20)	-3

1. $V(h,k) = (-3, 4)$

$4 = 9m + 18 - n + 6$

$-20 = 9m - n$

$x = \dfrac{-b}{2a}$, $-3 = \dfrac{-(-6)}{2m}$, $m = -1$

$-20 = 9(-1) - n$

$n = 11$

$m + n = 11 - 1 = 10$

Correct Answer : A

2. $F(x) = x^2 - 2mx + n$

$V(3, 2)$

$2 = 3^2 - 2m.2 + n$

$2 = 9 - 4m + n$

$-7 = -6m + n$

$x = \dfrac{-b}{2a} = \dfrac{-(-2m)}{2.1} = \dfrac{2m}{2}$

$3 = \dfrac{2m}{2}$, $m = 3$

$-7 = -6m + n$

$-7 = -6.3 + n$

$11 = n$

$m + n = 11 + 3 = 14$

Correct Answer : D

3. From the graph the Vertex Point is $(1, 4)$.

$V(x) = a(x - h)^2 + k$

$V(x) = a(x - 1)^2 + 4$

From the graph you can use $(0, 3)$ to find a.

$3 = a(0 - 1)^2 + 4$

$3 = a + 4$, $a = -1$

$V(x) = -1(x - 1)^2 + 4$

$V(x) = -x^2 + 2x + 3$

Correct Answer : A

4. $V(x) = -2x^2 + 4x - 6$

$V(x) = a(x - h)^2 + k$

$V(x) = -2(x - 1)^2 - 4$

Correct Answer : A

5. From the graph the Vertex Point is $(0, -4)$

Correct Answer : B

6. $F(x) = x^2 - 6x + 4$

Vertex Form

$V(x) = a(x - h) + k$

$V(x) = (x - 3)^2 - 9 + 4$

$V(x) = (x - 3)^2 - 5$

$V(h, k) = (3, -5)$

Correct Answer : B

7. $y = x^{\frac{1}{3}}$

$(y)^3 = (\sqrt[3]{x})^3$

$y^3 = x$

Correct Answer : C

8. Since $x = 2$ in the graph, only choice D can be correct.

Correct Answer : D

9. $x^2 + 6x - 16 = 0$

   $x \cdot x \quad -2 \cdot 8$

   $(x - 2) \cdot (x + 8) = 0$

   $x = 2 \quad or \quad x = -8$

   Correct Answer : A

10. Choice D does not represent linear relation because the domain is repeating.

   Correct Answer : D

11. From the graph the Vertex Point is $(2, 1)$.

   $V(x) = a(x - h)^2 + k$

   $V(x) = a(x - 2)^2 + 1$

   From the graph you can use $(0, -3)$

   $-3 = a(a - 2)^2 + 1$

   $-3 = 4a + 1$

   $-4 = 4a, \quad a = -1$

   $V(x) = -(x - 2)^2 + 1$

   $V(x) = -(x^2 - 4x + 4) + 1$

   $= -x^2 + 4x - 4 + 1$

   $= -x^2 + 4x - 3$

   Correct Answer : D

12. $x^2 + 12x - 45 = 0$

   $x^2 + 12x = 45$

   $(x + 6)^2 - 36 = 45$

   $(x + 6)^2 = 81$

   $x + 6 = \mp 9$

   $x + 6 = 9, \quad x = 3$

   $x + 6 = -9, \quad x = -15$

   since $x > 0, x = 3$

   Correct Answer : A

13. $x^2 + 4x - 12 = 0$

   $(x + 2)^2 - 4 = 12$

   $(x + 2)^2 = 16$

   $x + 2 = \mp 4$

   $x + 2 = 4 \quad or \quad x + 2 = -4$

   $x = 2 \quad or \quad x = -6$

   Correct Answer : A

14. $x^2 + 4x - 8 = 0$

   $x^2 + 4x = 8$

   $(x + 2)^2 - 4 = 8$

   $(x + 2)^2 = 12$

   $x + 2 = \mp \sqrt{12}$

   $x + 2 = \mp 2\sqrt{3}$

   $x + 2 = 2\sqrt{3} \quad or \quad x + 2 = -2\sqrt{3}$

   $x = 2\sqrt{3} - 2 \quad or \quad x = -2\sqrt{3} - 2$

   Correct Answer : A

15. $a^3 - a = 0$

   $a(a^2 - 1) = 0$

   $a(a - 1) \cdot (a + 1) = 0$

   $a = 0, \quad a = 1, \quad a = -1$

   Correct Answer : A

16. $x^2 - 8x + 16 = 0$

   $(x - 4)^2 = 0$

   $x = 4$

   $x \cdot m = \dfrac{4}{3}$

   $4m = \dfrac{4}{3}$

   $m = \dfrac{1}{3}$

   Correct Answer : C

17. $F(x) = x^2 - 3x - \frac{27}{4} = 0$

$(x - \frac{9}{2})(x + \frac{3}{2}) = 0$

$x = \frac{9}{2}$ or $x = \frac{-3}{2}$

Correct Answer : B

18. $F(x) = x^2 + 4x - 12$

$F(0) = -12$

$F(1) = 1 + 4 - 12 = -7$

$F(2) = 2^2 + 4.2 - 12 = 0$

$F(3) = 3^2 + 4.3 - 12 = 9$

$F(4) = 4^2 + 4.4 - 12 = 20$

Correct Answer : - 12, - 7, 0, 9, 20

19. $x^2 - 4ax - 12 = 0$

If 4 is one of the solutions

$4^2 - 4a.4 - 12 = 0$

$16 - 16a - 12 = 0$

$16a = 4$

$a = \frac{1}{4} = 0.25$

Correct Answer : 0.25

20. $x^2 + 12x - 13 = 0$

$(x + 13).(x - 1) = 0$

$x = -13$ or $x = 1$

since $x < 0$

$x + 10 = -13 + 10$

$= -3$

Correct Answer : - 3

Solving for Variables

1. If $a(b+c)=d$, solve for c in terms of a,b,d.

   A) $\frac{d}{a}-b$

   B) $ab-d$

   C) $\frac{b}{d}-a$

   D) $a-bd$

2. The area of the trapezoid is $A = \frac{(b_1 + b_2)h}{2}$. What is the height in terms of the base and the area.

   A) $\frac{A}{b_1 + b_2}$

   B) $\frac{2A}{b_1 + b_2}$

   C) $\frac{b_1 + b_2}{A}$

   D) $A(b_1 + b_2)$

3. $V = \pi r^2 h$ find r in terms of π, h and V.

   A) $v \times \pi \times h$

   B) $\frac{v}{\pi h}$

   C) $\sqrt{\frac{v}{\pi h}}$

   D) $\sqrt{\frac{\pi h}{v}}$

4. $\frac{1}{a} = \frac{1}{b} + \frac{1}{c}$ Find b in terms of a and c.

   A) $b = \frac{ac}{c-a}$

   B) $b = \frac{ac}{a-c}$

   C) $b = ac$

   D) $b = \frac{1}{c-a}$

5. If $2x-3y=10$, find x in terms of y.

   A) $\frac{10-3y}{2}$

   B) $\frac{10+3y}{2}$

   C) $\frac{5-3y}{2}$

   D) $10-3y$

6. The perimeter of a rectangle is $P=2L+2W$. What is the width in terms of the length and perimeter?

   A) $\frac{P}{2}+L$

   B) $\frac{P}{2}-L$

   C) $P+L$

   D) $P-2L$

Solving for Variables

Test 14

7. Two-points slope formula is $m = \dfrac{y_2 - y_1}{x_2 - x_1}$. What is x_2 in terms of the variables x_1, y_2, y_1 and m?

A) $x_2 = \dfrac{y_2 - y_1}{mx_1}$

B) $x_2 = \dfrac{y_2 - y_1 + mx_1}{m}$

C) $x_2 = y_2 - y_1 + mx_1$

D) $x_2 = y_2 + y_1 + mx_1$

8. $y = \dfrac{x^2}{3}$ solve the formula for x.

A) $3y$

B) $\sqrt{3y}$

C) $\dfrac{1}{3y}$

D) $-3y$

9. $xy + 6 = a$. Solve for x.

A) $\dfrac{a+6}{y}$

B) $\dfrac{y+6}{a}$

C) $\dfrac{a-6}{y}$

D) $\dfrac{y-6}{a}$

10. The slope intercept form is $y = mx + b$. Find x in terms of y, m and b.

A) $\dfrac{y-b}{m}$

B) $\dfrac{y+b}{m}$

C) $\dfrac{y-m}{b}$

D) $\dfrac{m-b}{y}$

11. $\dfrac{x+a}{4} = \dfrac{x-a}{3}$ Find a in terms of x.

A) $\dfrac{7}{x}$

B) $\dfrac{x}{7}$

C) $7x$

D) $7-x$

$$\frac{x+a}{4} = \frac{x-a}{3}$$

$$4x - 4a = 3x + 3a$$
$$-4y \quad -3a \quad -4x \quad -3a$$
$$\frac{-7a}{-7} = \frac{-x}{-7}$$

12. Which of the following expressions is not a factor of $x(x^2 - 25)$?

A) x

B) $x - 5$

C) $x + 5$

D) 5

Solving for Variables

13. What is the range of the following quadratic equation?

$$f(y) = -(x - 4)^2 + 10$$

A) $y \geq 10$

B) $y \leq 10$

C) $y \geq 4$

D) $y \geq -4$

14. For what value of x is the equation $x^2 - 3x - 5 = 0$ true?

A) $\dfrac{3 \pm \sqrt{29}}{2}$

B) $\dfrac{1 \pm \sqrt{19}}{2}$

C) $\dfrac{-3 \pm \sqrt{26}}{4}$

D) $\dfrac{-3 \pm \sqrt{29}}{6}$

(handwritten):
$x^2 - 3x = 5$

$\left(x - \dfrac{3}{2}\right)^2 - \dfrac{9}{4} = 5$

$x - \dfrac{3}{2} = \pm\sqrt{\dfrac{29}{4}}$

$x = \dfrac{\pm\sqrt{29}}{2} + \dfrac{3}{2}$

$x = \pm\dfrac{\sqrt{29}+3}{2}$

15. If $x^2 + 4x - 21 = (x + a)(x + b)$ for all values of x, what is one possible value of a + b?

A) -4

B) 4

C) 1

D) 5

Grid Questions

16. Find the sum of the roots of the quadratic equation, given below.

$$\frac{3}{4}(x - 2)^2 - 4 = \frac{15}{4}$$

Answer: ....

17. If x - 4 is a factor of if $x^2 - ax + 30$, where a is a constant, what is the value of a?

Answer: ....

18. $C = \dfrac{5}{9}(F - 32)$. Find F in terms of C.

Answer: ....

19. A=P+nrt. Find t in terms of P,r,n and A.

Answer: ....

Test 14
Answer Key

1)	A
2)	B
3)	C
4)	A
5)	B
6)	B
7)	B
8)	B
9)	C
10)	A
11)	B
12)	D
13)	B
14)	A
15)	A
16)	4
17)	$\dfrac{23}{2}$
18)	$f = \dfrac{9c + 160}{5}$
19)	$t = \dfrac{A - P}{nr}$

1. $a(b + c) = d$

$ab + ac = d$

$ac = d - ab$

$c = \dfrac{d - ab}{a} = \dfrac{d}{a} - b$

Correct Answer : A

2. $A = \dfrac{(b_1 + b_2)h}{2}$

$2A = (b_1 + b_2)h$

$\dfrac{2A}{b_1 + b_2} = h$

Correct Answer : B

3. $V = \pi r^2 h$

$\dfrac{V}{\pi h} = r^2$

$\sqrt{\dfrac{V}{\pi h}} = r$

Correct Answer : C

4. $\dfrac{1}{a} = \dfrac{1}{b} + \dfrac{1}{c}$

$\dfrac{1}{a} = \dfrac{c + b}{bc}$

$ac + ab = bc$

$ac = bc - ab$

$ac = b(c - a)$

$\dfrac{ac}{c - a} = b$

Correct Answer : A

5. $2x - 3y = 10$

$2x = 10 + 3y$

$x = \dfrac{10 + 3y}{2}$

Correct Answer : B

6. $P = 2L + 2W$

$W = \dfrac{P - 2L}{2} = \dfrac{P}{2} - L$

Correct Answer : B

7. $m = \dfrac{y_2 - y_1}{x_2 - x_1}$

$x_2 m - x_1 m = y_2 - y_1$

$x_2 = \dfrac{y_2 - y_1 + mx_1}{m}$

Correct Answer : B

8. $y = \dfrac{x^2}{3}$

$x^2 = 3y$

$x = \sqrt{3y}$

Correct Answer : B

9. $xy + 6 = a$

$xy = a - 6$

$x = \dfrac{a - 6}{y}$

Correct Answer : C

10. $y = mx + b$

$y - b = mx$

$\dfrac{y - b}{m} = x$

Correct Answer : A

11. $\dfrac{x + a}{4} = \dfrac{x - a}{3}$

$4x - 4a = 3x + 3a$

$\dfrac{x}{7} = a$

Correct Answer : B

12. $x(x^2 - 25)$

$x(x - 5) \cdot (x + 5)$

factors : x, $x - 5$, $x + 5$

Correct Answer : D

13. $F(x) = -(x - 4)^2 + 10$

when $x = 4$, y is max

$y \leq 10$

Correct Answer : B

14. $x^2 - 3x - 5 = 0$

$x^2 - 3x = 5$

$(x - \frac{3}{2})^2 - \frac{9}{4} = 5$

$(x - \frac{3}{2})^2 = \frac{29}{4}$

$x - \frac{3}{2} = \mp\sqrt{\frac{29}{4}}$

$x = \mp\frac{\sqrt{29}}{2} + \frac{3}{2}$

$x = \frac{\mp\sqrt{29} + 3}{2}$

Correct Answer : A

15. $x^2 + 4x - 21 = (x + a)(x + b)$

$\overset{\wedge}{x \quad x} \quad \overset{\wedge}{-3 \quad +7}$

$(x - 3) \cdot (x + 7) = (x + a)(x + b)$

$x = 3$ or $a = 3$ or $a = -7$

$x = -7 \qquad b = -7$ or $b = 3$

$a + b = -7 + 3 = -4$

Correct Answer : A

16. $\frac{3}{4}(x - 2)^2 - 4 = \frac{15}{4}$

$\frac{3}{4}(x - 2)^2 = \frac{31}{4}$

$x - 2 = \pm\sqrt{\frac{31}{3}}$

$x = \pm\sqrt{\frac{31}{3}} + 2$

$= 2 + \sqrt{\frac{31}{3}} + 2 - \sqrt{\frac{31}{3}}$

$= 4$

Correct Answer : 4

17. $x - 4 = 0$, $x = 4$

$x^2 - ax + 30 = 0$

$4^2 - 4a + 30 = 0$

$16 - 4a + 30 = 0$

$46 - 4a = 0$

$a = \frac{46}{4} = \frac{23}{2}$

Correct Answer : $\frac{23}{2}$

18. $C = \frac{5}{9}(F - 32)$

$9C = 5F - 160$

$\frac{9C + 160}{5} = F$

Correct Answer : $F = \frac{9C + 160}{5}$

19. $A = P + nrt$

$A - P = nrt$

$\frac{A - P}{nr} = t$

Correct Answer : $t = \frac{A - P}{nr}$

Scatter Plots

Type of Scatter Plots

> **Positive linear correlation**

> **Negative linear correlation**

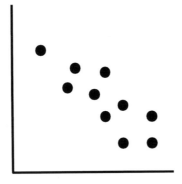

> **No correlation**

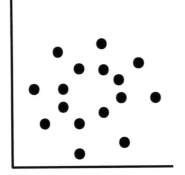

> Curvilinear correlation

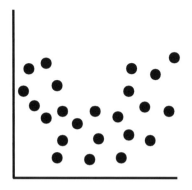

Bar Graph

A bar graph is used to show relationships between groups. The bar can be horizontal or veritical.

Example:

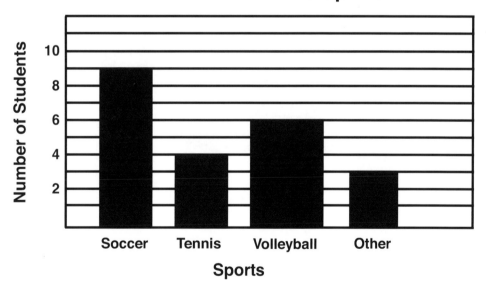

Circle Graph

A circle graph is used to show how a part of something relates to the whole. Mostly, circle graphs are needed to show percentages effectively.

Students Favorite Subjects

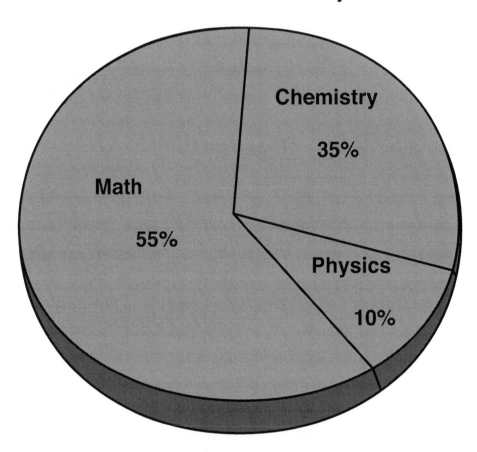

1. What type of correlation is the scatter plot?

   A) Positive Correlation
   B) No Correlation
   C) Negative Correlation
   D) Curvilinear Correlation

2. Which of following graphs has no correlation?

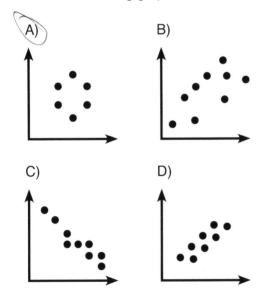

3. If the following circle graph has 5 different equal pizza slices, what percent of pizza is the cheese pizza?

Favorite pizza toppings

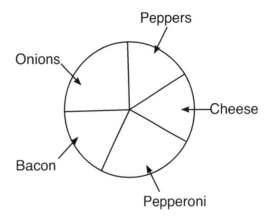

   A) 20%
   B) 25%
   C) 40%
   D) 45%

4. In Mr. Tony's math class, everyone has to do a math project. Out of the 25 students, 40% have completed their projects. How many students have completed their projects?

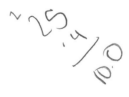

   A) 10 students
   B) 15 students
   C) 20 students
   D) 25 students

5. Students were asked whether they spend a long time or short time to complete their math test. The circle graph shows the responses of 90 students. How many students thought they completed in a short time?

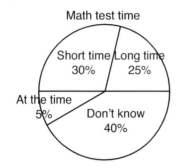

Math test time

Short time 30%

Long time 25%

At the time 5%

Don't know 40%

A) 3 students

B) 6 students

C) 9 students

D) 27 students

6. The table below shows the number of students who attended the Science Olympiad team last year. The data is displayed in the graph. What percent of the graph represents the 10th graders?

Grade	Number of Students
7th	30
8th	60
9th	90
10th	120

A) 20%

B) 25%

C) 35%

D) 40%

7. The table below shows the results of a survey on how students get to school. A circle graph is used to display the data. What percent of the graph represents the bus transportation?

Number of Students	Transportation
180	School Bus
60	Car
20	Walk
40	Bike

A) 40%

B) 45%

C) 55%

D) 60%

Use the graph to answer questions 8 to 10.

Students Favorite Sports

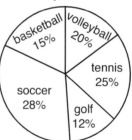

basketball 15%

volleyball 20%

tennis 25%

soccer 28%

golf 12%

8. What percent of the students like Volleyball?

A) 5%

B) 15%

C) 15%

D) 20%

9. What percent of the students like Basketball?

   A) 12%
   B) 15%
   C) 28%
   D) 30%

10. What percent of the students like Golf?

   A) 6%
   B) 9%
   C) 12%
   D) 18%

Use the graph to answer questions 11 and 12.

Library Visits

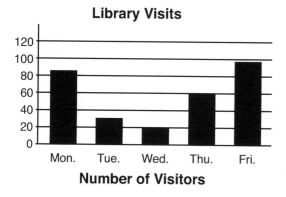

Number of Visitors

11. On which day did the library receive the most visitors?

   A) Monday
   B) Thursday
   C) Friday
   D) Tuesday

12. Approximately how many visitors came to the library on Friday?

   A) 120
   B) 100
   C) 80
   D) 60

Use the graph to answer questions 13 to 15.

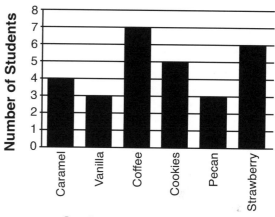

Students Favorite Ice Cream

13. How many people's favorite ice cream is vanilla?

   A) 1
   B) 2
   C) 3
   D) 4

14. From the above graph which type of ice cream is most favorable?

   A) Caramel
   B) Coffee
   C) Cookies
   D) Strawberry

15. What is the total number of people whose favorite ice cream is Strawberry and Vanilla?

   A) 3
   B) 5
   C) 7
   D) 9

Use the graph to answer questions 16 to 18.

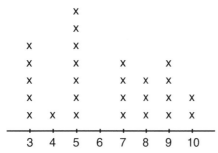

Number of Books Read

16. What is the greatest number of books read?

   A) 3
   B) 5
   C) 7
   D) 10

17. From the above graph how many students read 5 books?

   A) 6
   B) 7
   C) 8
   D) 9

18. From the above graph how many students read at least 5 books?

   A) 6
   B) 8
   C) 10
   D) 20

Use the graph to answer questions 19 to 20.

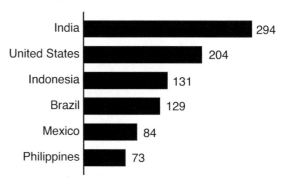

19. Which two countries have the closest Facebook users?

   A) India and Mexico
   B) U.S. and Philippines
   C) Indonesia and Brazil
   D) India and Brazil

20. About how many more people have Facebook accounts in India than in the U.S.?

    A) 70

    B) 80

    C) 90

    D) 100

Test 15
Answer Key

1)	C
2)	A
3)	A
4)	A
5)	D
6)	D
7)	D
8)	D
9)	B
10)	C
11)	C
12)	B
13)	C
14)	B
15)	D
16)	B
17)	B
18)	D
19)	C
20)	C

1. Negative Correlation

   Correct Answer : C

2. No Correlation

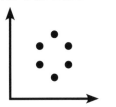

   Correct Answer : A

3. From graph $\frac{100}{5} = 20\%$

   Correct Answer : A

4. $25 \times \frac{40}{100} = 10$ students

   Correct Answer : A

5. From graph

   $x = \frac{30 \times 90}{100} = 27$

   Correct Answer : D

6. Total # of students

   $= 120 + 90 + 60 + 30 = 300$ students

   10th grade 120 students.

   $\frac{120}{300} = \frac{12}{30} = \frac{2 \times 20}{5 \times 20} = \frac{40}{100}$

   $= 40\%$

   Correct Answer : D

7. $\frac{Bus}{Total} = \frac{180}{300} = \frac{18}{30}$

   $= \frac{3 \times 20}{5 \times 20} = \frac{60}{100}$

   $= 60\%$

   Correct Answer : D

8. Total   100%
   Volleyball   20%

   Correct Answer : 20

9. Basketball   15%

   Correct Answer : B

10. Golf   12%

    Correct Answer : C

11. From the graph Friday had the most visitors.

    Correct Answer : C

12. From the graph approximately 100 visitors came to the library on Friday.

    Correct Answer : B

13. From the graph 3 students favorite ice cream is vanilla.

    Correct Answer : C

14. From the graph coffee ice cream is the most favorable.

    Correct Answer : B

15. From the graph the total number of peoples favorite ice cream is 9.

    Correct Answer : D

16. From the graph the greatest number of books is 5.

    Correct Answer : B

17. From the graph 7 students read 5 books.

    Correct Answer : B

18. From the graph 20 students read at least 5 books.

    Correct Answer : D

19. From the graph Indonesia and Brazil have the closest number of Facebook users.

    Correct Answer : C

20. 294 - 204 = 90

    Correct Answer : C

Statistics and Probability

Statistic: A statistic is a quantity that is calculated from a sample of data.

Mean (Average): The sum of the numbers divided by how many numbers there are.

$$\text{Mean} = \frac{\text{Sum of the numbers}}{\text{How many numbers there are}}$$

Example: Find the mean of 3,5,7,9.

Solution:

$$\text{Mean} = \frac{\text{Sum of the numbers}}{\text{How many numbers there are}}$$

$$\text{Mean} = \frac{3+5+7+9}{4} = \frac{24}{4} = 6$$

Median: Median is the middle number.

> Put all of the numbers in order.
> The median is the middle number.
> If there are two middle numbers, find the middle of those two numbers.

Example: Find the median of 3,10,20,8,18,30.

Solution: Put all of the numbers into order.

3, 8, 10, 18, 20, 30. Middle numbers are 10 and 18. The middle of these two number is $\frac{10+18}{2} = 14$

Mode: The mode is the most frequent value.

Example: A, B, D, A, B, A, C, D, A find the mode.

Solution: The most repetitive letter is A.

Range: The range is the difference between the lowest and highest value.

Example: Find the range of 2, 4, 20, 30, 50, 75.

Solution:

Range = 75-2 = 73

Probability: Probability is a fraction or decimal comparing the number of favorable (desired) outcomes to total numbers of possible outcomes. It is a number between and includes the numbers 0 and 1.

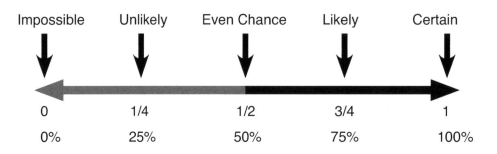

$$\text{Probability} = \frac{\text{Number of Desired Outcomes}}{\text{Total number of Possible Outcomes}}$$

Example: A letter is chosen at random from the word Solenoe. What is the probability of choosing the letter of e?

Solution:

$$\text{Probability} = \frac{\text{Number of Desired Outcomes}}{\text{Total number of Possible Outcomes}}$$

Answer: $\frac{2}{7}$

Statistics and Probability

Test 16

1. A math team has 6 students, 4 of which are girls and 2 of which are boys. In how many ways can the math team choose a team captain and team representative?

   A) 120
   B) 240
   C) 360
   D) 480

2. What is the mean of the following numbers?
   12,18,24,36,20

   A) 11
   B) 13
   C) 15
   D) 22

3. The mean of 5 numbers is 48. If 4 of the numbers are 64, 72, 54 and 34 then what is the value of the fifth number?

   A) 4
   B) 8
   C) 12
   D) 16

4. What measure of central tendency is calculated by a difference between the lowest and highest the number of values?

   A) Median
   B) Mean
   C) Mode
   D) Range

5. Vera has 10 green and 6 blue marbles in a bag. What is the probability of choosing a blue marble from the bag?

   A) $\frac{3}{8}$
   B) 8
   C) $\frac{5}{8}$
   D) $\frac{8}{3}$

6. Vera has 8 nickels, 4 dimes, and 6 quarters in her bag. What is the probability that she will randomly select nickels from her bag?

   A) 3
   B) 9
   C) $\frac{4}{9}$
   D) 4

7. Vera is taking an SAT math test that has 56 math questions. Each question has 4 answer choices. If she guesses randomly on every question, how many questions should she expect to answer correctly?

   A) 8
   B) 14
   C) 18
   D) 20

8. A letter is chosen at random from the word mathematician. What is the probability of choosing either an A or I ?

   A) $\frac{5}{13}$

   B) $\frac{4}{13}$

   C) $\frac{13}{5}$

   D) 13

9. What is the median of the following numbers?
   12,13,18,18,20,22,30,35,40

   A) 13
   B) 18
   C) 20
   D) 22

10. What is the median score achieved by a class who recorded the following scores on 6 science tests?
    74,80,78,65,90,92

    A) 76
    B) 77
    C) 78
    D) 79

11. What is the mode of the following numbers?
    11,11,13,15,15,20,25,32,40,32,60,70,32,70

    A) 11
    B) 15
    C) 32
    D) 70

12. What is the range of the following numbers?
    18,20,4,60,90,120,12

    A) 100
    B) 102
    C) 108
    D) 116

Statistics and Probability

Test 16

Use the data to answer question 13 to 15.

The temperature in Celsius (C°) in the first week of October was a follows.

$25C°, 21C°, 20C°, 25C°, 23C°, 14C°, 32C°$

13. What is the mode of the temperatures for the first week of October?

    A) $20C°$
    B) $21C°$
    C) $23C°$
    D) $25C°$

14. From the above data, what is the median of the temperatures for the first week of October?

    A) $14C°$
    B) $21C°$
    C) $23C°$
    D) $32C°$

15. From the above data, what is the range of the temperatures for the first week of October?

    A) $12C°$
    B) $16C°$
    C) $18C°$
    D) $21C°$

16. What is the average test score for the class if 6 students received scores of: 78, 82, 97, 66, 73 and 84?

    A) 72
    B) 78
    C) 80
    D) 82

17. If a is the average of 4k and 6, b is the average of 2k and 12 and c is the average 6k and 18, then what is the average of a, b, c in terms of k?

    A) $k + 6$
    B) $2k + 6$
    C) $k + 12$
    D) $2k + 12$

18. If the average of k+2 and 3k+6 is m and if the average of 5k and 7k-12 is n, what is the average of m and n?

    A) $2k + 1$
    B) $4k - 1$
    C) $3k - 1$
    D) $5k - 1$

19. Two classes have taken a science test. The first class had 20 students and the average test score of that class was 90%. The second class had 24 students and their average score was 85%. If the teacher combined the test scores of both classes, what is the average of both classes together if you round your answer to the nearest ones?

A) 82%
B) 83%
C) 86%
D) 87%

20. The average of five consecutive positive integers is 28. What is the greatest possible value of one of these integers?

A) 24
B) 26
C) 30
D) 32

Test 16
Answer Key

1)	C
2)	D
3)	D
4)	D
5)	A
6)	C
7)	B
8)	A
9)	C
10)	D
11)	C
12)	D
13)	D
14)	C
15)	C
16)	C
17)	B
18)	B
19)	D
20)	C

1. $P_{6,2} = \dfrac{6!}{2!} = \dfrac{6 \times 5 \times 4 \times 3 \times 2!}{2!}$

   $= 6 \times 5 \times 4 \times 3$

   $= 360$

   Correct Answer : C

2. $\text{Mean} = \dfrac{\text{Sum of members}}{\text{How many members there are}}$

   $\text{Mean} = \dfrac{12 + 18 + 24 + 36 + 20}{5}$

   $\text{Mean} = 22$

   Correct Answer : D

3. $\text{Mean} = \dfrac{64 + 72 + 54 + 34 + x}{5}$

   $48 = \dfrac{x + 224}{5}$

   $5 \times 48 = x + 224$

   $240 - 224 = x$

   $16 = x$

   Correct Answer : D

4. Range means the difference between the lowest and highest number values.

   Correct Answer : D

5. $P = \dfrac{\text{blue}}{\text{total}} = \dfrac{6}{16} = \dfrac{3}{8}$

   Correct Answer : A

6. $P = \dfrac{\text{nickels}}{\text{total}} = \dfrac{8}{18} = \dfrac{4}{9}$

   Correct Answer : C

7. $\dfrac{1}{4} \times 56 = \dfrac{56}{4} = 14$

   Correct Answer : B

8. Probability of A or I

   total A = 3

   total I = 2

   $\dfrac{\text{total A and I}}{\text{total letters}} = \dfrac{5}{13}$

   Correct Answer : A

9. Median : least to greatest of all numbers and find the middle number.

   12, 13, 18, 18, (20) 22, 30, 35, 40

   Correct Answer : C

10. Median :

    65, 74, 78, 80, 90, 92

    $\dfrac{78 + 80}{2} = 79$

    Correct Answer : D

11. Mode : most repeated number.

    Correct Answer : C

12. Range = Biggest number - smallest number

    Range = 120 - 4 = 116

    Correct Answer : D

13. Mode : most repeated number.

Correct Answer : D

14. Median :

$14°C, 20°C, 21°C, 23°C, 25°C, 25°C, 32°C$

(23°C circled)

Correct Answer : C

15. Range = max - min

$R = 32°C - 14°C$

$R = 18°C$

Correct Answer : C

16. Mean $= \dfrac{18 + 82 + 97 + 66 + 73 + 84}{6}$

$M = \dfrac{480}{6} = 80$

Correct Answer : C

17. $\dfrac{a + b + c}{3} = \dfrac{2k + 3 + k + 6 + 3k + 9}{3}$

$= \dfrac{6k + 18}{3} = 2k + 6$

Correct Answer : B

18. $m = \dfrac{k + 2 + 2k + 6}{2}$

$m = \dfrac{4k + 8}{2} = 2k + 4$

$n = \dfrac{12k - 12}{2}$

$n = 6k - 6$

$\dfrac{m + n}{2} = \dfrac{2k + 4 + 6k - 6}{2}$

$= \dfrac{8k - 2}{2} = 4k - 1$

Correct Answer : B

19. $\dfrac{sum}{\text{\#of students}} = .90$

$\dfrac{sum}{20} = .90$, sum = 18

$\dfrac{sum}{\text{\#of students}} = .85$

$\dfrac{sum}{24} = .85$, sum = 20.4

total sum $= 18 + 40.4 = 38.4$

total students $= 20 + 24 = 44$

Estimated Average $= \dfrac{38.4}{44}$

$\cong .87$

$\cong 87\%$

Correct Answer : D

20. $\dfrac{x + x + 1 + x + 2 + x + 3 + x + 4}{5} = 28$

$\dfrac{5x + 10}{5} = 28$

$x + 2 = 28$

$x = 26$

The greatest one $= x + 4$

$= 26 + 4$

$= 30$

Correct Answer : C

Imaginary Numbers

An imaginary number is a complex number that can be written as a real number multiplied by the imaginary number. It's defined by $i^2 = -1$

Example: 10i is an imaginary number and its square is -100.

Tips: Zero is considered to be both a real number and an imaginary number.

$$i^1 = i \quad i^2 = -1 \quad i^3 = -i \quad i^4 = 1$$
$$i^5 = i \quad i^6 = -1 \quad i^7 = -i \quad i^8 = 1$$
$$i^9 = i \quad i^{10} = -1 \quad i^{11} = -i \quad i^{12} = 1_f$$
$$i^2 = -1 \text{ or } i = \sqrt{-1}$$

Complex Numbers

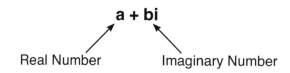

a + bi

Real Number   Imaginary Number

Complex number in standard form: a + bi

Example:

Complex number: $-3\sqrt{-4}$

Standard form: $-3 + 2i$

$$-3 + \sqrt{-4} = -3 + \sqrt{(-1(2^2))} = -3 + 2\sqrt{(i^2)} = -3 + 2i$$

Operations and Real Numbers

Adding and Subtracting Complex Numbers

Example: (3+2i) + (4+3i) = 3+2i+4+3i = 7+5i

Example: (6+4i) - (5+3i) = 6+4i-5-3i = 1+i

Multiplying and Dividing Complex Numbers

1) $(x+yi)(a+bi) = x(a+bi) + yi(a+bi)$
$= xa + (xb)i + (ya)i + (yb)i^2$
$= xa + (xb)i + (ya)i + (yb)(-1)$
$= (xa-yb) + (xb+ya)i$

2) $(x+yi)(x-yi) =$
$= x^2 - xyi + xyi - y^2i^2 = x - y^2(-1)$
$= x^2 - y^2$

Example: $(2+i)(4-i) = ?$

Solution:

$2 \times 4 - 2i + 4i - i^2 = 8 + 2i - (-1) = 8 + 2i + 1 = 9 + 2i$

3) When $b \neq 0$ and $c \neq 0$, always multiply the numerator and denominator by the opposite of the denominator.

$$\frac{a+bi}{c+di} = \frac{a+bi}{c+di}\left(\frac{c-di}{c-di}\right) = \frac{(ac+bd)+(bc-ad)i}{c^2+d^2}$$

Example: $\frac{2+3i}{2-i} = ?$

Solution:

$$\frac{2+3i}{2+i} = \frac{2+3i}{2+i} \times \left(\frac{2-i}{2-i}\right) = \frac{(2 \times 2)+(3 \times 1)+(6-2)i}{2^2+1^2} = \frac{7+4i}{5}$$

1. Which of the following is equivalent to the complex numbers $\frac{4+5i}{2+3i}$?

   A) $\frac{23-2i}{13}$

   B) $\frac{23+2i}{13}$

   C) $\frac{2-23i}{13}$

   D) $\frac{13-2i}{23}$

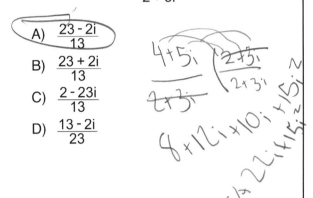

4. Which one of the following complex numbers is equivalent to $\frac{3-2i}{5+2i}$?

   A) $\frac{11}{29} - \frac{16i}{29}$

   B) $\frac{29}{11} - \frac{16i}{11}$

   C) $\frac{11}{29} + \frac{16i}{29}$

   D) $\frac{5}{19} - \frac{11i}{19}$

2. Which of the following is equivalent to the complex numbers $(2+4i)(5-3i)$?

   A) $22+14i$

   B) $14+22i$

   C) $22-14i$

   D) $14-22i$

5. $i^{15} + i^{21} + i^{48}$

   Which of the following is equivalent to the complex number shown above?

   A) $1-2i$

   B) $1+2i$

   C) $2i$

   D) 1

3. Which of the following is equivalent to the complex numbers $\frac{2}{3} - \frac{i}{6}$?

   A) $\frac{4-i}{6}$

   B) $\frac{6-i}{4}$

   C) $\frac{4+i}{6}$

   D) $\frac{6+i}{4}$

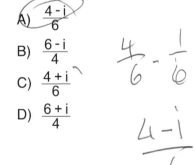

6. Which expressions are equivalent to $x^2 - 2x + 2 = 0$?

   A) $1 \pm 2i$

   B) $1 \pm i$

   C) $2 \pm i$

   D) $2 \pm 2i$

7. If a=3-2i and b=4+2i then which of the following is equal to ab?

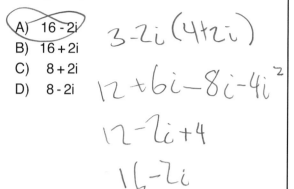

A) 16 - 2i

B) 16 + 2i

C) 8 + 2i

D) 8 - 2i

8. $i^{2018} \times i^{2019}$

Which of the following is equivalent to the complex number shown above?

A) 0

B) 1

C) -i

D) i

9. Which of the following complex numbers are equivalent to (i-2)(i+6)?

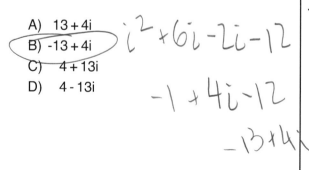

A) 13 + 4i

B) -13 + 4i

C) 4 + 13i

D) 4 - 13i

10. Which of the following complex numbers are equivalent to $\frac{4}{i} + i$?

A) $\frac{3}{i}$

B) $\frac{i}{3}$

C) 3

D) i

11. Which of the following complex numbers are equivalent to $\frac{a - bi}{a + bi}$?

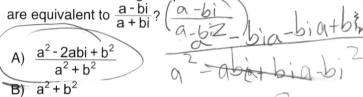

A) $\frac{a^2 - 2abi + b^2}{a^2 + b^2}$

B) $a^2 + b^2$

C) $\frac{a^2 - 2abi + b^2}{a^2 - b^2}$

D) $\frac{a^2 - 2abi - b^2}{a^2 + b^2}$

12. Which of the following complex numbers are equivalent to $(\frac{1 + i}{1 - i})^{2018}$?

A) 1

B) -1

C) i

D) -i

Imaginary Numbers

Test 17

13. Which of the following is equal to (12+8i) - (8-5i)?

A) 4 + 13i
B) 4 - 13i
C) 13 - 4i
D) 13 + 4i

Handwritten: 12+8i - 8 +5i   4+13i

16. Which of the following is equal to $\frac{4}{1+i\sqrt{3}}$?

A) $1 - i\sqrt{3}$
B) $1 + i\sqrt{3}$
C) 1
D) 3i

Handwritten: $\frac{4}{1+i\sqrt{3}}\left(\frac{1-i\sqrt{3}}{1-i\sqrt{3}}\right)$ $\frac{4-4i\sqrt{3}}{3}$ $\frac{4-4i\sqrt{3}}{4}$ $1-i\sqrt{3}$

14. What is the simplest form of $\sqrt{-5} \times \sqrt{75}$?

A) $5i\sqrt{15}$
B) $5\sqrt{15}$
C) 5
D) $-5\sqrt{15i}$

17. Which of the following complex numbers are equivalent to $(\sqrt{2} + i\sqrt{2}) \times (\sqrt{2} - i\sqrt{2})$?

A) 4i
B) 4
C) -4i
D) -4

15. Which of the following is a solution to the equation $x^2 = 6x - 11$?

A) $3 \pm i\sqrt{2}$
B) $-3 \pm i\sqrt{2}$
C) $2 \pm i\sqrt{3}$
D) $-2 \pm i\sqrt{3}$

Handwritten: $x^2 - 6x = -11$ $(x-3)^2 = -9$ $\sqrt{(x-3)^2} = \mp 2$ $(x-3) = \sqrt{2}i$

18. $24 = -4x^2$. Solve for x.

A) $\pm i\sqrt{6}$
B) $-i\sqrt{6}$
C) 6i
D) -6

Handwritten: $x - 3 = \pm i\sqrt{2}$

19. Which of the following complex numbers is equivalent to $(\frac{1}{2} - \frac{i}{2}) \times (\frac{1}{2} + \frac{i}{2})$?

A) $\frac{i}{2}$

B) $\frac{2}{2i}$

C) $\frac{1}{2}$

D) $-\frac{1}{2}$

$\left(\frac{1}{2} - \frac{i}{2}\right)\left(\frac{1}{2} + \frac{i}{2}\right)$

$\frac{1}{4} + \frac{i}{4} - \frac{i}{4} - \frac{i^2}{4}$

$\frac{1}{4} - \frac{i^2}{4}$

20. Simplify $\sqrt{-5} + \sqrt{-20} + \sqrt{-125}$?

A) $-8i\sqrt{5}$

B) $8i\sqrt{5}$

C) $8i$

D) $-8i$

$i\sqrt{5} + 2i\sqrt{5} + 5i\sqrt{5}$

$8i\sqrt{5}$

21. Evaluate $7i^{20} + 10i^2 + 15i^{12}$?

A) 4

B) 6

C) 12i

D) 12

Test 17
Answer Key

1)	A
2)	A
3)	A
4)	A
5)	D
6)	B
7)	A
8)	D
9)	B
10)	A
11)	A
12)	B
13)	A
14)	A
15)	A
16)	A
17)	B
18)	A
19)	C
20)	B
21)	D

Imaginary Numbers

Test 17 Solutions

1. $\dfrac{4 + 5i}{2 + 3i}\left(\dfrac{2 - 3i}{2 - 3i}\right) = \dfrac{8 - 12i + 10i + 15}{4 + 9}$

$= \dfrac{23 - 2i}{13}$

Correct Answer : A

2. $(2 + 4i)(5 - 3i)$

$= 10 - 6i + 20i + 12$

$= 22 + 14i$

Correct Answer : A

$\boxed{i^2 = -1}$

3. $\dfrac{2}{3} - \dfrac{i}{6} = \dfrac{4}{6} - \dfrac{i}{6}$

$= \dfrac{4 - i}{6}$

Correct Answer : A

4. $\dfrac{3 - 2i}{5 + 2i}$

$= \dfrac{3 - 2i}{5 + 2i}\left(\dfrac{5 - 2i}{5 - 2i}\right)$

$= \dfrac{15 - 6i - 10i - 4}{25 + 4}$

$= \dfrac{11 - 16i}{29}$

Correct Answer : A

5. $i^{15} + i^{21} + i^{48}$

Rule : $i^2 = -1$

$= (i^2)^7 . i + (i^2)^{10} . i + (i^2)^{24}$

$= (-1)^7 . i + (-1)^{10} . i + (-1)^{24}$

$= -i + i + 1$

$= 1$

Correct Answer : D

6. $x^2 - 2x + 2 = 0$

$x^2 - 2x = -2$

$(x - 1)^2 - 1 = -2$

$(x - 1)^2 = -1$

$(x - 1)^2 = i^2$

$x - 1 = \mp i$

$x = 1 \mp i$

Correct Answer : B

7. $a = 3 - 2i$

$b = 4 + 2i$

$a.b = (3 - 2i)(4 + 2i)$

$= 12 + 6i - 8i + 4$

$= 16 - 2i$

Correct Answer : A

8. $i^{2018} \times i^{2019}$

Rule : $i^2 = -1$

$= (i^2)^{1009} \times (i^2)^{1009} \times i$

$= (-1)^{1009} \times (-1)^{1009} \times i$

$= (-1) \times (-1) \times i$

$= i$

Correct Answer : D

9. $(i - 2)(i + 6)$

$= i^2 + 6i - 2i - 12$

$= -1 + 4i - 12$

$= -13 + 4i$

Correct Answer : B

10. $\dfrac{4}{i} + i = \dfrac{4 + i^2}{i} = \dfrac{4 - 1}{i} = \dfrac{3}{i}$

Correct Answer : A

.

11. $\dfrac{a - bi}{a + bi} = \dfrac{(a - bi)(a - bi)}{(a + bi)(a - bi)}$

$= \dfrac{a^2 - abi - bai + b^2 i^2}{a^2 - b^2 i^2}$

$= \dfrac{a^2 - 2abi - b^2}{a^2 + b^2}$

Correct Answer : D

12. $\left(\dfrac{1 + i}{1 - i}\right)^{2018}$

$= \left(\dfrac{(1 + i)(1 + i)}{(1 - i)1 + i}\right)^{2018}$

$= \left(\dfrac{1 + i + i + i^2}{1 - i^2}\right)^{2018}$

$= \left(\dfrac{1 + 2i - 1}{1 + 1}\right)^{2018} = \left(\dfrac{2i}{2}\right)^{2018}$

$= i^{2018}$

$= (i^2)^{1009} = (-1)^{1009} = -1$

Correct Answer : B

13. $(12 + 8i) - (8 - 5i)$

$= 12 + 8i - 8 + 5i$

$= 4 + 13i$

Correct Answer : A

14. $\sqrt{-5} \times \sqrt{75}$

Rule : $i^2 = -1$

$\sqrt{5i^2} \times \sqrt{75}$

$= \sqrt{5 \times 75i^2}$

$= \sqrt{15 \times 25i^2}$

$= 5i\sqrt{15}$

Correct Answer : A

15. $x^2 = 6x - 11$ $\qquad$ ⬭ $i^2 = -1$

$x^2 - 6x = -11$

$(x - 3)^2 - 9 = -11$

$(x - 3)^2 = -2$

$\sqrt{(x - 3)^2} = \sqrt{2i^2}$

$x - 3 = \mp i\sqrt{2}$

$x = 3 \mp i\sqrt{2}$

Correct Answer : A

16. $\dfrac{4}{1 + i\sqrt{3}} = \dfrac{4}{1 + i\sqrt{3}}\left(\dfrac{1 - i\sqrt{3}}{1 - i\sqrt{3}}\right)$

$= \dfrac{4 - 4i\sqrt{3}}{1 - i^2 . 3} = \dfrac{4 - 4i\sqrt{3}}{1 + 3}$

$= \dfrac{4 - 4i\sqrt{3}}{4} = 1 - i\sqrt{3}$

Correct Answer : A

17. $(\sqrt{2} + i\sqrt{2}) . (\sqrt{2} - i\sqrt{2})$

$= 2 - 2i + 2i - i^2 . 2$

$= 2 - 2i^2$

$= 2 + 2$

$= 4$

Correct Answer : B

18. $i^2 = -1$

$24 = -4x^2$

$-6 = x^2$

$6i^2 = x^2$

$\mp i\sqrt{6} = x$

Correct Answer : A

19. $\left(\dfrac{1}{2} - \dfrac{i}{2}\right) \times \left(\dfrac{1}{2} + \dfrac{i}{2}\right)$

$= \dfrac{1}{4} + \dfrac{i}{4} - \dfrac{i}{4} - \dfrac{i^2}{4}$

$= \dfrac{1}{4} - \dfrac{i^2}{4}$

$= \dfrac{1}{4} + \dfrac{1}{4} = \dfrac{2}{4} = \dfrac{1}{2}$

Correct Answer : C

20. $\sqrt{-5} + \sqrt{-20} + \sqrt{-125}$

$= i\sqrt{5} + 2i\sqrt{5} + 5i\sqrt{5}$

$= 8i\sqrt{5}$

Correct Answer : B

21. $7i^{20} + 10i^2 + 15i^{12}$

$= 7\left(i^2\right)^{10} + 10i^2 + 15\left(i^2\right)^6$

$= 7(-1)^{10} + 10(-1) + 15(-1)^6$

$= 7 - 10 + 15$

$= 12$

Correct Answer : D

1. $12x - ay + 12 = 0$ if the slope of equation is $\frac{3}{4}$, what is the value of a=?

   A) 16

   B) $\frac{1}{16}$

   C) -16

   D) $-\frac{1}{16}$

2. The line M passes the coordinate points (-2,3) and (1,6). What is the slope of line M?

   A) 1

   B) -1

   C) 2

   D) -2

3. Which of the following equations represents a line that is **parallel** to the line that passes through point A(2,6) and point B(4,8)?

   A) y = x + 4

   B) y = -x + 4

   C) y = x - 4

   D) y = -x - 4

4. If the sum of three consecutive integers is 96, which one of the following is the highest one?

   A) 31

   B) 32

   C) 33

   D) 34

5. What is the solution to the equation below?

   $2(y-6) = 3(2y-12)$

   A) -6

   B) 6

   C) 1

   D) $\frac{1}{6}$

6. How many solutions does the system of equations shown below have?

   $a = 3b + 10$
   $2a - 6b = 20$

   A) Zero

   B) 1

   C) 2

   D) Many / Infinity

7.
$$x - 2y = 12$$
$$3x - 4y = 18$$
In the system of equations above, solve for the x value.

A) 1

B) 6

C) -6

D) 8

8. $\frac{2x + 4}{3} - \frac{x}{2} = \frac{3}{2}$ Find the value of x.

A) 1

B) 3

C) 6

D) 9

9. A cleaning company charges $150 to clean 15 classrooms. What is the company's price for cleaning a single class?

A) $10

B) $15

C) $20

D) $25

10. What is the value of $\frac{m}{n}$?

$$\frac{18}{24} = \frac{n}{m}$$

A) $\frac{2}{3}$

B) $-\frac{2}{3}$

C) $\frac{4}{3}$

D) $\frac{3}{4}$

11. What is the ratio of $\frac{1}{3}$ to $\frac{4}{5}$?

A) $\frac{1}{12}$

B) $\frac{1}{5}$

C) $\frac{5}{12}$

D) $\frac{12}{5}$

12. 30% of 60 is equal to what percentage of 60?

A) 25%

B) 30%

C) 35%

D) 40%

13. If x and y are positive integers and 2x-4y=3 then find $\dfrac{16^x}{256^y}$

- A) 16
- B) 32
- C) 64
- D) 128

14. Convert $\dfrac{1}{5}$ kilograms to grams. (1kg=1000gr)

- A) 2
- B) 20
- C) 200
- D) 2000

15. If y varies inversely as x and x=6 when y=24, find y when x=9.

- A) 4
- B) 8
- C) 16
- D) 24

16. Find y when $x = \dfrac{1}{4}$, if y varies directly as x and y=4 when x=6.

- A) 6
- B) -6
- C) $\dfrac{1}{6}$
- D) 3

17. Which of the following equations is an example of direct variation?

- A) $y = kx$
- B) $y = \dfrac{k}{x}$
- C) $y = \dfrac{x}{k}$
- D) $y = \dfrac{1}{x}$

18. Evaluate $3^{15} \times 3^2 = 3^{-n} \times 3^m \times 3^7$ then find m - n = ?

- A) 10
- B) 12
- C) 14
- D) 16

19. If P(x-1) = 3x+1 then P(x+2)=?

    A) 3x+10

    B) 3x-10

    C) -3x+10

    D) -3x-10

20. Which of the following is equal to $16x^2 - 9y^2$?

    A) (4x-3y)(4x+3y)

    B) (4x+3y)

    C) (4x+3y)(4x+3y)

    D) (4x-3y)(4x-3y)

21. What are the factors of $x^2 - 13x + 40$?

    A) (x-5)(x+8)

    B) (x+5)(x+8)

    C) (x-5)(x-8)

    D) (x+5)(x-8)

22. In the polynomial below, a is the constant. If the polynomial is divisible by P(x-2) then find the value of a.

$$P(x) = x^3 + ax^2 - 2x$$

    A) 1

    B) -1

    C) 2

    D) -2

Mixed Review
Test 4
Answer Key

1)	A
2)	A
3)	A
4)	C
5)	B
6)	D
7)	C
8)	A
9)	A
10)	C
11)	C
12)	B
13)	C
14)	C
15)	C
16)	C
17)	A
18)	A
19)	A
20)	A
21)	C
22)	B

1. Slope of equation $= \dfrac{12}{a}$

$\dfrac{12}{a} = \dfrac{3}{4}$, then a = 16

Correct Answer : A

2. (-2, 3) and (1, 6)

slope $= \dfrac{y_2 - y_1}{x_2 - x_1}$

slope $= \dfrac{6 - 3}{1 - (-2)} = \dfrac{3}{3} = 1$

Correct Answer : A

3. Slope $= \dfrac{y_2 - y_1}{x_2 - x_1} = \dfrac{8 - 6}{4 - 2} = 1$

A (2, 6)

y = mx + b

y = x + b

6 = 2 + b

4 = b

y = x + 4

Correct Answer : A

4. The sum of three consecutive integers

x + x + 1 + x + 2 = 96

3x + 3 = 96

3x = 93

x = 31

The highest one x + 2 = 31 + 2 = 33

Correct Answer : C

5. 2(y - 6) = 3(2y - 12)

2y - 12 = 6y - 36

24 = 4y

6 = y

Correct Answer : B

6. a = 3b + 10

2a - 6b = 20

a - 3b = 10

a = 3b + 10

3b + 10 = 3b + 10

10 = 10

Correct Answer : D

7. $-2 \diagup$ x - 2y = 12

            3x - 4y = 18

        -2x + 4y = -24

 +   3x - 4y = 18

             x = -6

Correct Answer : C

8. $\dfrac{2x + 4}{3} - \dfrac{x}{2} = \dfrac{3}{2}$

$\dfrac{4x + 8 - 3x}{6} = \dfrac{9}{6}$

x + 8 = 9

x = 1

Correct Answer : A

9. $x = \dfrac{\$150}{15} = \$10$

Correct Answer : A

10. $\dfrac{18}{24} = \dfrac{n}{m}$

$\dfrac{24}{18} = \dfrac{m}{n}$

$\dfrac{4}{3} = \dfrac{m}{n}$

Correct Answer : C

11. Ratio of $\dfrac{1}{3}$ to $\dfrac{4}{5}$

$\dfrac{1}{3} \div \dfrac{4}{5} = \dfrac{1}{3} \times \dfrac{5}{4} = \dfrac{5}{12}$

Correct Answer : C

12. $30 \times \dfrac{60}{100} = 18$

$\dfrac{18}{60} = \dfrac{30}{100} = 30\%$

Correct Answer : B

13. $\dfrac{16^x}{256^y} = \dfrac{4^{2x}}{4^{4y}} = 4^{2x-4y}$

$= 4^3 = 64$

Correct Answer : C

14. 1kg = 1000gr

$\dfrac{1}{5}$kg $= \dfrac{1}{5} \times 1000 = 200$gr

Correct Answer : C

15. $yx = k$ (inverse)

$6 \times 24 = k$

$144 = k$

$y \times 9 = 144$

$y = \dfrac{144}{9} = 16$

Correct Answer : C

16. $y = kx$ (directly)

$4 = 6k$

$\dfrac{2}{3} = k$

$y = kx$

$y = \dfrac{2}{3} \times \dfrac{1}{4} = \dfrac{1}{6}$

Correct Answer : C

17. Direct variation

$y = kx$

Correct Answer : A

18. $3^{15} \times 3^2 = 3^{-n} \times 3^m \times 3^7$

$3^{15+2} = 3^{m-n+7}$

$17 = m - n + 7$

$10 = m - n$

Correct Answer : A

19. $P(x - 1) = 3x + 1$

$P(x + 2) = ?$

$P(x + 3 - 1) = 3(x + 3) + 1$

$P(x + 2) = 3x + 9 + 1 = 3x + 10$

Correct Answer : A

20. $16x^2 - 9y^2 = (4x - 3y)(4x + 3y)$

Correct Answer : A

21.

$x^2 - 13x + 40$

x   x   -5 -8

$(x - 5) . (x - 8)$

Correct Answer : C

22. $P(x) = x^3 + ax^2 - 2x$

if polynomial is divisible by

$P(x - 2)$ then $x - 2 = 0$ $x = 2$

$P(2) = 2^3 + a.2^2 - 2.2$

$0 = 8 + 4a - 4$

$0 = 4 + 4a$

$-4 = 4a$

$-1 = a$

Correct Answer : B

1. Which of following is equivalent to $x^{\frac{3}{4}}$?

   A) $\sqrt{x}$

   B) $\sqrt[3]{x^4}$

   C) $\sqrt[4]{x^3}$

   D) x

2. Which of following has the same value as $\sqrt{6} \times \sqrt{12}$?

   A) $6\sqrt{2}$

   B) $-6\sqrt{2}$

   C) $2\sqrt{2}$

   D) $-2\sqrt{2}$

3. $x = \dfrac{2^3}{\sqrt{64}}$ Find x.

   A) 1

   B) -1

   C) 2

   D) 4

4. $P(x) = x^3 - x^2 + 3$ and $Q(x) = -2x^3 + 2x^2 - 6$. Find $P(x) + Q(x)$.

   A) $x^3 - x^2 + 3$

   B) $x^3 + x^2 - 3$

   C) $x^3 - x^2 - 3$

   D) $-x^3 + x^2 - 3$

5. Simplify the following equation:

$$\dfrac{x^2 - 81}{x + 9} ?$$

   A) $\dfrac{x - 3}{x + 3}$

   B) $\dfrac{x - 9}{x + 9}$

   C) $x - 9$

   D) $x + 9$

6. Simplify $\sqrt[3]{0.008}$

   A) 1

   B) 5

   C) $\dfrac{1}{5}$

   D) -5

7. Simplify $\sqrt{32} - \sqrt{8} + \sqrt{128}$.

   A) $-10\sqrt{2}$

   B) 10

   C) $\sqrt{2}$

   D) $10\sqrt{2}$

8. If $2x^2 - 3x + 2 = 0$, then find $x^2 + \dfrac{1}{x^2}$.

   A) $\dfrac{1}{4}$

   B) 4

   C) 6

   D) 8

9. Simplify $\dfrac{x^2 - 6x - 16}{x^2 + 4x + 4}$.

   A) $x - 8$

   B) $\dfrac{x - 8}{x + 2}$

   C) $x + 9$

   D) $\dfrac{x + 8}{x - 2}$

10. Simplify $\dfrac{x^2 - y^2}{x^2 - xy} \div \dfrac{x^2 + xy}{xy - x}$.

   A) $x + 2$

   B) $y + 1$

   C) $\dfrac{x - y}{x}$

   D) $\dfrac{y - 1}{x}$

11. If $x = 1 + \sqrt{2}$ and $y = 1 - \sqrt{2}$, then find $x \cdot y$?

   A) -2

   B) 2

   C) 1

   D) -1

12. If $x > 0$, what is the value of x in $|2x-3| = 7$?

   A) -1

   B) 1

   C) 2

   D) 5

13. If 5a - 3b = -16 and a=-2, then find b.

    A) 2

    B) -2

    C) 3

    D) -3

14. If $2^{2x-3} = 8^{x-6}$, what is the value of x?

    A) 12

    B) 15

    C) 18

    D) 21

15. According to the formula $F = \frac{9}{5}C + 32$ the temperature in degrees Fahrenheit can be converted to degrees Celsius C. Find F when $C = 40°$

    A) 104F

    B) -104F

    C) 100F

    D) 150F

16. For the function below, m>0 is a constant and f(5)=110. What is the value of f(6)?
$$f(x) = mx^2 + 10$$

    A) 124

    B) 134

    C) 144

    D) 154

17. What is the value of $g(f(-1))$ when $f(x) = 2x^2 + 1$ and $g(x) = 3x^2 - 9$?

    A) 12

    B) 18

    C) 24

    D) 36

18. If $g(x - 2) = \frac{3x + 3}{2x - 3}$, then $g(2)$?

    A) 1

    B) 3

    C) -3

    D) 5

19. $f(x)=\begin{cases} -2x + 5, & x < 0 \\ x^2 + 5, & x \geq 0 \end{cases}$

From the above function, find f (2)+f (-3)?

A) 15

B) 20

C) 25

D) -25

22. What is the simplest form of $\sqrt{-8} \times \sqrt{32}$?

Answer: ....

20. What is the vertex, of the parabola
$y = 2x^2 + 4x - 6$?

A) $f(x) = 2(x + 1)^2 - 8$

B) $f(x) = 2(x + 2)^2 - 3$

C) $f(x) = -2(x - 2)^2 + 4$

D) $f(x) = 3(x - 1)^2 - 6$

Grid Questions

21. If $\dfrac{x + a}{8} = \dfrac{x - a}{7}$, find a in terms of x.

Answer: ....

Mixed Review
Test 5
Answer Key

1)	C
2)	A
3)	A
4)	D
5)	C
6)	C
7)	D
8)	A
9)	B
10)	D
11)	D
12)	D
13)	A
14)	B
15)	A
16)	D
17)	B
18)	B
19)	B
20)	A
21)	$\frac{x}{15}$
22)	16i

Mixed Review

Test 5 Solutions

1. $x^{\frac{3}{4}} = \sqrt[4]{x^3}$

   Correct Answer : C

2. $\sqrt{6} \times \sqrt{12}$

   $= \sqrt{72} = \sqrt{36 \times 2}$

   $= 6\sqrt{2}$

   Correct Answer : A

3. $x = \dfrac{2^3}{\sqrt{64}} = \dfrac{8}{8} = 1$

   Correct Answer : A

4. $P(x) + Q(x)$

   $= x^3 - x^2 + 3 - 2x^3 + 2x^2 - 6$

   $= -x^3 + x^2 - 3$

   Correct Answer : D

5. $\dfrac{x^2 - 81}{x + 9} = \dfrac{(x - a)(x + 4)}{(x + 4)}$

   $= x - 9$

   Correct Answer : C

6. $\sqrt[3]{0.008} = \sqrt[3]{\dfrac{8}{1000}} = \sqrt[3]{\left(\dfrac{2}{10}\right)^3}$

   $= \dfrac{2}{10} = \dfrac{1}{5}$

   Correct Answer : C

7. $\sqrt{32} - \sqrt{8} + \sqrt{128}$

   $= 4\sqrt{2} - 2\sqrt{2} + 8\sqrt{2}$

   $= 10\sqrt{2}$

   Correct Answer : D

8. $\dfrac{2x^2}{2x} - \dfrac{3x}{2x} + \dfrac{2}{2x} = 0$

   $x - \dfrac{3}{2} + \dfrac{1}{x} = 0$

   $x + \dfrac{1}{x} = \dfrac{3}{2}$, $\quad x^2 + \dfrac{1}{x^2} + 2 = \dfrac{9}{4}$

   $x^2 + \dfrac{1}{x^2} = \dfrac{1}{4}$

   Correct Answer : A

9. $\dfrac{x^2 - 6x - 16}{x^2 + 4x + 4}$

   $\dfrac{(x + 2)(x - 8)}{(x + 2)(x + 2)} = \dfrac{x - 8}{x + 2}$

   Correct Answer : B

10. $\dfrac{x^2 - y^2}{x^2 - xy} \div \dfrac{x^2 + xy}{xy - x}$

    $\dfrac{(x - y)(x + y)}{x(x - y)} \cdot \dfrac{x(y - 1)}{x(x + y)}$

    $= \dfrac{y - 1}{x}$

    Correct Answer : D

11. $x = 1 + \sqrt{2}$

    $y = 1 - \sqrt{2}$

    $xy = (1 + \sqrt{2})(1 - \sqrt{2})$

    $= 1 - 2$

    $= -1$

    Correct Answer : D

12. $|2x - 3| = 7$

    if $x > 0$ then

    $2x - 3 = 7$

    $2x = 10$, $x = 5$

    Correct Answer : D

13. $5a - 3b = -16$

if $a = -2$

$5(-2) - 3b = -16$

$-10 - 3b = -16$

$-3b = -6$

$b = 2$

Correct Answer : A

14. $2^{2x-3} = 8^{x-6}$

$2^{2x-3} = 2^{3x-18}$

$2x - 3 = 3x - 18$

$15 = x$

Correct Answer : B

15. $F = \frac{9}{5}^{\circ} C + 32$

$F = \frac{9}{5} \times 40 + 32$

$F = \frac{360}{5} + 32$

$F = 72 + 32$

$F = 104^{\circ}F$

Correct Answer : A

16. $F(x) = mx^2 + 10$

$F(5) = 25m + 10$

$110 = 25m + 10$

$100 = 25m$

$4 = m$

$F(x) = 4x^2 + 10$

$F(6) = 4 \times 6^2 + 10$

$F(6) = 4 \times 36 + 10$

$= 144 + 10$

$= 154$

Correct Answer : D

17. $f(-1) = 2(-1)^2 + 1$

$= 2 + 1 = 3$

$g(3) = 3(3)^2 - 9$

$= 3 \times 9 - 9$

$= 27 - 9 = 18$

Correct Answer : B

18. $g(x - 2) = \frac{3x + 3}{2x - 3}$

$g(2) = ?$

$g(4 - 2) = \frac{3.4 + 3}{2.4 - 3}$

$g(2) = \frac{12 + 3}{8 - 3}$

$g(2) = \frac{15}{5} = 3$

Correct Answer : B

19. $F(2) = x^2 + 5 = 2^2 + 5 = 4 + 5 = 9$

$F(-3) = -2x + 5 = -2(-3) + 5 = 6 + 5 = 11$

$9 + 11 = 20$

Correct Answer : B

20. Vertex Form

$V(x) = a(x - h)^2 + k$

$V(x) = 2(x^2 + 2x) - 6$

$V(x) = 2(x + 1)^2 - 8$

Correct Answer : A

21. $\frac{x + a}{8} = \frac{x - a}{7}$

$8x - 8a = 7x + 7a$

$a = \frac{x}{15}$

Correct Answer : $\frac{x}{15}$

22. $i^2 = -1$

$\sqrt{-8} \times \sqrt{32}$

$= \sqrt{8i^2} \times \sqrt{32}$

$= \sqrt{8 \times 32 . i^2}$

$= \sqrt{4 \times 64 \times i^2}$

$= 2 \times 8 \times i$

$= 16i$

Correct Answer : 16i

Lines, Angles, and Triangles

Vocabulary	Definition	Pictures
Point	A dot or location	●
Line	A line extended forever in both directions	←———→
Line Segment	A part of a line with two endpoints	•———•
Ray	A line that starts at one point and continues on forever in one direction	•———→
Parallel Lines	Parallel lines never intersect and stay the same distance apart	←———→ ←———→
Perpendicular Lines	Perpendicular lines are lines that intersect at a right angle	
Intersecting Lines	Intersecting lines are two lines that share exactly one point	
Acute Angle	An angle that is less than 90° but greater then 0°	
Right Angle	An angle that is exactly 90°	
Obtuse Angles	An angle that is greater than 90° but less than 180°	
Straight Angle	An angle that is exactly 180°	180° x o y

Corresponding Angles

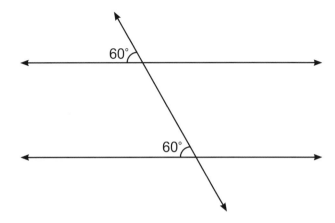

Alternate Interior Angles

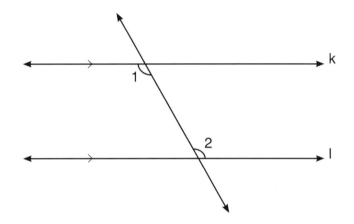

if k // l, then
∠1 ≅ ∠2

Alternate Exterior Angles

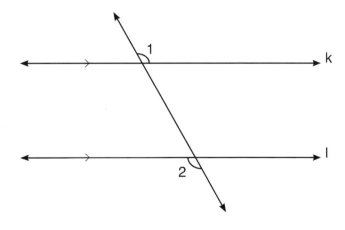

if k // l, then
∠1 ≅ ∠2

191

Triangle Angles

The sum of the interior angles of a triangle is equal to 180

Example:

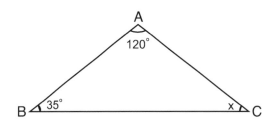

Solution: $35° + 120° + x = 180°$. Then, $x = 180° - 155° = 25°$

Pythagorean Theorem

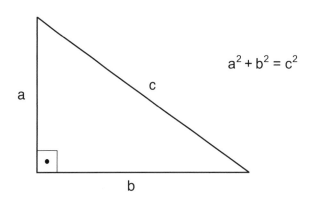

$$a^2 + b^2 = c^2$$

Special Right Triangles

▶ 45° : 45° : 90°

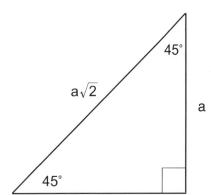

▶ 30° : 60° : 90°

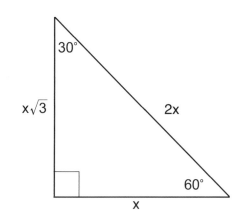

► 60° : 60° : 60° **(Equilateral Triangle)**

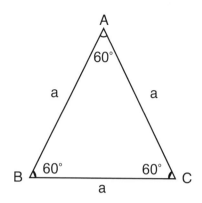

Area Formulas

Parallelogram	Area = base × height	 Height Base
Triangle	Area = $\dfrac{\text{base} \times \text{height}}{2}$	 h b
Rectangle	Area = base × height	 Height Base
Equilateral triangle	Area = $\dfrac{\sqrt{3}}{4} \times a^2$	 a a a
Square	Area = width × length	s s Area = s^2
Trapezoid	Area = $\dfrac{(b_1 + b_2)}{2} \times h$	b_1 h b_2

193

1. If |AC| = |CD|, Δ(ACD) = Δ(DCB) and ∠(BAC) = 70°

Find x = ?

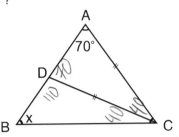

A) 30°

B) 40°

C) 50°

D) 60°

3. Find the value of x in the diagram.

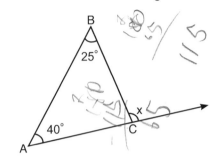

A) 40°

B) 55°

C) 65°

D) 75°

2. Find the value of x in the diagram.

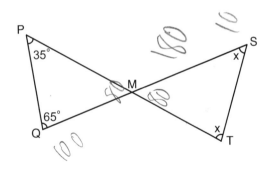

A) 25°

B) 35°

C) 45°

D) 50°

4.

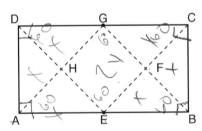

A B C D is a Rectangle.

Δ(GAB) and Δ(ECD) are equilateral triangles,

find $\dfrac{\text{Area (EFB)}}{\text{Area (AGB)}}$ = ?

A) $\dfrac{1}{2}$ B) $\dfrac{1}{3}$ C) $\dfrac{1}{4}$ D) $\dfrac{1}{5}$

5.

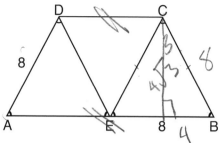

ABCD Trapezoid, △(AED) Equilateral triangle.
DC // AB, $\overline{CE} = \overline{CB}$, $\overline{AD} = 8cm$ $\overline{BE} = 8cm$

Find the area of A(ABCD) Trapezoid.

A) $12\sqrt{3}$ B) $24\sqrt{3}$ C) $18\sqrt{3}$ D) $48\sqrt{3}$

6.

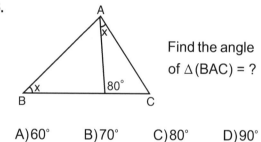

Find the angle
of △(BAC) = ?

A) 60°   B) 70°   C) 80°   D) 90°

7.

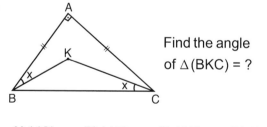

Find the angle
of △(BKC) = ?

A) 110°   B) 115°   C) 135°   D) 120°

8.

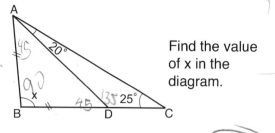

Find the value
of x in the
diagram.

A) 60°   B) 70°   C) 80°   D) 90°

9.

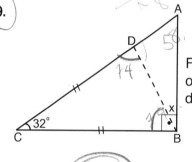

Find the value
of x in the
diagram.

A) 13°   B) 16°   C) 36°   D) 38°

10. What is the area of the figures A(ABC)?

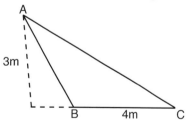

A) 3m² (actually $3m^2$)   B) $6m^2$ C) $9m^2$ D) $12m^2$

11.

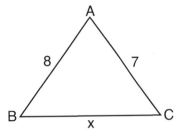

What is the possible value of x?

A) 1   B) 15   C) 16   D) 12

14. Below are similar triangles. If AB=10, BC=12, DF=48. What is the length of DE?

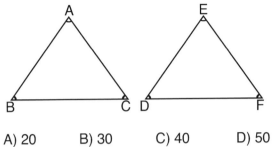

A) 20   B) 30   C) 40   D) 50

12.

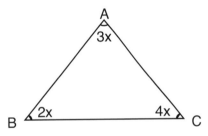

What is the value of x ?

A) 10°   B) 20°   C) 30°   D) 40°

15.

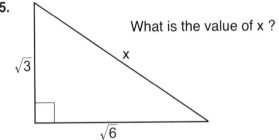

What is the value of x ?

A) $\sqrt{6}$ B) $\sqrt{3}$ C) 3   D) 6

13.

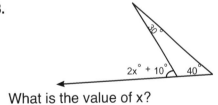

What is the value of x?

A) 10°   B) 20°   C) 30°   D) 40°

16. What are the values of x and y ?

A) 2, 4   B) 4, 2   C) $\sqrt{3}$, 2   D) 4, $\sqrt{3}$

17. Find the area of A(ABC).

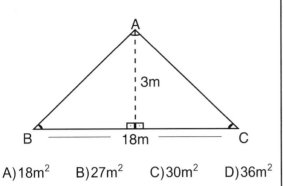

A) $18m^2$ B) $27m^2$ C) $30m^2$ D) $36m^2$

19.

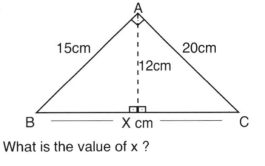

What is the value of x ?

A) 15cm   B) 20cm   C) 25cm   D) 30cm

18. What is the area of an equilateral triangle with a side of 4?

A) $\sqrt{3}$
B) $2\sqrt{3}$
C) $4\sqrt{3}$
D) $6\sqrt{3}$

Test 18
Answer Key

1)	A
2)	D
3)	C
4)	C
5)	D
6)	C
7)	C
8)	D
9)	B
10)	B
11)	D
12)	B
13)	C
14)	C
15)	C
16)	B
17)	B
18)	C
19)	C

1.

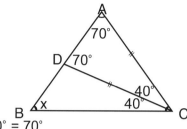

$x + 40° = 70°$

$x = 30°$

Correct Answer : A

2.

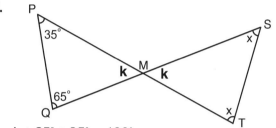

$k + 65° + 35° = 180°$

$k + 100° = 180°$

$k = 80°$

$2x + k = 180°$

$2x + 80° = 180°$

$2x = 100°$

$x = 50°$

Correct Answer : D

3.

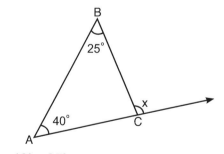

$x = 40° + 25°$

$x = 65°$

Correct Answer : C

4.

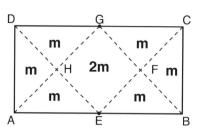

$$\frac{\text{Area (EFB)}}{\text{Area (AGB)}} = \frac{m}{4m} = \frac{1}{4}$$

Correct Answer : C

5.

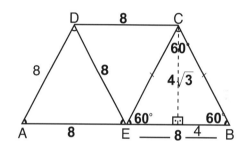

$$\text{Area of Trapezoid} = \frac{(b_1 + b_2)h}{2}$$

$$\text{Area} = \frac{(8 + 16)4\sqrt{3}}{2} = 48\sqrt{3}$$

Correct Answer : D

6.

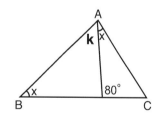

$80° = x + k$

Angle of $\triangle$ (BAC) $= x + k = 80°$

Correct Answer : C

7.

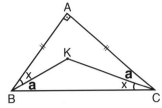

$2x + 2a + 90° = 180°$

$x + a = 45°$

$m(k) + x + a = 180°$

$m(k) + 45° = 180°$

$m(k) = 135°$

Correct Answer : C

8.

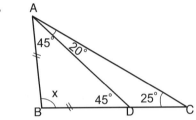

$m(D) = 45°$

$x + 45° + 20° + 25° = 180°$

$x + 90° = 180°$ $x = 90°$

Correct Answer : D

9.

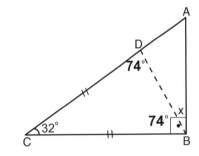

$\dfrac{180° - 32°}{2} = \dfrac{148°}{2} = 74°$

$x + 74° = 90°$ $x = 16°$

Correct Answer : B

10.

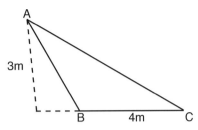

$\text{Area of } A(ABC) = \dfrac{3m \times 4m}{2}$

$= \dfrac{12m^2}{2} = 6m^2$

Correct Answer : B

11.

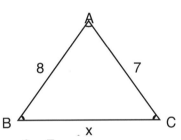

$8 - 7 < x < 8 + 7$

$1 < x < 15$

Correct Answer : D

12.

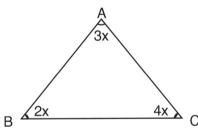

$3x + 2x + 4x = 180°$

$9x = 180°$

$x = 20°$

Correct Answer : B

13.

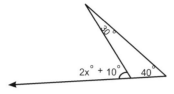

$2x + 10° = 40° + 30°$

$2x = 70° - 10°$

$2x = 60°$

$x = 30°$

Correct Answer : C

14.

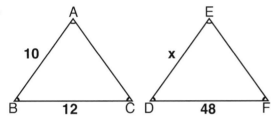

$\frac{10}{12} = \frac{x}{48}$

$x = 40$

Correct Answer : C

15.

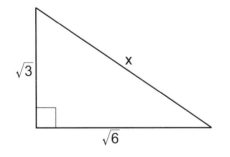

$(\sqrt{3})^2 + (\sqrt{6})^2 = x^2$

$3 + 6 = x^2$

$9 = x^2$

$3 = x$

Correct Answer : C

16.

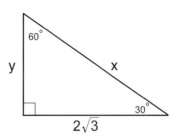

if $60° \longrightarrow 2\sqrt{3}$

       $30° \longrightarrow 2$, $y = 2$

       $90° \longrightarrow 4$, $x = 4$

Correct Answer : B

17.

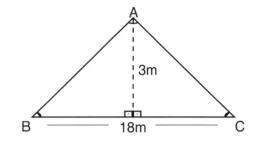

Area (ABC) = $\frac{3m \times 18m}{2}$

= $27m^2$

Correct Answer : B

18.

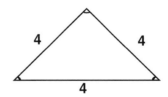

Area = $\frac{a^2\sqrt{3}}{4}$

Area = $\frac{(4)^2\sqrt{3}}{4}$

= $\frac{16\sqrt{3}}{4} = 4\sqrt{3}$

Correct Answer : C

19.

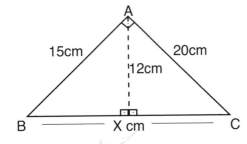

Rule: $12cm \cdot x = 15cm \cdot 20cm$

$x = \dfrac{15cm \cdot 20cm}{12cm}$

$x = 25cm$

Correct Answer : C

$180 - 2x + 80 = 180$

$180 - 2x + 80 + 180 - x + 70 = 90$

$360 - 2x + 80 - x + 70$

$360 - 3x + 130 = 90$

$490 - 3x = 90$
-490

$3\overline{)400}$
$\underline{3}$
20

$4 \, 0 \, 1 \, 8$

$180 - x \oplus 70 \quad 180 - 2x - 90$

$180 - (x + 70)$

$110 - x + 100 - 2x = 90$

$210 - 3x = 90$

$\dfrac{-3x}{-3} = \dfrac{-120}{-3}$

$x = 40$

Lines, Angles, and Triangles

Test 19

1.

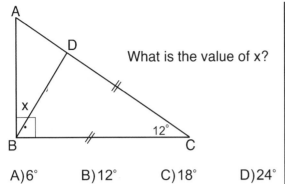

What is the value of x?

A) 6°   B) 12°   C) 18°   D) 24°

2.

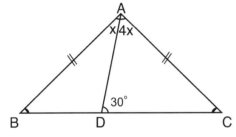

What is the value of x?

A) 20°   B) 40°   C) 60°   D) 80°

3.

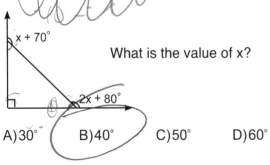

What is the value of x?

A) 30°   B) 40°   C) 50°   D) 60°

4.

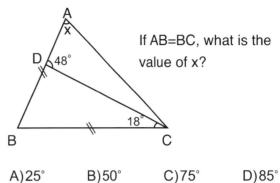

If AB=BC, what is the value of x?

A) 25°   B) 50°   C) 75°   D) 85°

5.

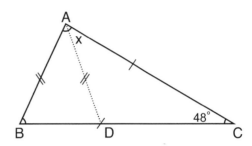

From the following figure, if AB=AD and BC=AC, then what is the value of x?

A) 9°   B) 18°   C) 27°   D) 36°

6.

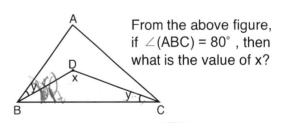

From the above figure, if ∠(ABC) = 80° , then what is the value of x?

A) 80°   B) 90°   C) 100°   D) 110°

7.

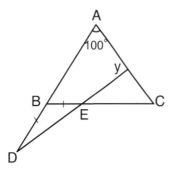

From the above figure if $|\overline{AB}| = |\overline{AC}|$ and $|\overline{BD}| = |\overline{BE}|$, What is the value of y?

A) 15°   B) 30°   C) 45°   D) 60°

9.

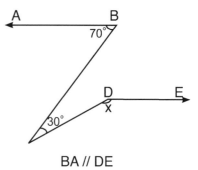

BA // DE

What is the value of x ?

A) 120°   B) 140°   C) 150°   D) 160°

8.

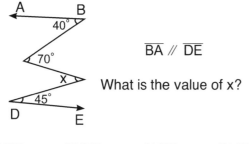

$\overline{BA}$ // $\overline{DE}$

What is the value of x?

A) 75°   B) 80°   C) 85°   D) 95°

10.

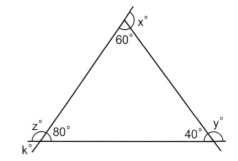

İn the figure above, wich of the following is greatest?

A) x°   B) y°   C) z°   D) k°

11.

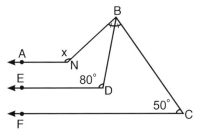

AN // ED // FC
From the figure, what is the value of x?

A) 50°   B) 80°   C) 110°   D) 120°

13.

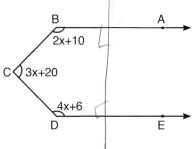

From the figure BA // DE,
what is the value of x?

A) 8°   B) 16°   C) 32°   D) 36°

$2x+10 + 3x+20 + 4x+6 + 180 = 540$

$9x + 900 = 360$

12.

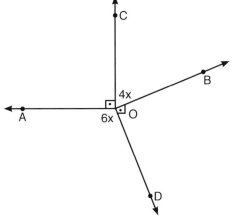

From the figure ∠(BOC) = 6x, ∠(AOD) = 4x
what is the value of x?

A) 10°   B) 18°   C) 30°   D) 40°

14.

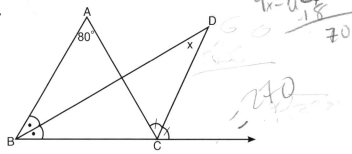

From the figure, what is the value of x?

A) 10°   B) 20°   C) 30°   D) 40°

15.

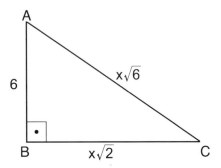

What is the value of x ?

A)1   B)3   C)5   D)9

$$(x\sqrt{6})^2 = 6^2 + (x\sqrt{2})^2$$
$$6x^2 = 36 + 2x^2$$
$$-2x^2$$
$$\frac{4x^2}{4} = \frac{36}{4}$$
$$x^2 = \sqrt{9}$$

16.

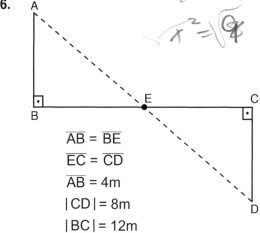

$$\overline{AB} = \overline{BE}$$
$$\overline{EC} = \overline{CD}$$
$$\overline{AB} = 4m$$
$$|CD| = 8m$$
$$|BC| = 12m$$

What is the value of $|\overline{AD}| = $?

A)$8\sqrt{2}$ B)$12\sqrt{2}$ C)$16\sqrt{2}$ D)$20\sqrt{2}$

17.

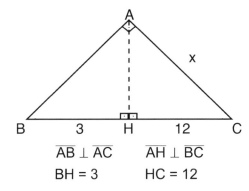

$$\overline{AB} \perp \overline{AC} \qquad \overline{AH} \perp \overline{BC}$$
$$BH = 3 \qquad HC = 12$$

What is the value of x?

A)10   B)$\sqrt{12}$ C)$6\sqrt{5}$ D)5

18.

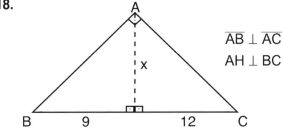

$$\overline{AB} \perp \overline{AC}$$
$$AH \perp BC$$

What is the value of x?

A)$3\sqrt{3}$ B)$6\sqrt{3}$ C)$8\sqrt{3}$ D)$12\sqrt{3}$

19.

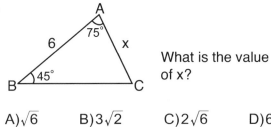

What is the value of x?

A)$\sqrt{6}$ B)$3\sqrt{2}$ C)$2\sqrt{6}$ D)6

Test 19
Answer Key

1)	A
2)	B
3)	B
4)	C
5)	B
6)	C
7)	D
8)	A
9)	B
10)	B
11)	C
12)	B
13)	D
14)	D
15)	B
16)	B
17)	C
18)	B
19)	C

1.

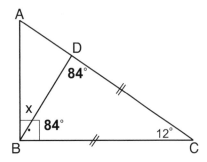

$$\frac{180° - 12°}{2} = \frac{168°}{2} = 84°$$
$$x + 84° = 90° \qquad x = 6°$$
Correct Answer : A

2.

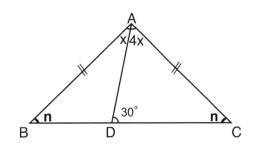

$$x + n = 30°$$
$$5x + 2n = 180° \qquad x = 40°$$
Correct Answer : B

3.

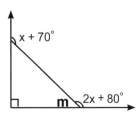

$$m = 180° - 2x + 80° \qquad m = 100° - 2x$$
$$90° + m = x + 70°$$
$$90° + 100° - 2x = x + 70°$$
$$120° = 3x$$
$$40° = x$$
Correct Answer : B

4.

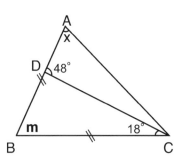

$$m + 18° = 48°, \quad m = 30°$$
$$\frac{180° - 30°}{2} = \frac{150°}{2} = 75°$$
Correct Answer : C

5.

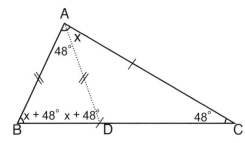

$$2x + 144° = 180°$$
$$x = 18°$$
Correct Answer : B

6.

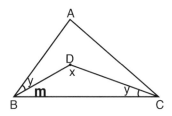

$$y + m = 80°$$
$$x + y + m = 180°$$
$$x + 80° = 180°$$
$$x = 100°$$
Correct Answer : C

7.

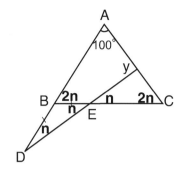

$2n + 2n + 100° = 180°$

$4n + 100° = 180°$

$4n = 80°$

$n = 20°$

$y = 3n$

$y = 60°$

Correct Answer : D

8.

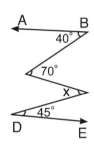

$40° + x = 70° + 45°$

$x = 75°$

Correct Answer : A

9.

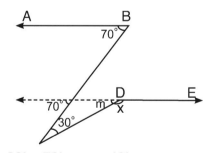

$m + 30° = 70°$ $m = 40°$

$m + x = 180°$

$40° + x = 180°$ $x = 140°$

Correct Answer : B

10.

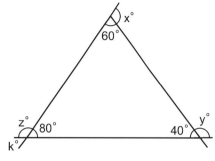

$x = 120°$

$y = 140°$

$z = 100°$

$k = 80°$

Correct Answer : B

11.

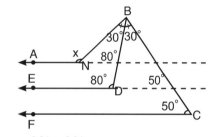

$x = 80° + 30°$

$x = 110°$

Correct Answer : C

12.

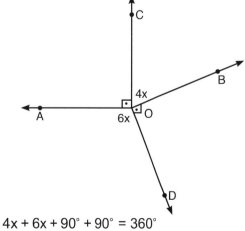

$4x + 6x + 90° + 90° = 360°$

$10x + 180° = 360°$

$x = 18°$

Correct Answer : B

13.

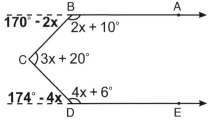

$170° - 2x + 174° - 4x = 3x + 20°$

$344° - 6x = 3x + 20°$

$324° = 9x$

$36° = x$

Correct Answer : D

14.

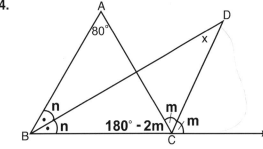

$180° - 2m + 2n + 80° = 180°$

$2n - 2m + 80° = 0°$

$2m - 2n = 80°$

$m - n = 40°$

$x + n = m$

$x = m - n = 40°$

Correct Answer : D

15.

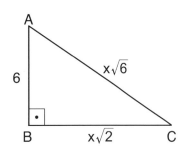

$6^2 + 2 \cdot x^2 = 6 \cdot x^2$

$36 + 2x^2 = 6x^2$

$36 = 4x^2, \quad 9 = x^2, \quad 3 = x$

Correct Answer : B

16.

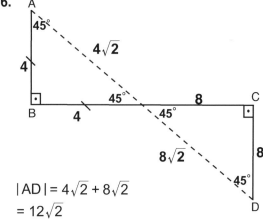

$|AD| = 4\sqrt{2} + 8\sqrt{2}$

$= 12\sqrt{2}$

Correct Answer : B

17.

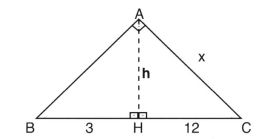

$h^2 = 3 \times 12, \quad h^2 = 36 \quad h = 6$

$h^2 + 12^2 = x^2$

$6^2 + 12^2 = x^2$

$36 + 144 = x^2$

$x = 6\sqrt{5}$

Correct Answer : C

18.

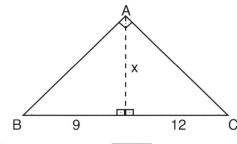

$x^2 = 9 \times 12, \quad x = \sqrt{9 \times 12}$

$x = 6\sqrt{3}$

Correct Answer : B

19.

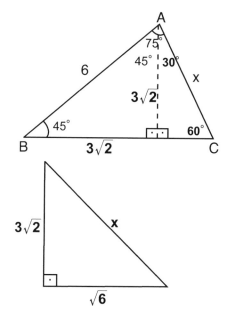

$x^2 = (3\sqrt{2})^2 + (\sqrt{6})^2$

$x^2 = 18 + 6$

$x^2 = 24$

$x = 2\sqrt{6}$

Correct Answer : C

1.

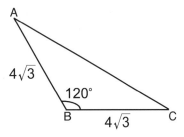

From the figure, what is the area of △(ABC)?

A) $12\sqrt{3}$ B) $8\sqrt{3}$ C) $9\sqrt{3}$ D) $18\sqrt{3}$

3.

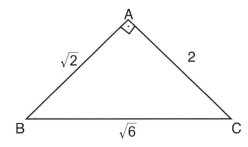

What is the area of △(ABC)?

A) 2   B) $\sqrt{2}$ C) $2\sqrt{2}$ D) $3\sqrt{2}$

2.

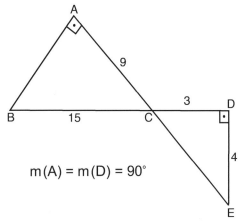

m(A) = m(D) = 90°

Find the area of △(ABC).

A) 27   B) 36   C) 54   D) 72

4.

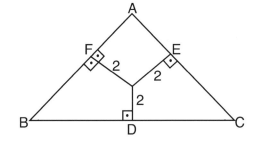

If △(ABC) is an equilateral triangle,
m(D) = m(F) = m(E) = 90. What is the area
of △(ABC)?

A) 48   B) $48\sqrt{3}$ C) $12\sqrt{3}$ D) $36\sqrt{3}$

5.

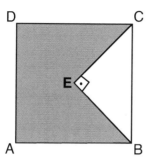

Square ABCD has a perimeter of 32m, and the perimeter of the triangle EBC is 18m. Find the area of the shaded part.

A)18m²   B)52m²   C)55m²   D)64m²

7.

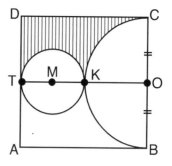

In the figure above ABCD is a square and AB = 4 feet. What is the area of the shaded part?

A)$8-\frac{3\pi}{2}$ B)$4-\frac{3\pi}{2}$ C)$\frac{3\pi}{2}-2$ D)$\frac{3\pi}{2}$

6.

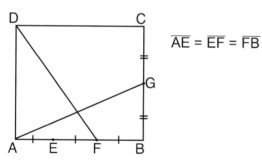

$\overline{AE} = \overline{EF} = \overline{FB}$

In square ABCD find $\frac{\overline{AE}}{\overline{BG}}$

A)1   B)3   C)$\frac{2}{3}$ D)6

8

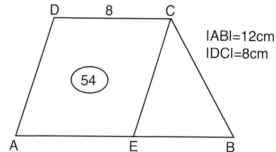

|ABI=12cm
|DCI=8cm

In the above figure, ABCD is a trapezoid and AECD is parallelogram.
If the area A(AECD)= 54cm² then what is the area of triangle CBE?

A)7.5cm²   B)13.5cm²   C)27cm²   D)54cm²

9.

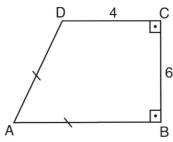

In the above trapezoid ABCD, DC=4, BC=6, and AD=AB.

What is the value of |AB| ?

A) $\frac{13}{4}$ B) $\frac{13}{2}$ C) 13   D) 4

10.

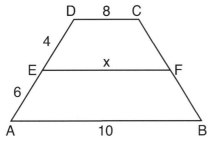

In the above trapezoid ABCD, DC=8, EF=x, and AB=10.

What is the value of x ?

A) 2.2   B) 4.4   C) 8.8   D) 9.8

11.

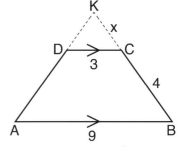

In the above figure, what is the value of x?

A) 2   B) 4   C) 6   D) 8

12.

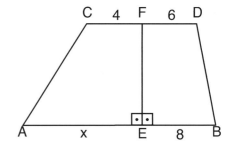

In the above figure, if the area of AEFC is equal to the area of EBDF,

what is the value of x ?

A) 6   B) 8   C) 10   D) 12

13.

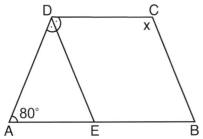

In the above figure, DC//EB and DE//CB.

What is the value of x?

A) 100°   B) 120°   C) 130°   D) 150°

15. The figure ABCD is rectangular and AKB is an equilateral triangle. If the area of the rect - angle is $8\sqrt{3}$, then find the AB.

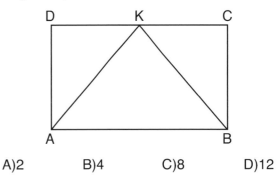

A) 2   B) 4   C) 8   D) 12

14. In the figure below, ABCD is a square and AE ⊥ EB. EB=8, AE=6. What is the area of the shaded part?

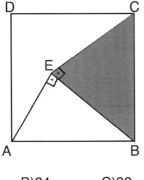

A) 16   B) 24   C) 32   D) 48

16. In the figure below, O is the center of the circle. If OB=AO=10 and BC=12, what is the area of A(ABC)?

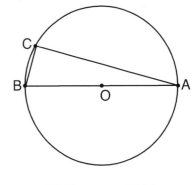

A) 24   B) 48   C) 64   D) 96

17. What is the area of the following square if the length of AD is $6\sqrt{2}$?

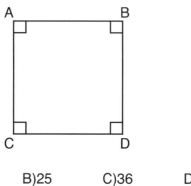

A)16   B)25   C)36   D)47

19.

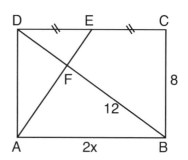

In the above figure, $\triangle(AFB)$ is similar to $\triangle(DEF)$,
what is the value of x?

A)$\sqrt{15}$ B)$\sqrt{35}$ C)$\sqrt{55}$ D)$\sqrt{65}$

18. Which of the following could not be the third side of the triangle if a triangle has sides of lengths 4 and 10?

A)6   B)8   C)10   D)13

Test 20
Answer Key

1)	A
2)	C
3)	B
4)	C
5)	C
6)	C
7)	A
8)	B
9)	B
10)	C
11)	A
12)	C
13)	C
14)	B
15)	B
16)	D
17)	C
18)	A
19)	D

1.

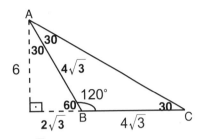

$$30° \longrightarrow 2\sqrt{3}$$
$$60° \longrightarrow 6$$
$$\text{Area} = \frac{h \times b}{2} = \frac{6 \times 4\sqrt{3}}{2}$$
$$= 12\sqrt{3}$$

Correct Answer : A

2.

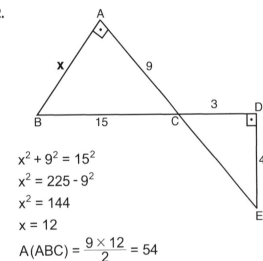

$$x^2 + 9^2 = 15^2$$
$$x^2 = 225 - 9^2$$
$$x^2 = 144$$
$$x = 12$$
$$A(ABC) = \frac{9 \times 12}{2} = 54$$

Correct Answer : C

3.

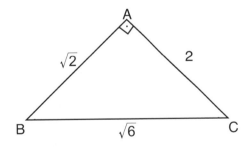

$$A(ABC) = \frac{b \times h}{2} = \frac{|AB| . |AC|}{2}$$
$$= \frac{\sqrt{2} \times 2}{2} = \sqrt{2}$$

Correct Answer : B

4.

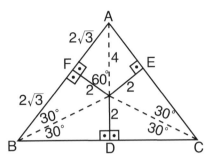

$$AB = 4\sqrt{3}$$
$$\triangle(ABC) = \frac{a^2\sqrt{3}}{4}$$
$$= \frac{(4\sqrt{3})^2 . \sqrt{3}}{4} = \frac{48\sqrt{3}}{4}$$
$$= 12\sqrt{3}$$

Correct Answer : C

5.

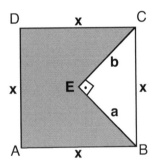

Perimeter of ABCD = 32m
$$4x = 32m \quad x = 8m$$
$$a + b + x = 18m$$
$$a^2 + b^2 = x^2 \quad a^2 + b^2 = 64$$
$$(a + b)^2 - 2ab = 64$$
$$a + b = 10, \quad 100 - 2ab = 64 \quad ab = 18$$
$$A(BEC) = \frac{18}{2} = 9m^2$$
Shaded Area = 64 - 9
$$= 55m^2$$

Correct Answer : C

6.

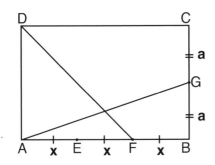

$3x = 2a$

$\dfrac{3x}{2} = a$

$\dfrac{AE}{BG} = \dfrac{x}{\frac{3x}{2}} = \dfrac{x}{1} \times \dfrac{2}{3x} = \dfrac{2}{3}$

Correct Answer : C

8.

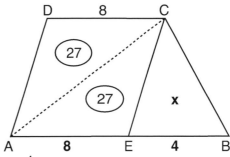

$\dfrac{x}{27} = \dfrac{4}{8}$

$\dfrac{x}{27} = \dfrac{1}{2}$

$x = 13.5\text{cm}^2$

Correct Answer : B

9.

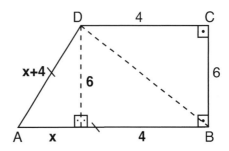

Pythagorean theorem

$(x + 4)^2 = x^2 + 6^2$

$x^2 + 8x + 16 = x^2 + 36$

$8x + 16 = 36$

$8x = 20 \quad x = \dfrac{5}{2}$

$AB = x + 4 = \dfrac{5}{2} + 4 = \dfrac{13}{2}$

Correct Answer : B

7.

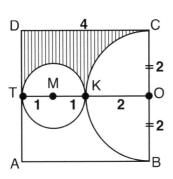

$A(ABCD) = 4^2 = 16\text{ft}^2$

$A(DTOC) = 4 \times 2 = 8\text{ft}^2$

Area of small half circle $= \dfrac{\pi r^2}{2} = \dfrac{\pi}{2}$

Area of quarter of big circle $= \dfrac{\pi r^2}{4}$

$= \dfrac{\pi \cdot 2^2}{4} = \pi$

Shaded part area $= 8 - (\dfrac{\pi}{2} + \pi) = 8 - \dfrac{3\pi}{2}$

Correct Answer : A

10.

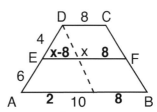

From similarity theorem

$\dfrac{x - 8}{2} = \dfrac{4}{10}$

$10(x - 8) = 8$

$10x - 80 = 8 \quad 10x = 88 \quad x = 8.8$

Correct Answer : C

11.

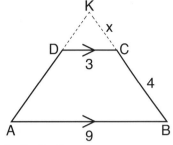

From similarity theorem

$$\frac{x}{x+4} = \frac{3}{9}$$

$$x = 2$$

Correct Answer : A

12.

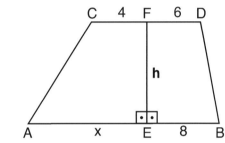

if A(AEFC) = A(EBDF)

$$\frac{(6+8)\not{h}}{2} = \frac{(4+x)\not{h}}{2}$$

$$\frac{14}{\not{2}} = \frac{4+x}{\not{2}}$$

$$14 = 4 + x \quad 10 = x$$

Correct Answer : C

13.

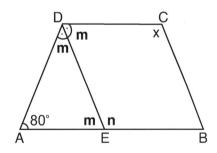

$$2m + 80 = 180°$$

$$2m = 100° \quad m = 50°$$

$$m + n = 180° \quad 50 + n = 180°$$

$$n = 130° \quad x = n = 130°$$

Correct Answer : C

14.

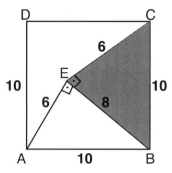

Shaded area $= \frac{6 \times 8}{2} = 24$

Correct Answer : B

15.

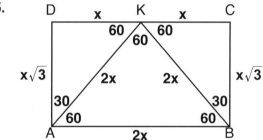

$$A(ABCD) = x\sqrt{3} \cdot 2x = 8\sqrt{3}$$

$$= 2x^2 = 8 \quad x^2 = 4 \quad x = 2$$

$$AB = 2x = 4$$

Correct Answer : B

16.

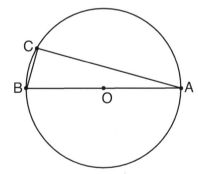

Pythogorean theorem

$$(BC)^2 + (AC)^2 = (BA)^2$$

$$12^2 + (AC)^2 = 20^2 \quad AC = 16$$

$$A(ABC) = \frac{12 \times 16}{2} = 96$$

Correct Answer : D

17.

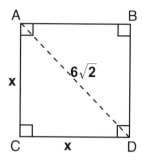

$x^2 + x^2 = (6\sqrt{2})^2$

$2x^2 = 72$

$x^2 = 36, \quad x = 6$

$A(ABCD) = 6^2 = 36$

Correct Answer : C

18.

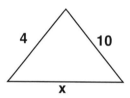

$10 - 4 < x < 10 + 4$

$6 < x < 14$

Correct Answer : A

19.

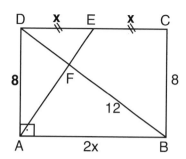

From similarity theorem

$\dfrac{AF}{EF} = \dfrac{FB}{FD} = \dfrac{AB}{ED}$

$\dfrac{12}{FD} = \dfrac{2x}{x} \qquad FD = 6$

Pythagorean theorem

$(AD)^2 + (AB)^2 = (BD)^2$

$8^2 + (2x)^2 = (18)^2$

$64 + 4x^2 = 324$

$x^2 = 65, \quad x = \sqrt{65}$

Correct Answer : D

Circle

Radius	The distance from the center of the circle to the edge.	
Chord	A line segment whose endpoints are on a circle.	
Diameter	A **chord** that passes through the center of the circle.	
Tangent	A line which intersects a circle in exactly one point.	
Segment	A region of a circle which is "cut off" from the rest of the circle by a secant or a chord.	

Area of Circle	$A = \pi r^2$
Circumference	$C = 2\pi r$
Semi-Circle	$A = \frac{1}{2}\pi r^2$
Area of the Sector	$A = \frac{n°}{360°}\pi r^2$
Central Angle	$m(AOB)=m(AB)=\alpha$
Equations of a Circle	$(x-h)^2 + (y-k)^2 = r^2$
Inscribed Angle	$m(BAC) = \frac{m(BC)}{2} = \alpha$
Tangent Chord Angle	$m(ATB) = \frac{m(TA)}{2} = \alpha$
Angle Formed by Two Intersecting Chords	$m(APB) = \frac{m(BA)+m(DC)}{2} = \alpha$
Angle Formed Outside of Circle by Intersection	$m(APB) = \frac{m(AB)-m(DC)}{2} = \alpha$
Length of an Arc Formula	$\overset{\frown}{AB} = 2\pi r\frac{\alpha}{360°}$

Circle

Test 21

1. In the following figure, O is the center of circle, what is the measure of angle $\angle(ACB)$?

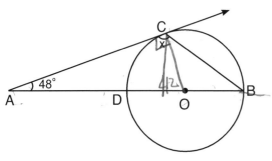

A) 111°   B) 112°   C) 115°   D) 118°   E) 120°

2. In the following figure, what is the measure of x?

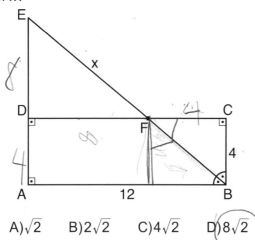

A) $\sqrt{2}$ B) $2\sqrt{2}$ C) $4\sqrt{2}$ D) $8\sqrt{2}$

3. In the following figure, what is the measure of x?

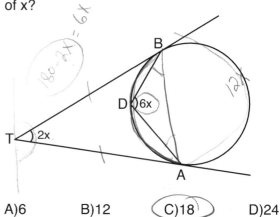

A) 6   B) 12   C) 18   D) 24

$$180 - 2x + 12\varphi = 360$$
$$10x = 480$$

4. Find the area of the shaded part of the triangle (BEC).

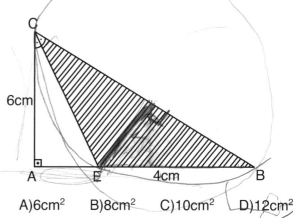

A) 6cm²   B) 8cm²   C) 10cm²   D) 12cm²

5. In the following figure O is the center of circle, what is the measure of x?

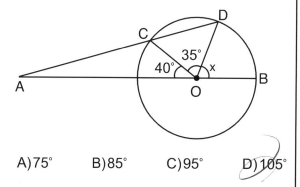

A) 75°   B) 85°   C) 95°   D) 105°

7. In the following figure O is the center of circle, what is the measure of x?

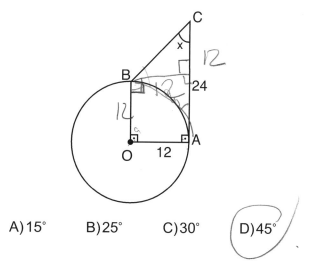

A) 15°   B) 25°   C) 30°   D) 45°

6. In the following figure, what is the measure of x?

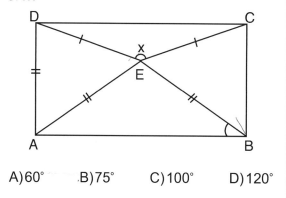

A) 60°   B) 75°   C) 100°   D) 120°

8. In the figure below, AB and CE are diameters of the circles. What is the measure of x?

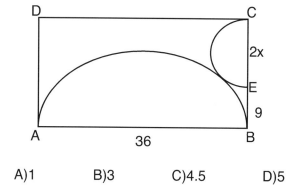

A) 1   B) 3   C) 4.5   D) 5

9. In the following figure, what is the measure of x?

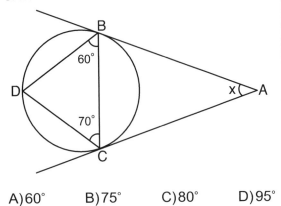

A) 60°   B) 75°   C) 80°   D) 95°

10. Equilateral triangle AEB is inscribed in the rectangle. If AB=12, what is the measure of x?

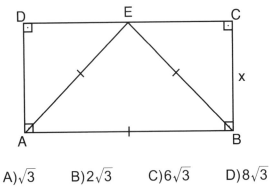

A) $\sqrt{3}$ B) $2\sqrt{3}$ C) $6\sqrt{3}$ D) $8\sqrt{3}$

11. In the following figure, what is the measure of a?

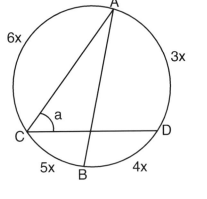

A) 15°   B) 25°   C) 30°   D) 45°

12. In the following figure △(AEB) is an equilateral triangle. What is the value of x?

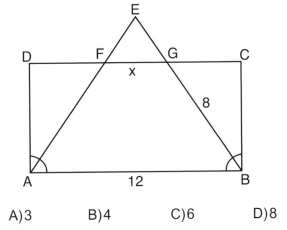

A) 3   B) 4   C) 6   D) 8

13. In the following figure O is the center of circle, what is the measure of x?

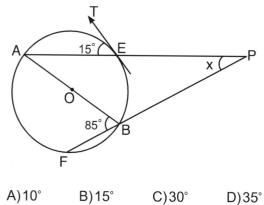

A) 10°   B) 15°   C) 30°   D) 35°

15. In the following figure O is the center of circle, what is the measure of $\angle(ABC)$?

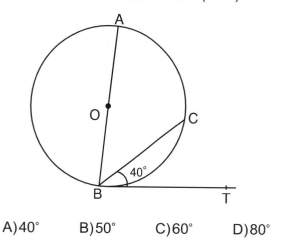

A) 40°   B) 50°   C) 60°   D) 80°

14. Find the area of the shaded part in the following rectangle.

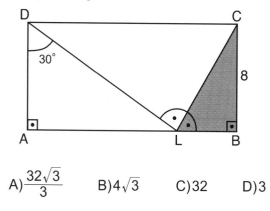

A) $\dfrac{32\sqrt{3}}{3}$ B) $4\sqrt{3}$ C) 32   D) 3

16. In the following figure O is the center of circle, what is the value of x?

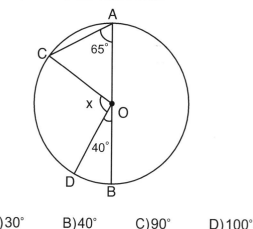

A) 30°   B) 40°   C) 90°   D) 100°

17. In the following circle O is the center of circle, what is the value of x?

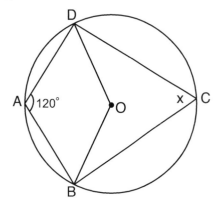

A) 50°   B) 60°   C) 120°   D) 140°

18. If the area of a circle is 36π, then find the circumference of the circle.

A) 8π
B) 10π
C) 12π
D) 16π

19. If the circumference of a circle is 12π, what is the area of the circle?

A) 6π
B) 12π
C) 24π
D) 36π

20. The angles of a triangle are in the ratio of 4:5:9. What is the degree measure of the smallest angle?

A) 40°
B) 30°
C) 25°
D) 20°

Test 21
Answer Key

1)	A
2)	D
3)	C
4)	D
5)	D
6)	D
7)	D
8)	C
9)	C
10)	C
11)	C
12)	B
13)	A
14)	A
15)	B
16)	C
17)	B
18)	C
19)	D
20)	A

1.

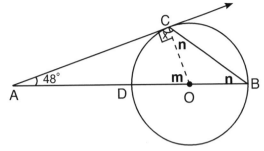

$90° + 48° + m = 180°$

$m = 42°$

$2n = m,\quad 2n = 42°,\quad n = 21°$

$x = 90° + n = 90° + 21° = 111°$

Correct Answer : A

2.

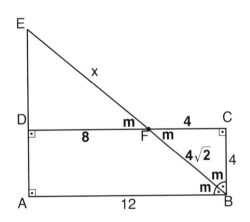

From similarity theorem

$\triangle(EDF) \cong \triangle(BCF)$

$\dfrac{x}{8} = \dfrac{4\sqrt{2}}{4}$

$x = 8\sqrt{2}$

Correct Answer : D

3.

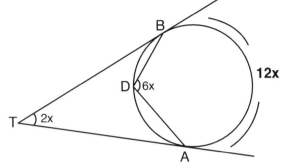

ArcADB $= 180° - 2x$

ArcAB $= 12x$

$12x + 180° - 2x = 360°$

$10x + 180° = 360°$

$10x = 180°\quad x = 18°$

Correct Answer : C

4.

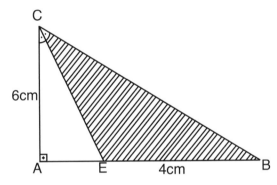

Area of shaded part $= \dfrac{6cm \cdot 4cm}{2}$

$= \dfrac{24cm^2}{2} = 12cm^2$

Correct Answer : D

5.

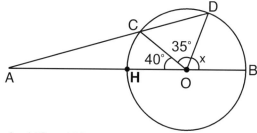

ArcHC = 40°
ArcCD = 35°
ArcBD = x
40° + 35° + x = 180°
x = 180° - 75°
x = 105°

Correct Answer : D

6.

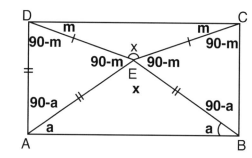

x + 2m = 180°
x + 2a = 180°
x + 2a = x + 2m
a = m
90 - m + 90 - m + 90 - m = 180°
270° - 3m = 180°
30 = m
x + 2m = 180°
x + 60 = 180°
x = 120°

Correct Answer : D

7.

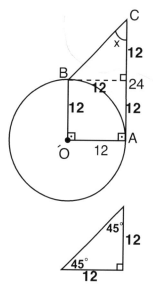

Correct Answer : D

8.

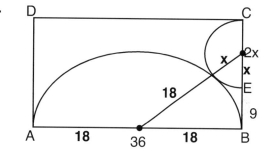

Pythagorean theorem
$(x + 9)^2 + 18^2 = (x + 18)^2$
$x^2 + 18x + 81 + 324 = x^2 + 36x + 324$
81 = 18x
$\frac{81}{18}$ = x
$\frac{9}{2}$ = x,   4.5 = x

Correct Answer : C

9.

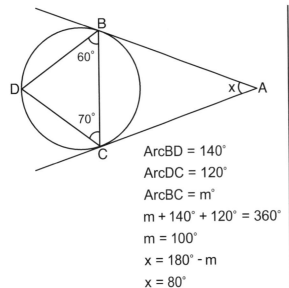

ArcBD = 140°

ArcDC = 120°

ArcBC = m°

m + 140° + 120° = 360°

m = 100°

x = 180° - m

x = 80°

Correct Answer : C

10.

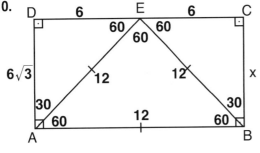

x = 6√3

Correct Answer : C

11.

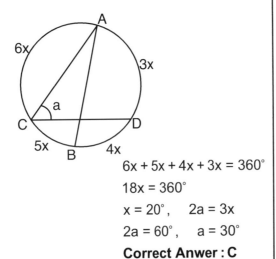

6x + 5x + 4x + 3x = 360°

18x = 360°

x = 20°,   2a = 3x

2a = 60°,   a = 30°

Correct Anwer : C

12.

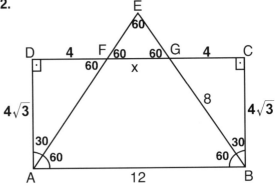

4 + x + 4 = 12

x = 4

Correct Answer : B

13.

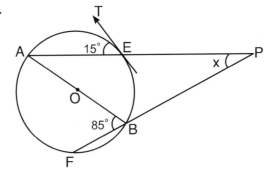

ArcFB = 10°

ArcAT = 30°

ArcAF = 170°

ArcEB = m

m + 170° + 30° + 10° = 360°

m = 150°

$x = \dfrac{ArcAF - ArcEB}{2}$

$x = \dfrac{170° - 150°}{2} = 10°$

Correct Answer : A

14.

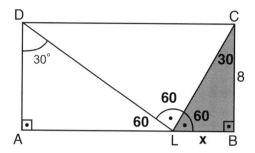

Rule

If $x\sqrt{3} = 8$, $x = \dfrac{8\sqrt{3}}{3}$

$A(LBC) = \dfrac{x \cdot 8}{2} = \dfrac{8 \times \dfrac{8\sqrt{3}}{3}}{2}$

$= \dfrac{64\sqrt{3}}{6} = \dfrac{32\sqrt{3}}{3}$

Correct Answer : A

15.

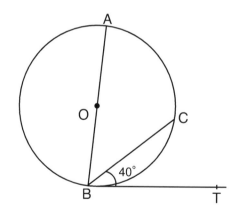

ArcBC = 80°

ArcAC = 100°

$\triangle(ABC) = \dfrac{100°}{2} = 50°$

Correct Answer : B

16.

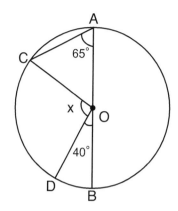

ArcDB = 40°

ArcDC = x

ArcBDC = 130°

x + 40 = 130°

x = 90°

Correct Answer : C

17.

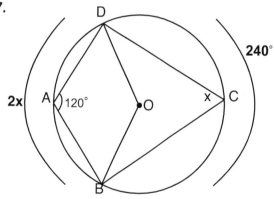

ArcBCD = 240°

ArcBAD = 2x

2x + 240° = 360°

2x = 120°

x = 60°

Correct Answer : B

18. $A = \pi r^2$

$36\pi = \pi r^2$

$36 = r^2$

$6 = r$

$C = 2\pi r = 12\pi$

Correct Answer : C

19. $C = 2\pi r$

$2\pi r = 12\pi$

$2r = 12$

$r = 6$

$A = \pi r^2 = 36\pi$

Correct Answer : D

20. $4k + 5k + 9k = 180°$

$18k = 180°$

$k = 10°$

smallest angle = $4k$

$= 40°$

Correct Answer : A

Circle

1. In the following figure O is the center of circle, find the length of the arc AB.

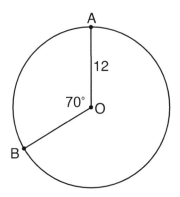

A)$\frac{14}{3}\pi$ B)$\frac{3}{14}\pi$ C)3π D)14π

2. In the following figure O is the center of circle and the radius is 4cm. Find the length of arc AB.

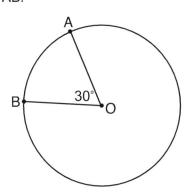

A)$\frac{2}{3}\pi$ B)$\frac{3}{2}\pi$ C)3π D)2π

3. In the following figure P is the center of circle, find the area of the shaded region.

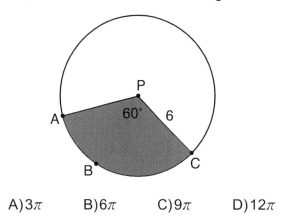

A)3π B)6π C)9π D)12π

4. In the following figure O is the center of circle, find the area of the shaded part.

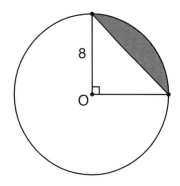

A)$16-32\pi$ B)$16\pi-32$ C)32π D)16π

5. If the center of a circle is at (3,6), and the radius of the circle is 4, what is the equation of that circle?

A) $(x-3)^2 + (y-6)^2 = 4$

B) $(x-3)^2 + (y-6)^2 = 8$

C) $(x-3)^2 + (y-6)^2 = 16$

D) $(x-6)^2 + (y-3)^2 = 4$

8. Find the equation of the circle centered at (3,-2) with a radius of 5.

A) $(x-3)^2 + (y-2)^2 = 5$

B) $(x-3)^2 + (y+2)^2 = 5$

C) $(x+3)^2 + (y+2)^2 = 5$

D) $(x-3)^2 + (y+2)^2 = 25$

6. What is the radius of a circle with the equation $(x-3)^2 + (y+2)^2 = 25$?

A) 3
B) 4
C) 5
D) 6

9. The two line segments are tangents to the circle. Find x.

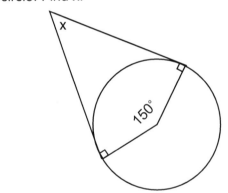

A) 10°   B) 20°   C) 30°   D) 50°

7. The endpoints of a diameter of circle M are located at points (3,5) and (7,8). What is the circumference of the circle?

A) 5π
B) 10π
C) 15π
D) 20π

10. In the following O is the center of circle, AC and AB are tangents of the circle. Find x.

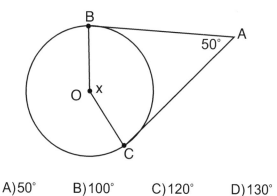

A) 50°   B) 100°   C) 120°   D) 130°

11. In the following circle AB = 3, BC = 6 and, B is the center of both circle. Find the shaded area.

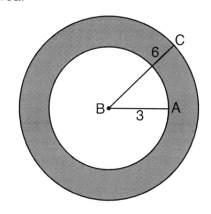

A) 9π   B) 12π   C) 18π   D) 27π

12. If the bigger circle has a center at O and a diameter of 16 inches, find the area of the shaded part.

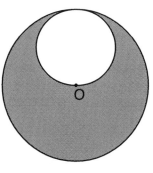

A) 12π   B) 24π   C) 32π   D) 48π

13. Find the area of the shaded region.

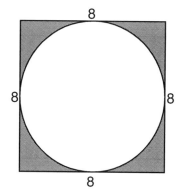

A) 64 - 32π
B) 64 - 16π
C) 32π - 64
D) 16 - 32π

14. In the following figures, ABC is an equilateral triangle and each side is $6\sqrt{3}$ cm. Find the shaded area.

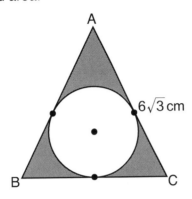

$6\sqrt{3}$ cm

A) $6-3\pi$ B) $27\sqrt{3}-9\pi$ C) $27-9\pi$ D) $36-12\pi$

15. In the following figure P is the center of circle, find the area of the shaded region.

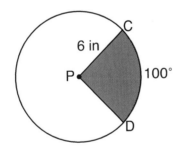

C
6 in
P
100°
D

A) 5π B) 10π C) 20π D) 30π

16. If the area of the circle is 36π, what is the diameter of the circle?

A) 3
B) 6
C) 9
D) 12

17. If the ratio of the circumference to the area of a circle is 4 to 6, what is the radius of the circle?

A) 1
B) 3
C) 4
D) 6

Test 22
Answer Key

1)	A
2)	A
3)	B
4)	B
5)	C
6)	C
7)	A
8)	D
9)	C
10)	D
11)	D
12)	D
13)	B
14)	B
15)	B
16)	D
17)	B

1.

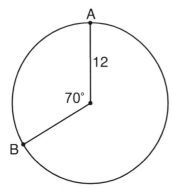

$\text{ArcAB} = \dfrac{2\pi r\, \alpha}{360}$

$= \dfrac{2\pi r 70°}{360°} = \dfrac{2\pi.12.70°}{360°}$

$= \dfrac{14}{3}\pi$

Correct Answer : A

2.

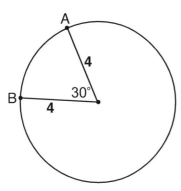

$\text{ArcAB} = \dfrac{2\pi r\, \alpha}{360}$

$= \dfrac{2.\pi.4.30}{360}$

$= \dfrac{2}{3}\pi$

Correct Answer : A

3.

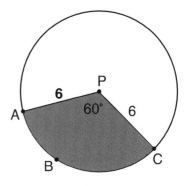

$\text{Shaded Area} = \dfrac{\pi r^2\, \alpha}{360}$

$= \dfrac{\pi 36.60}{360}$

$= 6\pi$

Correct Answer : B

4.

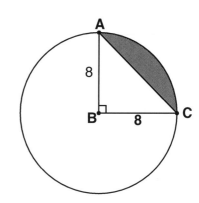

$A(ABC) = \dfrac{8 \times 8}{2} = 32$

Area of Quarter of Circle

$= \dfrac{\pi r^2}{4} = \dfrac{64\pi}{4} = 16\pi$

Shaded Area $= 16\pi - 32$

Correct Answer : B

5. $(x - h)^2 + (y - k)^2 = r^2$

$(x - 3)^2 + (y - 6)^2 = 16$

Correct Answer : C

6. $(x - h)^2 + (y - k)^2 = r^2$

$r^2 = 25$

$r = 5$

Correct Answer : C

7. $d = \sqrt{(x_2 - x_1)^2 + (y_2 - y_1)^2}$

$d = \sqrt{(7 - 3)^2 + (8 - 5)^2}$

$d = \sqrt{4^2 + 3^2}$

$d = 5$

$c = \pi d = 5\pi$

Correct Answer : A

8. $(x - h)^2 + (y - k)^2 = r^2$

$(x - 3)^2 + (y + 2)^2 = 5^2$

$r^2 = 25$

$r = 5$

Correct Answer : D

9.

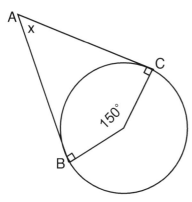

$x = 180° - 150°$

$x = 30°$

Correct Answer : C

10.

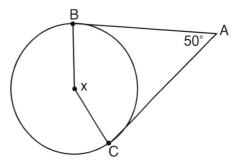

ArcBC = 180° - 50°

ArcBC = 130°

x = 130°

Correct Answer : D

11.

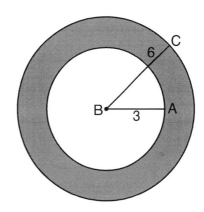

Small Circle Area = πr^2

= 9π

Big Circle Area = πr^2

= 36π

Shaded Part Area = $36\pi - 9\pi$

= 27π

Correct Answer : D

12.

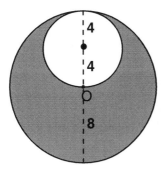

Small Circle Area = $\pi r^2 = 16\pi$

Big Circle Area = $\pi r^2 = 64\pi$

Shaded Area = $64\pi - 16\pi$

$= 48\pi$

Correct Answer : D

13.

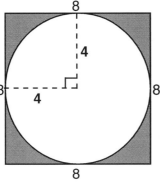

A(ABCD) = $8 \times 8 = 64$

Area of Circle = $\pi r^2 = 16\pi$

Shaded Area = $64 - 16\pi$

Correct Answer : B

14.

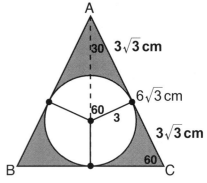

r = 3cm

Triangle Area = $\dfrac{a^2\sqrt{3}}{4} = \dfrac{(6\sqrt{3})^2\sqrt{3}}{4}$

$= \dfrac{108\sqrt{3}}{4} = 27\sqrt{3}\,\text{cm}^2$

Circle Area = $\pi r^2 = 3^2\pi = 9\pi$

Shaded Area = $27\sqrt{3} - 9\pi$

Correct Answer : B

15.

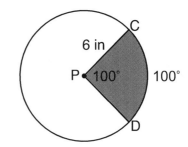

Shaded Area = $\dfrac{\pi r^2 \alpha}{360°}$

$= \dfrac{\pi.6^2.100°}{360°}$

$= \dfrac{36\pi.100°}{360°}$

$= 10\pi$

Correct Answer : B

16. Circle Area $= \pi r^2$

$\pi r^2 = 36\pi$

$r^2 = 36$

$r = 6$

$d = 2r$

$d = 12$

Correct Answer : D

17. $\dfrac{\text{ratio of circumference}}{\text{ratio of area}}$

$\dfrac{2\pi r}{\pi r^2} = \dfrac{4}{6}$

$\dfrac{2r}{r^2} = \dfrac{4}{6}$

$\dfrac{2}{r} = \dfrac{4}{6}$, $r = 3$

Correct Answer : B

Volume

Right rectangular prism	
	$V = l \times w \times h$
Cube	$V = a^3$
Cylinder	$V = \pi r^2 h$
Pyramid	$V = \frac{1}{3}(l \times w \times h)$
Cone	$V = \frac{1}{3}\pi r^2 h$
Sphere	$V = \frac{4}{3}\pi r^3$

Example: The radius of the sphare below is 6 cm. What is the volume of the sphere?

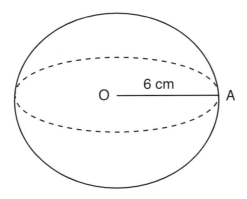

Solution :

$$V = \frac{4}{3}\pi r^3$$

$$V = \frac{4}{3}\pi (6)^3 = \frac{4}{3}\pi (6cm \times 6cm \times 6cm) = 288\pi cm^3$$

Example: The radius and the height of the cylinder below are respectively 3 cm and 4 cm. What is the volume of the Cylinder?

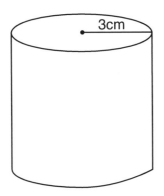

Solution : $V = \pi r^2 h$

$$V = \pi (3cm)^2 \times h = \pi (9cm^2 \times 4cm)$$

$$V = 36\pi cm^3$$

1. Find the volume of the following cylinder. (Give your answer in terms of π)

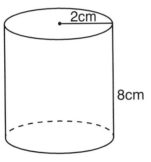

A)$4\pi cm^3$ B)$16\pi cm^3$ C)$24\pi cm^3$ D)$32\pi cm^3$

2. Find the volume of the following cube.

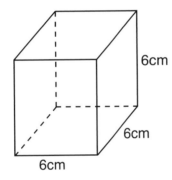

A)$36cm^3$ B)$116cm^3$ C)$216cm^3$ D)$322cm^3$

3. In the following cylinder shape, if the volume of the cylinder is $72\pi cm^3$ then find the radius of the cylinder.

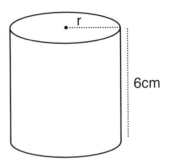

A)$\sqrt{3}$ cm   B)$2\sqrt{3}$ cm   C)$4\sqrt{3}$ cm   D)6cm

4. In the following figures, the volume of the Cone and the cylinder are equal. What is the value of a?

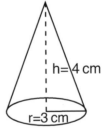 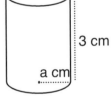

A)1cm   B)2cm   C)3cm   D)4cm

5. A cylinder has a height of 4 cm and a volume of $64\pi\,\text{cm}^3$. What is the radius of the cylinder?

A) 4 cm
B) 8 cm
C) 10 cm
D) 24 cm

6. Find the volume of the following cylinder shown below. (Give your answer in terms of π)

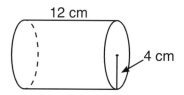

12 cm

4 cm

A)$32\pi\,\text{cm}^3$ B)$112\pi\,\text{cm}^3$ C)$154\pi\,\text{cm}^3$ D)$192\pi\,\text{cm}^3$

7. Find the volume of the sphere shown below. (Give your answer in terms of π)

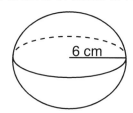

6 cm

A)$120\pi\,\text{cm}^3$ B)$150\pi\,\text{cm}^3$ C)$196\pi\,\text{cm}^3$ D)$288\pi\,\text{cm}^3$

8. A cone and a sphere have the same radius and volume. Find the radius r in terms of the height h of the sphere.

A)h   B)2h   C)$\dfrac{h}{2}$ D)$\dfrac{h}{4}$

9. The volume of a sphere is $36\pi\,\text{cm}^3$. Find the radius of the sphere.

A) 1 cm
B) 3 cm
C) 6 cm
D) 8 cm

10. In the following cone shape the diameter is 18ft and height 12ft. Find the volume of cone. (Give your answer in terms of π)

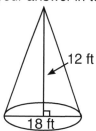

12 ft

18 ft

A) $150\pi\,\text{ft}^3$

B) $196\pi\,\text{ft}^3$

C) $324\pi\,\text{ft}^3$

D) $480\pi\,\text{ft}^3$

11. Find the volume of the following pyramid.

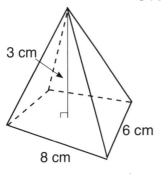

3 cm

6 cm

8 cm

A) 12cm^3 B) 24cm^3 C) 48cm^3 D) 60cm^3

12. Find the volume of a cone with a height of 10cm and a radius of 6cm. (Give your answer in terms of π)

A) 96πcm^3

B) 110πcm^3

C) 120πcm^3

D) 150πcm^3

13. The radius of a cylinder is increased by 25% and its height is decreased by 20%. What is the effect on the volume of cylinder?

A) It is decreased by 50%
B) It is decreased by 25%
C) It is increased by 25%
D) It is increased by 50%

14. A cylinder has a height that is four times as long as its radius. If the volume of the cylinder is 32πcm^3 then find the radius.

A) 1 cm
B) 2 cm
C) 3 cm
D) 4 cm

15. A cube has a volume of 64 ft^3 . What is one side of the cube?

A) 2ft
B) 3ft
C) 4ft
D) 6ft

16. Find the volume of a rectangular prism that has a length of 6cm, a width of 4cm, and a height of 10cm.

A) 60 cm^3
B) 120 cm^3
C) 240 cm^3
D) 480 cm^3

17. The volume of the following rectangular prism is 96cm^3. What is the value of h?

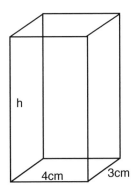

h

4cm   3cm

A)   4 cm

B)   8 cm

C) 12 cm

D) 16 cm

Test 23
Answer Key

1)	D
2)	C
3)	B
4)	B
5)	A
6)	D
7)	D
8)	D
9)	B
10)	C
11)	C
12)	C
13)	C
14)	B
15)	C
16)	C
17)	B

Volume

1.

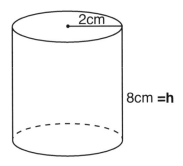

h = 8cm   r = 2cm

$V = \pi r^2 h$

$V = \pi.(2\text{cm})^2.8\text{cm}$

$V = 32\pi\text{cm}^3$

Correct Answer : D

2.

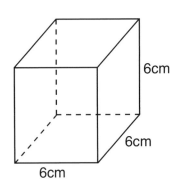

$V = a^3$, a = 6cm

$V = (6\text{cm})^3$

$V = 216\text{cm}^3$

Correct Answer : C

3.

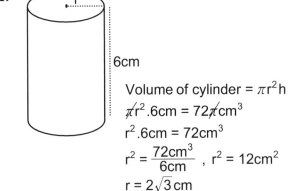

Volume of cylinder = $\pi r^2 h$

$\cancel{\pi} r^2.6\text{cm} = 72\cancel{\pi}\text{cm}^3$

$r^2.6\text{cm} = 72\text{cm}^3$

$r^2 = \dfrac{72\text{cm}^3}{6\text{cm}}$, $r^2 = 12\text{cm}^2$

$r = 2\sqrt{3}\,\text{cm}$

Correct Answer : B

4.

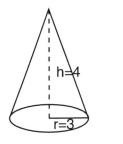 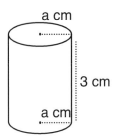

$V_{\text{cone}} = \dfrac{1}{3}\pi r^2 h = \dfrac{1}{3}\pi.9.4 = 12\pi$

$V_{\text{cylinder}} = \pi r^2 h = \pi.a^2.3$

$= \pi.a^2.3$

$V_{\text{cone}} = V_{\text{cylinder}}$

$12\cancel{\pi} = \cancel{\pi}.a^2.3$

$\dfrac{12}{3} = a^2$, $a^2 = 4$, $a = 2\text{cm}$

Correct Answer : B

5. h = 4cm

$V = 64\text{cm}^3$

$V = \pi r^2 h$

$64\cancel{\pi} = \cancel{\pi}.r^2.4$, $r^2 = 16\text{cm}^2$

r = 4cm

Correct Answer : A

6.

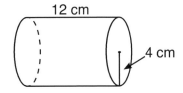

r = 4cm   h = 12cm

$V = \pi r^2 h$

$V = 12\text{cm}.(4\text{cm})^2.\pi = \pi \times 16 \times 12\text{cm}^3$

$V = 192\pi\text{cm}^3$

Correct Answer : D

7.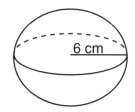

6 cm

$V = \frac{4}{3}\pi r^3$

$\frac{4}{3}\pi.216 cm^3$

$= 288\pi cm^3$

Correct Answer : D

8. $V_{cone} = \frac{1}{3}\pi r^2 h$ } $V_{cone} = V_{sphere}$

$V_{sphere} = \frac{4}{3}\pi r^3$ $\frac{1}{3}\pi r^2 h = \frac{4}{3}\pi r^3$

$\frac{1}{4}h = r$

Correct Answer : D

9. $V_{sphere} = \frac{4}{3}\pi r^3$

$36\pi cm^3 = \frac{4}{3}\pi r^3$

$r^3 = 27 cm^3$

$r = 3cm$

Correct Answer : B

10.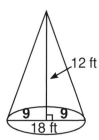

12 ft

9 9

18 ft

$V = \frac{1}{3}\pi r^2 h$

$V = \frac{1}{3}\pi.81.12$

$V = 324\pi ft^3$

Correct Answer : C

11.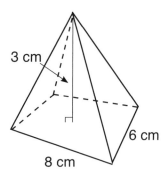

3 cm

6 cm

8 cm

$V_{pyramid} = \frac{l \times w \times h}{3}$

$V = \frac{3cm \times 6cm \times 8cm}{3}$

$V = 48cm^3$

Correct Answer : C

12. $V_{cone} = \frac{1}{3}\pi r^2 h$

$V = \frac{1}{3}\pi.36.10 = 120\pi cm^3$

Correct Answer : C

13. Suppose $r = 4$ $V = \pi r^2$

$h = 5$ $V = \pi.16.5 = 80\pi$

$r \longrightarrow 25\%$ increase $r = 5$

$h \longrightarrow 20\%$ decrease $h = 4$

$V = \pi r^2 = 25 \times 4 \times \pi = 100\pi$

$\frac{100\pi - 80\pi}{80\pi} = \frac{1}{4} = 25\%$ increase

Correct Answer : C

14. radius = r   } $V = \pi r^2 h$

  h = 4r

$V = \pi.r^2.4r = 4\pi r^3$

$4\pi r^3 = 32\pi cm^3$, $r^3 = 8cm^3$

$r = 2cm$

Correct Answer : B

15. $V_{cube} = a^3$

$a^3 = 64ft^3$

$a = 4ft$

Correct Answer : C

16. $V_{rectangular\,prism} = l \times w \times h$

$V = 4cm \times 6cm \times 10cm$

$= 240cm^3$

Correct Answer : C

17.

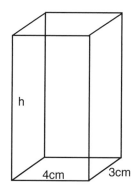

$V_{rectangular} = l \times w \times h$

$h.4cm.3cm = 96cm^3$

$h = \dfrac{96cm^3}{12cm^2}$

$h = 8cm$

Correct Answer : B

Trigonometry

Formulas for right triangles

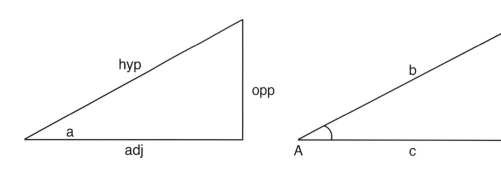

$$\sin \alpha = \frac{\text{opposite}}{\text{hypotenuse}}$$

$$\sin\widehat{A} = \frac{|BC|}{|AC|} = \frac{a}{b}$$

$$\sin\widehat{C} = \frac{|AB|}{|AC|} = \frac{c}{b}$$

$$\cos \alpha = \frac{\text{adjacent}}{\text{hypotenuse}}$$

$$\cos\widehat{A} = \frac{|AB|}{|AC|} = \frac{c}{b}$$

$$\cos\widehat{C} = \frac{|BC|}{|AC|} = \frac{a}{b}$$

$$\tan \alpha = \frac{\text{opposite}}{\text{adjacent}}$$

$$\tan\widehat{A} = \frac{|BC|}{|AB|} = \frac{a}{c}$$

$$\tan\widehat{C} = \frac{|AB|}{|BC|} = \frac{c}{a}$$

$$\cot \alpha = \frac{\text{adjacent}}{\text{opposite}}$$

$$\cot\widehat{A} = \frac{|AB|}{|BC|} = \frac{c}{a}$$

$$\cot\widehat{C} = \frac{|BC|}{|AB|} = \frac{a}{c}$$

Convert Radians to Degrees

D: Degrees

R: Radians

$$\frac{D}{180} = \frac{R}{\pi}$$

254

Trigonometry on the Unit Circle

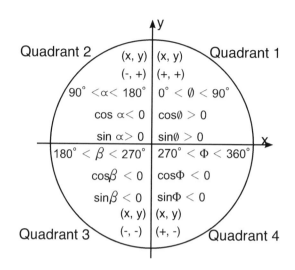

Trigonometric Values of Special Angles

Degrees	$0°$	$30°$	$45°$	$60°$	$90°$	$180°$	$360°$
Radians	0	$\dfrac{\pi}{6}$	$\dfrac{\pi}{4}$	$\dfrac{\pi}{3}$	$\dfrac{\pi}{2}$	π	2π
$\sin\emptyset$	0	$\dfrac{1}{2}$	$\dfrac{1}{\sqrt{2}}$	$\dfrac{\sqrt{3}}{2}$	1	0	0
$\cos\emptyset$	1	$\dfrac{\sqrt{3}}{2}$	$\dfrac{1}{\sqrt{2}}$	$\dfrac{1}{2}$	0	-1	1
$\tan\emptyset$	0	$\dfrac{1}{\sqrt{3}}$	1	$\sqrt{3}$	Und	0	0
$\cot\emptyset$	Und	$\sqrt{3}$	1	$\dfrac{1}{\sqrt{3}}$	0	Und	Und
$\sec\emptyset$	1	$\dfrac{2}{\sqrt{3}}$	$\sqrt{2}$	2	Und	-1	1
$\csc\emptyset$	Und	2	$\sqrt{2}$	$\dfrac{2}{\sqrt{3}}$	1	Und	Und

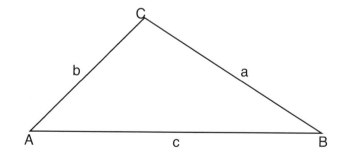

Law of Cosines

$$c^2 = a^2 + b^2 - 2ab\cos C$$

Law of Sines

$$\frac{\sin A}{a} = \frac{\sin B}{b} = \frac{\sin C}{c}$$

Trigonometry

Test 24

1. What is the radian measure of 120°?

A) $\frac{2}{3}\pi$

B) $\frac{3}{2}\pi$

C) 2π

D) 3π

2. Convert 60° into radians measure? (Give your answer in terms of π)

A) $\frac{1}{3}\pi$

B) 3π

C) 2π

D) $\frac{1}{2}\pi$

3. Find x.

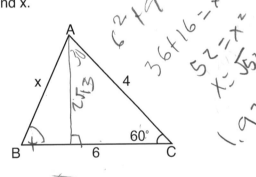

A) $\sqrt{7}$ B) $2\sqrt{7}$ C) $3\sqrt{7}$ D) $4\sqrt{7}$

4. For the following right triangle, what is the co-sine of angle C?

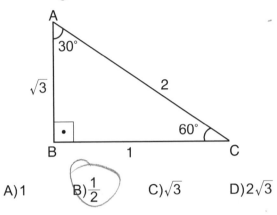

A) 1 B) $\frac{1}{2}$ C) $\sqrt{3}$ D) $2\sqrt{3}$

5. For the following right triangle, what is the sine of angle A?

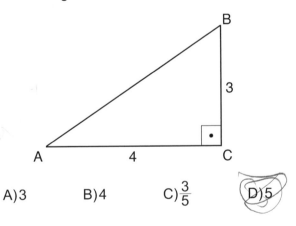

A) 3 B) 4 C) $\frac{3}{5}$ D) 5

6. From the following right triangle, if the sine$C = \frac{5}{13}$, then find cosine C?

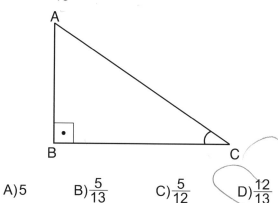

A) 5   B) $\frac{5}{13}$ C) $\frac{5}{12}$ D) $\frac{12}{13}$

7. In the right triangle below, which of the following is correct?

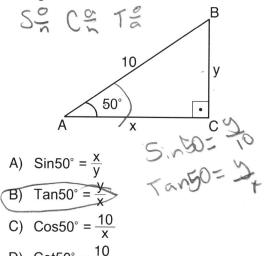

A) $Sin50° = \frac{x}{y}$

B) $Tan50° = \frac{y}{x}$

C) $Cos50° = \frac{10}{x}$

D) $Cot50° = \frac{10}{y}$

$Sin50 = \frac{y}{10}$

$Tan50 = \frac{y}{x}$

8. Simplify $Sin\theta \cdot Cot\theta$

A) $Tan\theta$ B) $Cot\theta$ C) $Sin\theta$ D) $Cos\theta$

9. In the two right triangles below, if Tan A=Cot D, find the value of EF.

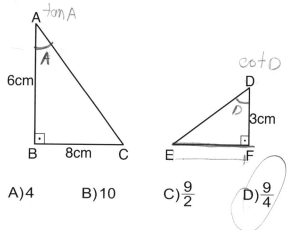

A) 4   B) 10   C) $\frac{9}{2}$ D) $\frac{9}{4}$

10. For the following right triangle, find the length of a. (Round your answer to the nearest tenth)

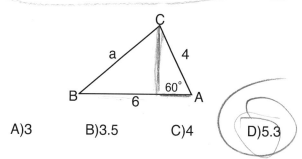

A) 3   B) 3.5   C) 4   D) 5.3

11. Convert the following radian measure into degrees.

$$\frac{2\pi}{3}$$

A) 40°   B) 90°   C) 120°   D) 150°

12. Given the right triangle ABC, find the value of Sine C?

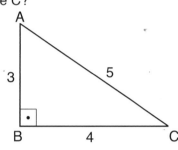

A) 3   B) $\frac{5}{3}$ C) 5   D) $\frac{3}{5}$

13. Given the right triangle ABC, find the value of cosx.

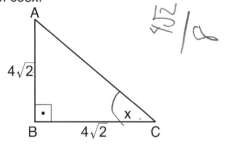

A) $\frac{\sqrt{2}}{2}$ B) 2   C) $\sqrt{2}$ D) $4\sqrt{2}$

14. Find $\cos30° \times \sin60° \times \tan60°$?

A) $\frac{\sqrt{3}}{3}$

B) $\frac{3}{4}$

C) $\sqrt{3}$

D) $\frac{3\sqrt{3}}{4}$

15. Find $\dfrac{\cos67° \times \cot16°}{\tan74° \times \sin23°}$?

A) $\frac{1}{3}$

B) 1

C) 2

D) 3

16. If $0° < x < 90°$ and $\sin x = \dfrac{3}{5}$, then find cotx?

A) $\frac{3}{4}$

B) $\frac{4}{3}$

C) $\frac{4}{5}$

D) 5

17. In the following table each square is equal to 1 unit. Find $\dfrac{\sin x}{\cos x}$.

A) $\dfrac{3}{2}$

B) 3

C) $\dfrac{2}{3}$

D) $\sqrt{10}$

3

$\dfrac{2}{\sqrt{3}} \cdot \dfrac{\sqrt{3}}{3}$

$2^2 + 3^2 = x^2$

$4 + 9 = x^2$

$\sqrt{13} = x$

18. Cos46° is equivalent to which of the following?

A) cos30°

B) sin60°

C) sin44°

D) sin30°

Test 24
Answer Key

1)	A
2)	A
3)	B
4)	B
5)	C
6)	D
7)	B
8)	D
9)	D
10)	D
11)	C
12)	D
13)	A
14)	D
15)	B
16)	B
17)	C
18)	C

1. $\dfrac{D}{180°} = \dfrac{R}{\pi}$

$\dfrac{120°}{180°} = \dfrac{R}{\pi}$

$\dfrac{2}{3} = \dfrac{R}{\pi}$, $R = \dfrac{2}{3}\pi$

Correct Answer : A

2. $\dfrac{60°}{180°} = \dfrac{R}{\pi}$, $R = \dfrac{1}{3}\pi$

Correct Answer : A

3.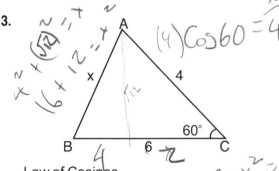

Law of Cosines

$x^2 = 6^2 + 4^2 - 2.4.6\,Cos60$

$x^2 = 36 + 16 - 48\,Cos60$

$x^2 = 52 - 48 \cdot \dfrac{1}{2}$

$x^2 = 52 - 24 = 28$

$x^2 = 28$, $x = 2\sqrt{7}$

Correct Answer : B

4.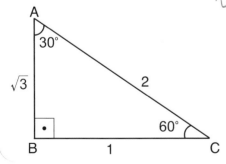

$CosineC = \dfrac{Adj}{Hypotenuse}$

$= \dfrac{1}{2}$

Correct Answer : B

5.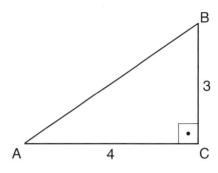

$SinA = \dfrac{Opposite}{Hypotenuse}$

$SinA = \dfrac{3}{5}$

Correct Answer : C

6.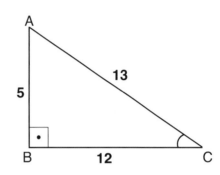

$SinC = \dfrac{5}{13}$

$5^2 + x^2 = 13^2$

$x^2 = 144$, $x = 12$

$CosineC = \dfrac{Adj}{Hypotenuse} = \dfrac{12}{13}$

Correct Answer : D

7.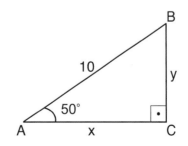

$Tan50° = \dfrac{Sin50°}{Cos50°} = \dfrac{y}{x}$

Correct Answer : B

8. $\text{Sin}\theta \cdot \text{Cot}\theta$

$\text{Cot}\theta = \dfrac{\text{Cos}\theta}{\text{Sin}\theta}$

$\cancel{\text{Sin}\theta} \cdot \dfrac{\text{Cos}\theta}{\cancel{\text{Sin}\theta}}$

$= \text{Cos}\theta$

Correct Answer : D

9.

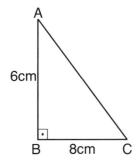

$\text{TanA} = \text{CotD}$

$\text{TanA} = \dfrac{8}{6}$

$\left.\begin{array}{l}\\ \\ \end{array}\right\}$ $\dfrac{8}{6} = \dfrac{3}{\text{EF}}$, $\text{EF} = \dfrac{18}{8} = \dfrac{9}{4}$

$\text{CotD} = \dfrac{3}{\text{EF}}$

Correct Answer : D

10.

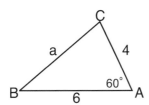

$a^2 = 36 + 16 - 2.4.6\text{Cos}60$

$\text{Cos}60 = 0.5$

$a^2 = 52 - 2.4.6(0.5)$

$a^2 = 52 - 24$

$a^2 = 28 \qquad a = 5.2915$

$a \approx 5 \cdot 3$

Correct Answer : D

11. $\dfrac{\text{D}}{180°} = \dfrac{\text{R}}{\pi}$

$\dfrac{\text{D}}{180°} = \dfrac{\frac{2\pi}{3}}{\pi}$

$\text{D} = 120°$

Correct Answer : C

12.

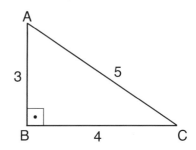

$\text{SinC} = \dfrac{\text{Opposite}}{\text{Hypotenuse}}$

$\text{SinC} = \dfrac{3}{5}$

Correct Answer : D

13.

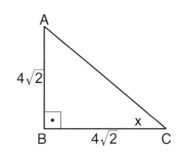

$\text{CosineX} = \dfrac{\text{Adj}}{\text{Hypotenuse}}$

$\text{CosX} = \dfrac{4\sqrt{2}}{8} = \dfrac{\sqrt{2}}{2}$

Correct Answer : A

14. $\text{Cos}30° \times \text{Sin}60° \times \text{Tan}60°$

$= \dfrac{\sqrt{3}}{2} \times \dfrac{\sqrt{3}}{2} \times \sqrt{3}$

$= \dfrac{3\sqrt{3}}{4}$

Correct Answer : D

15. $\cos 67° = \sin 23°$

$\cot 16° = \tan 74°$

$\dfrac{\sin 23° \times \tan 74°}{\tan 74° \times \sin 23°} = 1$

Correct Answer : B

16.

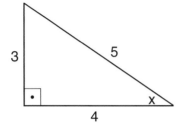

$\cot x = \dfrac{\text{Adj}}{\text{Opposite}}$

$\cot x = \dfrac{4}{3}$

Correct Answer : B

17.

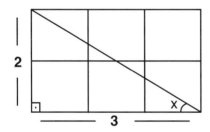

$\sin x = \dfrac{2}{\sqrt{13}}$

$\cos x = \dfrac{3}{\sqrt{13}}$

$\dfrac{\sin x}{\cos x} = \dfrac{\dfrac{2}{\sqrt{13}}}{\dfrac{3}{\sqrt{13}}} = \dfrac{2}{3}$

Correct Answer : C

18. $\cos 46° = \sin 44°$

Correct Answer : C

1. $2^x + 2^x + 2^x + 2^x = 64$. The equation is true for what value of x?

   A) 2
   B) 4
   C) 6
   D) 8

2. $\dfrac{x^8 \cdot x^{-4} \cdot x^6}{x^{10}}$ The expression is equivalent to which of the following integers?

   A) x^2
   B) 1
   C) 0
   D) x

   $x^{-4} \cdot x^4$

3. For what positive value of x is x^4 equivalent to 81?

   A) 1
   B) 2
   C) 3
   D) 4

   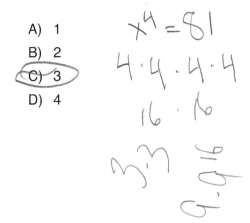

   $x^4 = 81$

   $4 \cdot 4 \cdot 4 \cdot 4$

   $16 \cdot 16$

4. What is the solution set to the equation $\sqrt{3a} = \sqrt{a^2 - 4}$?

   A) [1, 4]
   B) [-1, 4]
   C) [-1, -4]
   D) [1, -4]

   $3a = a^2 - 4$

   $-3a$

   $0 = a^2 - 3a - 4$

   $(a-4)$
   $(a+1)$

5. $\dfrac{x^2 - 11x + 24}{x - 3}$ Which of the following is equivalent to the expression?

   A) x - 3
   B) x + 3
   C) x - 8
   D) x + 8

   $(x-3)(x-8)$
   $(x-4)(x-?)$

6. $(x - 2)(x - 8) = x^2 - mnx + 16$. If m and n are positive integers which of the following could not be the value of m?

   A) 1
   B) 2
   C) 10
   D) 15

   $(x-2)(x-8) = x^2 - mnx + 16$

   $x^2 - 8x - 2x + 16$

   $x^2 - 10x + 16 = x^2 - mnx$

   $-10x = -mnx$

   $mn = 10$

7. Which of the following expressions in the form a+bi is equivalent to $\frac{3 + 2i}{2 - 5i}$?
(Note $i^2 = -1$)

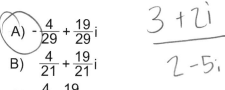

A) $-\frac{4}{29} + \frac{19}{29}i$

B) $\frac{4}{21} + \frac{19}{21}i$

C) $\frac{4}{6} - \frac{19}{6}i$

D) $\frac{4}{6} + \frac{19}{6}i$

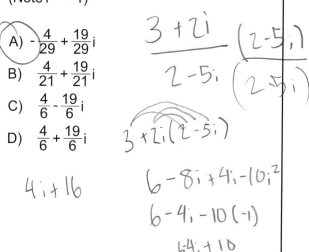

$4i + 16$

$6 - 8i + 4i - 10i^2$

$6 - 4i - 10(-1)$

$6 \cdot 4i + 10$

8. An angle that measures $\frac{\pi}{12}$ radians measures how many degrees?

A) 15°

B) 30°

C) 45°

D) 60°

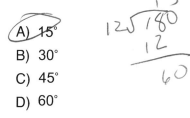

9. If 2x+10=6x-14, what is the value of x?

A) 3

B) 6

C) 9

D) 12

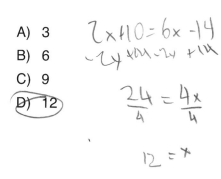

10. What is the area of the triangle below?

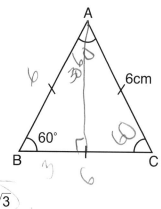

A) $3\sqrt{3}$

B) $6\sqrt{3}$

C) $9\sqrt{3}$

D) $12\sqrt{3}$

11. If $\frac{3x^2}{y^2} = 27y^2$, x = ?

A) y^2

B) $3y^2$

C) $6y^2$

D) $9y^2$

$(y^2)\frac{3x^2}{y^2} = 27y^2(y^2)$

$3x^2 = 27y^4$

$\frac{3x^2}{3} = \frac{27y^4}{3}$

$\sqrt{x^2} = \sqrt{9y^4}$

$x = 3y^2$

12. In the triangle ABC shown below, what is the value of x?

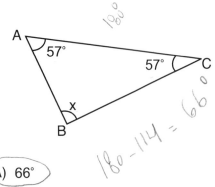

(handwritten: 180°)

A 57°
57° C
x
B

(handwritten: 180-114 = 66   66°)

A) 66°

B) 78°

C) 88°

D) 98°

13. Which of the following lines below are perpendicular to the equation of 3x-4y=12?

A) $y = \frac{3x}{4} + 12$

B) $y = \frac{-4x}{3} + 12$

C) $y = \frac{2x}{3} + 12$

D) $y = \frac{x}{3} + 12$

(handwritten work:)
$3x-4y=12$
$-3x \quad -3y$
$\frac{-4y}{-4} = \frac{-3x-12}{-4}$
$y = \frac{3}{4}x + 3$
$x = \frac{3}{4}y + 3$
$(\frac{4}{3}x - 3 = \frac{3}{4}y)(\frac{4}{3})$
$\frac{4x-12}{3}$

14. In the system of equations below, k and m are constant. If the system has many solutions, what is the value of k?

$4x-3ky=12$
$8x+6y=m$

A) 0

B) 1

C) -1

D) 2

15. Which of the following numbers is not a solution to the inequality?

$4y-12<8<y+7$

A) 1

B) 2

C) 3

D) 4

(handwritten: $-y+12-y$ +12   3y< 3y<)

16. What is the value of $\frac{1}{mn}$?

$\frac{8}{m} = \frac{n}{6}$

A) $\frac{1}{48}$

B) 48

C) $\frac{1}{24}$

D) 24

(handwritten: $(6)\frac{8}{m} = \frac{n}{6}(6)$ $\frac{48}{m} = n$ $\frac{8}{m} = \frac{48}{m} \cdot \frac{1}{6}$ $\frac{8}{m} = \frac{48}{6m}$ $\frac{8}{m} = \frac{48}{6m}$)

17. Simplify the following equation.

$$\frac{x^2 - 16}{x - 4} = ?$$

A) $\frac{x-4}{x+4}$

B) $\frac{x-2}{x+2}$

C) $x - 4$

D) $x + 4$

$$\frac{(x-4)(x+4)}{x-4}$$

$$4\left(\frac{m}{8} - \frac{6}{8}y\right) - 3k\left(\frac{m}{6} - \frac{4}{3}x\right) = 12$$

$$\frac{4m}{8} - \frac{24}{8}y - \frac{3km}{6} + \frac{12k}{3} = 12$$

$$2\left(\frac{m}{4} - 3y - \frac{k}{2} + 4k\right) = 12$$

$$\frac{2m}{4} - 6y - k + 8k = 24$$

$$(A)\ \frac{2m}{4} - 6y + 7k = 24$$

$$\frac{8}{m} = \frac{8}{m}$$

$$\left(\frac{6}{1}\right)\frac{8}{m} = \frac{n}{6}(6)$$

$$\left(\frac{m}{1}\right)\frac{48}{m} = n(m)$$

$$48 = nm$$

Mixed Review
Test 6
Answer Key

1)	B
2)	B
3)	C
4)	B
5)	C
6)	D
7)	A
8)	A
9)	B
10)	C
11)	B
12)	A
13)	B
14)	C
15)	A
16)	A
17)	D

1. $2^x + 2^x + 2^x + 2^x = 64$

$2^x(1 + 1 + 1 + 1) = 64$

$2^x \cdot 4 = 2^6$

$2^x \cdot 2^2 = 2^6$, $\cancel{2}^{x+2} = \cancel{2}^6$

$\quad\quad\quad x + 2 = 6$

$\quad\quad\quad\quad\quad x = 4$

Correct Answer : B

2. $\dfrac{x^8 \cdot x^{-4} \cdot x^6}{x^{10}} = \dfrac{x^{8-4+6}}{x^{10}}$

$= \dfrac{x^{10}}{x^{10}} = x^0 = 1$

Correct Answer : B

3. $x^4 = 81$

$x^4 = 3^4$

$x = 3$

Correct Answer : C

4. $\sqrt{3a} = \sqrt{a^2 - 4}$

$3a = a^2 - 4$

$0 = a^2 - 3a - 4$

$0 = (a - 4)(a + 1)$

$a = 4$ or $a = -1$

Correct Answer : B

5. $\dfrac{x^2 - 11x + 24}{x - 3} = \dfrac{(x - 3)(x - 8)}{(x - 3)}$

$= x - 8$

Correct Answer : C

6. $(x - 2)(x - 8) = x^2 - mnx + 16$

$\cancel{x}^2 - 10x + \cancel{16} = \cancel{x}^2 - mnx + \cancel{16}$

$-10x = -mnx$

$10 = mn$

$m = 5,$ or $n = 2$

$m = 2,$ or $n = 5$

$m = 10, \quad n = 1$

$m = 1 \quad\quad n = 10$

Correct Answer : D

7. $\dfrac{3 + 2i}{2 - 5i}\left(\dfrac{2 + 5i}{2 + 5i}\right) = \dfrac{6 + 15i + 4i - 10}{4 + 25}$

$= \dfrac{-4 + 19i}{29}$

Correct Asnwer : A

8. $\dfrac{D}{180^0} = \dfrac{R}{\pi}$

$\dfrac{D}{180^0} = \dfrac{\frac{\pi}{12}}{\frac{\pi}{1}}$

$\dfrac{D}{180^0} = \dfrac{1}{12}$

$D = \dfrac{180^0}{12} = 15^0$

Correct Answer : A

9. $2x + 10 = 6x - 14$

$24 = 4x$

$6 = x$

Correct Answer : B

10.

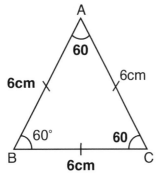

$$\text{Area} = \frac{a^2\sqrt{3}}{4}$$

$$= \frac{36\sqrt{3}}{4} = 9\sqrt{3}$$

Correct Answer : C

11. $\frac{3x^2}{y^2} = 27y^2$

$3x^2 = 27y^4$

$x = 3y^2$

Correct Answer : B

12. $x + 57^0 + 57^0 = 180^0$

$x + 114^0 = 180^0$

$x = 66^0$

Correct Answer : A

13. $m_1 = \frac{3}{4}$ from equation

$m_1 \times m_2 = -1$ (perpendicular)

$\frac{3}{4} \times m_2 = -1 \qquad m_2 = \frac{-4}{3}$

Only Choice B has slope of $\frac{-4}{3}$

Correct Answer : B

14. $4x - 3ky = 12$

$8x + 6y = m$

if the system of equations has many solutions, that means equations have the same slope.

$m_1 = \frac{4}{3k}, \qquad m_2 = \frac{-8}{6}$

$m_1 = m_2$

$\frac{4}{3k} = \frac{-8}{6}, \quad k = -1$

Correct Answer : C

15. $4y - 12 < 8 < y + 7$

$4y - 12 < 8$ or $8 < y + 7$

$4y < 20$ or $8 - 7 < y$

$y < 5$ or $1 < y$

$1 < y < 5$

Correct Answer : A

16. $\frac{8}{m} = \frac{n}{6}$

$mn = 48$

$\frac{1}{mn} = \frac{1}{48}$

Correct Answer : A

17. $\frac{x^2 - 16}{x - 4}$

$= \frac{(x - 4)(x + 4)}{x - 4}$

$= x + 4$

Correct Answer : D

1. If $\frac{1}{4} = m^n$, then $\frac{4^{-1}}{m} = ?$

A) m^n

B) m^{n-1}

C) m^{n+1}

D) 4

2. $\frac{a^{2m}}{a^{10}} = a^6$ and $a^{3n} = a^{30}$, then $m \times n = ?$

A) 50

B) 60

C) 70

D) 80

3. If $10^{m-2} = n$, then $10^{-m} = ?$

A) 10

B) 100n

C) $\frac{1}{10n}$

D) $\frac{1}{100n}$

4. If $3^4 \times 81^3 = 3^{4x}$, then $x = ?$

A) 3

B) 4

C) 8

D) 12

5. If $\frac{m}{n} = 3$, what is the value of $\frac{6n}{m}$?

A) 1

B) 2

C) 3

D) $\frac{1}{2}$

6. If $2x + 10 = 20$, what is the value of 2^{-x}?

A) 8

B) 32

C) $\frac{1}{8}$

D) $\frac{1}{32}$

7. If $\dfrac{a}{3} = \dfrac{28 - a}{4}$, what is the value of $\dfrac{32}{a} = ?$

A) 4

B) 8

C) 32

D) $\dfrac{8}{3}$

8. Which value of n satisfies the equation below?

$$\dfrac{3}{4}(n^2) = \dfrac{27}{64}$$

A) $\dfrac{3}{4}$

B) 3

C) 4

D) $\dfrac{4}{3}$

9. If $\dfrac{1}{2}a \times \dfrac{1}{2}a \times \dfrac{1}{2}a = \dfrac{1}{64}$, then a = ?

A) 1

B) 2

C) $\dfrac{1}{2}$

D) 4

10. If $\dfrac{a}{4} = 3$, then $\dfrac{a^{-1}}{12} = ?$

A) 12

B) 144

C) $\dfrac{1}{12}$

D) $\dfrac{1}{144}$

11. If $A = \dfrac{1}{2}tv^2$, what is v in terms of A and t?

A) $\dfrac{2A}{t}$

B) $\dfrac{A}{2t}$

C) $\sqrt{\dfrac{2A}{t}}$

D) $\sqrt{\dfrac{t}{2A}}$

12. If $a = \dfrac{3m + n}{k}$, then m = ?

A) $\dfrac{ak}{3n}$

B) $\dfrac{ak + n}{3}$

C) $\dfrac{ak - n}{3}$

D) $\dfrac{n}{ak - 3}$

13. $\frac{m-n}{n} = \frac{4}{5}$, what is the value of $\frac{m}{n}$?

A) $\frac{9}{5}$

B) $\frac{5}{9}$

C) 5

D) 9

14. If $(a+b)^2 = 36$ and $ab = 12$, what is the value of $a^2 + b^2$?

A) 6

B) 8

C) 12

D) 16

15. If $x=7y$ and $x-4y=24$, then $x=?$

A) 8

B) 12

C) 24

D) 56

16. After a 30% decrease, the new price of a shirt is $140. What was the original price?

A) $100

B) $150

C) $200

D) $210

17. If $16^x = 64^y$, what is the ratio of y to x?

A) $\frac{3}{2}$

B) $\frac{2}{3}$

C) 2

D) 3

18. A new copy machine can print 120 pages per hour, and an older copy machine can print 80 pages per hour. How many minutes will two copy machines working together take to copy a total of 360 pages?

A) 72

B) 96

C) 108

D) 120

19. If 3x-y=6 and 2x+3y=4, what is the average of x and y?

    A) 1

    B) 2

    C) 3

    D) 4

20. If $2^a \times 2^a \times 2^a \times 2^a = 8^{4b}$, then a = ?

    A) b

    B) 2b

    C) 3b

    D) 8b

21. If $2^a + 2^a + 2^a + 2^a = 8^{4b}$, then a = ?

    A) 12b

    B) 12-b

    C) b-12

    D) 12b-2

Mixed Review
Test 7
Answer Key

1)	B
2)	D
3)	D
4)	B
5)	B
6)	D
7)	D
8)	A
9)	C
10)	D
11)	C
12)	C
13)	A
14)	C
15)	D
16)	C
17)	B
18)	C
19)	A
20)	C
21)	D

1. $\frac{1}{4} = m^n$

$4^{-1} = m^n$

$\frac{4^{-1}}{m^1} = \frac{m^n}{m^1} = m^{n-1}$

Correct Answer : B

2. $\frac{a^{2m}}{a^{10}} = a^6$

$a^{2m-10} = a^6$

$2m - 10 = 6$

$m = 8$

$a^{3n} = a^{30}$ $3n = 30$ $n = 10$

$m \times n = 8 \times 10 = 80$

Correct Answer : D

3. $10^{m-2} = n$

$\frac{10^m}{100} = n$ $10^m = 100n$

$10^{-m} = \frac{1}{10^m} = \frac{1}{100n}$

Correct Answer : D

4. $3^4 \times 81^3 = 3^{4x}$

$3^4 \times (3^4)^3 = 3^{4x}$

$3^4 \times 3^{12} = 3^{4x}$

$3^{16} = 3^{4x}$, $4x = 16$, $x = 4$

Correct Answer : B

5. $m = 3n$

$\frac{6n}{m} = 6 \times \frac{n}{m}$

$6 \times \frac{n}{3n} = 6 \times \frac{1}{3} = 2$

Correct Answer : B

6. $2x + 10 = 20$

$2x = 10$

$x = 5$

$2^{-x} = \frac{1}{2^x} = \frac{1}{2^5} = \frac{1}{32}$

Correct Answer : D

7. $\frac{a}{3} = \frac{28 - a}{4}$

$4a = 84 - 3a$

$7a = 84$

$a = 12$

$\frac{32}{a} = \frac{32}{12} = \frac{8}{3}$

Correct Answer : D

8. $\frac{3}{4}n^2 = \frac{27}{64}$

$n^2 = \frac{27}{64} \times \frac{4}{3}$

$n^2 = \frac{9}{16}$

$n = \frac{3}{4}$

Correct Answer : A

9. $\frac{1}{2}a \times \frac{1}{2}a \times \frac{1}{2}a = \frac{1}{64}$

$\frac{1}{8}a^3 = \frac{1}{64}$

$a^3 = \frac{1}{8}$

$a = \frac{1}{2}$

Correct Answer : C

10. $\frac{a}{4} = 3$, then $\frac{a^{-1}}{12}$

$a = 12$, $\frac{1}{a^1 \times 12} = \frac{1}{12 \times 12} = \frac{1}{144}$

Correct Answer : D

11. $A = \frac{1}{2}tV^2$

$2A = tV^2$

$\sqrt{\frac{2A}{t}} = \sqrt{V^2}$

$\sqrt{\frac{2A}{t}} = V$

Correct Answer : C

12. $a = \frac{3m + n}{k}$

$ak = 3m + n$

$\frac{ak - n}{3} = m$

Correct Answer : C

13. $\frac{m - n}{n} = \frac{4}{5}$

$5m - 5n = 4n$

$5m = 9n$

$\frac{m}{n} = \frac{9}{5}$

Correct Answer : A

14. $ab = 12$

$(a + b)^2 = 36$

$a^2 + b^2 + 2ab = 36$

$a^2 + b^2 + 2.12 = 36$

$a^2 + b^2 = 36 - 24 = 12$

Correct Answer : C

15. $x = 7y$

$x - 4y = 24$

$7y - 4y = 24$

$3y = 24$

$y = 8$

$x = 7y = 7 \times 8 = 56$

Correct Answer : D

16. Original Price = 100x

30% decrease 100x - 30x = 70x

70x = \$140   x = \$2

Original Price = 100x

$= 100 . 2$

$= 200$

Correct Answer : C

17. $16^x = 64^y$

$2^{4x} = 2^{6y}$

$4x = 6y$

$\frac{y}{x} = \frac{2}{3}$

Correct Answer : B

18. $\left(\frac{120}{60} + \frac{80}{60}\right)t = 360$

$\left(\frac{200}{60}\right)t = 360$

$\frac{10t}{3} = 360$

$\frac{t}{3} = 36$, $t = 108$

Correct Answer : C

19. $3 \diagup 3x - y = 6$

$2x + 3y = 4$

$9x - 3y = 18$

$2x + 3y = 4$

$+ \underline{11x = 22}$

$x = 2 , y = 0$

Average of x and y $= \frac{x + y}{2}$

$= \frac{2 + 0}{2} = 1$

Correct Answer : A

20. $2^a \times 2^a \times 2^a \times 2^a = 8^{4b}$

$2^{a+a+a+a} = (2^3)^{4b}$

$2^{4a} = 2^{12b}$

$4a = 12b$

$a = 3b$

Correct Answer : C

21. $2^a + 2^a + 2^a + 2^a = 8^{4b}$

$2^a(1 + 1 + 1 + 1) = (2^3)^{4b}$

$2^a.4 = 2^{12b}$

$2^a.2^2 = 2^{12b}$

$a + 2 = 12b$

$a = 12b - 2$

Correct Answer : D

1. $(\frac{1}{18})^{-\frac{1}{2}} \times (\frac{1}{2})^{-\frac{1}{2}} \times 2^{-1} = ?$

A) 1
B) 2
C) 3
D) 4

2. Find $2011^2 - 2010^2$?

A) 2010
B) 2011
C) 4021
D) 4001

3. $\frac{1}{2^{3x}} = \frac{1}{32^2}$ Find x.

A) $\frac{1}{3}$
B) $\frac{3}{10}$
C) 10
D) $\frac{10}{3}$

4. If b is directly proportional to a, and b = 24 when a = 12, what is the value of b when a=36?

A) 12
B) 24
C) 36
D) 72

5. If $\frac{12}{a} = \frac{b}{4}$, what is the value of ab?

A) 3
B) 6
C) 12
D) 48

6. The ratio of 2 to 3 is equal to which of the following ratios?

A) 3:2
B) 4:6
C) 8:10
D) 12:8

7. $\frac{1}{3}(6x - 9) + (x - 12) = ax + x + b$ What is the value of a - b?

A) 6
B) 9
C) 12
D) 17

8. $\frac{3}{5}x + ny = 25$ If the slope of the equation is $\frac{1}{25}$, what is the value of n?

A) 3
B) 5
C) 12
D) -15

9. Line K passes through the coordinate (4,8) and (10,14). What is the slope of line K?

A) 1
B) 2
C) 3
D) 4

10. If A=2(B+C), what is B in terms of A and C?

A) 2A - 2C
B) $\frac{A - 2C}{2}$
C) $\frac{A - 2}{2C}$
D) A - 2C

11. 3x+48=12x+12 What is the value of x?

A) 3
B) 4
C) 8
D) 12

12.
$$x+2ky=12$$
$$3x+4y=18$$
In the system of equations above, k is a constant. For what value of k will the system of equations have no solutions?

A) $\frac{1}{3}$
B) $\frac{2}{3}$
C) $\frac{3}{2}$
D) $-\frac{3}{2}$

13. The price of a book has been discounted 20%. The sale price is $68. What is the original price?

A) $12

B) $24

C) $36

D) $85

14. If $x = \dfrac{2^3}{\sqrt{12}}$, then find $x = ?$

A) $4\sqrt{3}$

B) $\sqrt{3}$

C) $\dfrac{4\sqrt{3}}{3}$

D) $\dfrac{3\sqrt{3}}{4}$

15. If $9^{2x-2} = 81^{2x-3}$ then what is the value of x?

A) 2

B) 3

C) $\dfrac{2}{3}$

D) $\dfrac{3}{2}$

16. If $k(x) = 3x - 2$, then find $k^{-1}(x) = ?$

A) $k^1(x) = \dfrac{x+2}{3}$

B) $k^1(x) = \dfrac{x-1}{3}$

C) $k^1(x) = \dfrac{x+1}{3}$

D) $k^1(x) = \dfrac{x-2}{3}$

17. $x^2 - 8x - 12 = 0$ Solve for x.

A) $x = 4 \pm 2\sqrt{7}$

B) $x = -4 \pm i\sqrt{7}$

C) $x = i\sqrt{7} \pm 4$

D) $x = \sqrt{7}$

18. What is the median of the following numbers?

$$12,\ 14,\ 18,\ 18,\ 18$$

A) 12

B) 13

C) 16

D) 18

19.
$$i^{2001} + i^{2012} + i^{2013}$$

Which of the following is equivalent to the complex number shown above?

A) 1 - i
B) 1 + 2i
C) i
D) 1

20. What is the area of the following square if the length of AC is $2\sqrt{2}$?

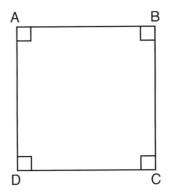

A) 4
B) 8
C) 12
D) 16

Mixed Review
Test 8
Answer Key

1)	C
2)	C
3)	D
4)	D
5)	D
6)	B
7)	D
8)	D
9)	A
10)	B
11)	B
12)	B
13)	D
14)	C
15)	A
16)	A
17)	A
18)	D
19)	B
20)	A

Mixed Review

Test 8 Solutions

1. $\left(\frac{1}{18}\right)^{\frac{-1}{2}} \cdot \left(\frac{1}{2}\right)^{\frac{-1}{2}} \cdot 2^{-1}$

$= \left(\frac{1}{18} \cdot \frac{1}{2}\right)^{\frac{-1}{2}} \cdot 2^{-1}$

$= \left(\frac{1}{36}\right)^{\frac{-1}{2}} 2^{-1}$

$= \left(\frac{1}{6}\right)^{-1} \cdot \frac{1}{2}$

$= 6 \cdot \frac{1}{2} = 3$

Correct Answer : C

2. $2011^2 - 2010^2$

$= (2011 + 2010) \cdot (2011 - 2010)$

$= (4021) \cdot 1$

$= 4021$

Correct Answer : C

3. $\frac{1}{2^{3x}} = \frac{1}{32^2}$

$\frac{1}{2^{3x}} = \frac{1}{(2^5)^2}$

$\frac{1}{2^{3x}} = \frac{1}{2^{10}}$

$2^{3x} = 2^{10}$

$3x = 10$

$x = \frac{10}{3}$

Correct Answer : D

4. $b = ak$

$24 = 12 \cdot k$

$2 = k$

$b = ak$

$b = 36 \cdot 2$

$b = 72$

Correct Answer : D

5. $\frac{12}{a} = \frac{b}{4}$

$ab = 48$

Correct Answer : D

6. The ratio of 2 to 3 is equivalent to 4 to 6

Correct Answer : B

7. $\frac{1}{3}(6x - 9) + (x - 12) = ax + x + b$

$2x - 3 + x - 12 = ax + x + b$

$3x - 15 = ax + x + b$

$3x - 15 = x(a + 1) + b$

$b = -15$

$a + 1 = 3 \quad a = 2$

$a - b = 2 - (-15)$

$= 17$

Correct Answer : D

8. $\frac{3}{5}x + ny = 25$

$\text{Slope} = -\frac{\frac{3}{5}}{\frac{n}{1}} = \frac{-3}{5n}$

$-\frac{3}{5n} = \frac{1}{25}$, $n = -15$

Correct Answer : D

9. $\text{slope} = \frac{y_2 - y_1}{x_2 - x_1} = \frac{14 - 8}{10 - 4} = \frac{6}{6}$

$\text{slope} = 1$

Correct Answer : A

10. $A = 2(B + C)$

$A = 2B + 2C$

$\dfrac{A - 2C}{2} = B$

Correct Answer : B

11. $3x + 48 = 12x + 12$

$36 = 9x$

$4 = x$

Correct Answer : B

12. $x + 2ky = 12$

$3x + 4y = 18$

$m_1 = -\dfrac{1}{2k}$ $\left.\begin{array}{l} \\ \\ \\ \end{array}\right\}$ $m_1 = m_2$

system of equations

$m_2 = -\dfrac{3}{4}$ has no solutions

$\dfrac{-1}{2k} = \dfrac{-3}{4}$, $\dfrac{1}{2k} = \dfrac{3}{4}$

$6k = 4$, $k = \dfrac{2}{3}$

Correct Answer : B

13. Discounted 20% sale price $68

sale price $= 100x - 20x$

$\$68 = 80x$

$\dfrac{68}{80} = x$

$\dfrac{17}{20} = x$

Original Price $= 100x$

$= 100 \cdot \dfrac{17}{20} = \$85$

Correct Answer : D

14. $x = \dfrac{2^3}{\sqrt{12}}$

$x = \dfrac{8}{2\sqrt{3}} = \dfrac{4 \cdot \sqrt{3}}{\sqrt{3} \cdot \sqrt{3}}$

$x = \dfrac{4\sqrt{3}}{3}$

Correct Answer : C

15. $9^{2x-2} = 81^{2x-3}$

$9^{2x-2} = 9^{2(2x-3)}$

$9^{2x-2} = 9^{4x-6}$

$2x - 2 = 4x - 6$

$4 = 2x$

$2 = x$

Correct Answer : A

16. $k(x) = 3x - 2$

$k^{-1}(x) = ?$

$3x - 2 = y$

$3x = y + 2$

$x = \dfrac{y + 2}{3}$

change x to y

$y = \dfrac{x + 2}{3}$

$k^{-1}(x) = \dfrac{x + 2}{3}$

Correct Answer : A

17. $x^2 - 8x - 12 = 0$

$x^2 - 8x = 12$

$(x - 4)^2 - 16 = 12$

$(x - 4)^2 = 28$

$x - 4 = \mp\sqrt{28}$

$x = 4 \mp \sqrt{28}$

$x = 4 \mp 2\sqrt{7}$

Correct Answer : A

18. Median : 12 14 ⑱ 18 18

Median : 18

Correct Answer : D

19. $i^{2001} + i^{2012} + i^{2013}$

Rule $\quad i^2 = -1$

$= (i^2)^{1000} \cdot i + (i^2)^{1006} + (i^2)^{1006} \cdot i$

$= (-1)^{1000} \cdot i + (-1)^{1006} + (-1)^{1006} \cdot i$

$= 1 \cdot i + 1 + 1 \cdot i$

$= i + 1 + i$

$= 2i + 1$

Correct Answer : B

20.

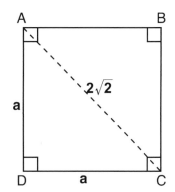

$a^2 + a^2 = (2\sqrt{2})^2$

$2a^2 = 8$

$a^2 = 4$

$a = 2$

Area of square $= a^2 = 4$

Correct Answer : A

1. $f(x) = x^3 - 2x^2 + 2x - 1$. Find $f(x + 1)$.

A) $x^3 + x^2 + x$

B) $x^3 - x^2 - x$

C) $2x^3 + x^2 - x$

D) $3x^3 + x^2 - x$

2. What is the sum of $(4i+3)+(3-3i)$? $(i = \sqrt{-1})$?

A) $i+3$
B) $i-3$
C) $i+6$
D) $i-6$

3. If $\frac{x-1}{4} = y$ and $y = 6$, what is the value of x?

A) 20
B) 23
C) 25
D) 27

4. Which of the following is equivalent to the expression below?
$$(x^2y - 2x^2 + 6xy) - (xy^2 - 2x^2 + 4xy)$$

A) $x^2y - xy^2 + 2xy$

B) $x^2y - xy^2 - 2xy$

C) $x^2y + xy^2 + 2xy$

D) $-x^2y - xy^2 - 2xy$

5. If $\frac{x}{y} = 3$, what is the value of $\frac{5y}{x}$?

A) 3

B) 5

C) $\frac{3}{5}$

D) $\frac{5}{3}$

6. What is the solution (x, y) to the system of equations below?
$$x + 4y = -23$$
$$y - x = 18$$

A) $(-1,19)$
B) $(-19,-1)$
C) $(-19,1)$
D) $(1,-19)$

7. A line in the xy plane passes through the origin and has a slope of $\frac{1}{3}$. Which of the following points lies on the line?

   A) (0,3)
   B) (3,0)
   C) (1,3)
   D) (3,1)

8. $f(x) = ax^3 + 8$

   For the function f defined above, a is a constant and f(2) = 6. What is the value of f(-2)?

   A) 4
   B) 8
   C) 10
   D) 24

9. If 2x - y = 3, what is the value of $\frac{4^x}{2^y}$?

   A) 4
   B) 6
   C) 8
   D) 12

10. If x > 0 and $x^2 - 25 = 0$, what is the value of x?

    A) 0
    B) -5
    C) 5
    D) 25

11. According to the system of equations below, what is the value of x?
    $$x + y = 10$$
    $$x + 2y = 6$$

    A) 4
    B) 6
    C) 8
    D) 14

12. If $a = 2\sqrt{3}$ and $3a = \sqrt{3x}$, what is the value of x?

    A) 18
    B) 24
    C) 36
    D) 72

13. For what value of x is |x-3| - 2x equal to 0?

A) 0
B) 1
C) -1
D) -2

14. What is the solutions to $x^2 + 2x + 3 = 0$?

A) -1
B) -2
C) $1 \pm \sqrt{2}\,i$
D) $-1 \pm \sqrt{2}\,i$

15. If $\frac{3}{4}x - \frac{1}{8}x = \frac{1}{12} + \frac{2}{3}$, what is the value of x?

A) 6
B) 7
C) $\frac{6}{7}$
D) $\frac{6}{5}$

16. If $\frac{6}{5}x = \frac{4}{9}$, what is the value of x?

A) 10
B) 2
C) $\frac{10}{27}$
D) $\frac{27}{16}$

17. Which of the following equations passes through the coordinates (1,2) and (-1, -2)?

A) $y = x$

B) $y = 2x$

C) $y = \frac{1}{2}x + 1$

D) $y = 2x - 1$

18. What is the value of k in the equation shown below?

$$2k-3+3k=6(k-4)$$

A) 11
B) 14
C) 19
D) 21

19.

$$2(x-3)>3(x-6)$$

Which of the following numbers is NOT a solution of the above inequality?

   A) 12
   B) 11
   C) 10
   D) 9

20. If x and y are positive integers and x-4y=3 then find $\dfrac{3^x}{81^y}$.

   A) 3
   B) 6
   C) 9
   D) 27

Mixed Review
Test 9
Answer Key

1)	A
2)	C
3)	C
4)	A
5)	D
6)	B
7)	D
8)	C
9)	C
10)	C
11)	D
12)	C
13)	B
14)	D
15)	D
16)	C
17)	B
18)	D
19)	A
20)	D

1. $F(x) = x^3 - 2x^2 + 2x - 1$
   $F(x + 1) = (x + 1)^3 - 2(x + 1)^2 + 2(x + 1) - 1$
   $= x^3 + 2x^2 + x + x^2 + 2x + 1 - 2x^2 - 4x - 2 + 2x + 2 - 1$
   $= x^3 + x^2 + x$
   Correct Answer : A

2. Sum of $(4i + 3) + (3 - 3i)$
   $= 4i - 3i + 3 + 3$
   $= i + 6$
   Correct Answer : C

3. $\dfrac{x - 1}{4} = y$
   $x - 1 = 4y$
   $x = 4y + 1$
   Since $y = 6$
   $x = 4.6 + 1$
   $x = 24 + 1 = 25$
   Correct Answer : C

4. $(x^2 y - 2x^2 + 6xy) - (xy^2 - 2x^2 + 4xy)$
   $= x^2 y - 2x^2 + 6xy - xy^2 + 2x^2 - 4xy$
   $= x^2 y - xy^2 + 2xy$
   Correct Answer : A

5. $\dfrac{x}{y} = 3$, $x = 3y$
   $\dfrac{5y}{x} = \dfrac{5y}{3y} = \dfrac{5}{3}$
   Correct Answer : D

6. $x + 4y = -23$
   $+\ \dfrac{y - x = 18}{5y = -5 \quad y = -1}$
   $x = -19$
   Correct Answer : B

7. xy plane passes through the origin
   $(0,0)$ and has a slope of $\dfrac{1}{3}$.
   $(0,0)$ and (x, y)
   $m = \dfrac{y - 0}{x - 0}$
   $\dfrac{1}{3} = \dfrac{y}{x} \Rightarrow x = 3y$
   $y = 1 \quad x = 3 \quad (3, 1)$
   Correct Answer : D

8. $F(x) = ax^3 + 8$
   $F(2) = 6$
   $F(2) = a \times 2^3 + 8$
   $6 = 8a + 8$
   $-2 = 8a$
   $\dfrac{-1}{4} = a$
   $F(x) = \dfrac{-1}{4} x^3 + 8$
   $F(-2) = \dfrac{-1}{4} (-2)^3 + 8$
   $= \dfrac{8}{4} + 8 = 2 + 8 = 10$
   Correct Answer : C

9. $2x - y = 3$
   $\dfrac{4^x}{2^y} = \dfrac{2^{2x}}{2^y} = 2^{2x-y}$
   $= 2^3 = 8$
   Correct Answer : C

10. $x > 0$ and $x^2 - 25 = 0$
    $(x - 5)(x + 5) = 0$
    $x = 5$ or $x = -5$
    since $x > 0$, then $x = 5$
    Correct Answer : C

11. $x + y = 10$

$\quad\;\; x + 2y = 6$

$-x - y = -10$

$\underline{+\; x + 2y = 6}$

$y = -4 \, , \; x = 14$

Correct Answer : D

12. $a = 2\sqrt{3}$

$3a = \sqrt{3x}$

$6\sqrt{3} = \sqrt{3x}$

$\sqrt{36 \times 3} = \sqrt{3x}$

$(\sqrt{108})^2 = (\sqrt{3x})^2$

$108 = 3x$

$\dfrac{108}{3} = x$

$36 = x$

Correct Answer : C

13. $|x - 3| - 2x = 0$

$x - 3 - 2x = 0 \, , \; x = -3 \, , \; (\text{x can not be -3})$

$\qquad\qquad \text{or}$

$-x + 3 - 2x = 0 \, , \; x = 1$

Correct Answer : B

14. $x^2 + 2x = -3$

$(x + 1)^2 - 1 = -3$

$(x + 1)^2 = -2$

$x + 1 = \mp i\sqrt{2}$

$x = -1 \mp i\sqrt{2}$

Correct Answer : D

15. $\dfrac{3}{4}x - \dfrac{1}{8}x = \dfrac{1}{12} + \dfrac{2}{3}$

$\dfrac{6x - x}{8} = \dfrac{9}{12}$

$\dfrac{5x}{8} = \dfrac{3}{4} \qquad x = \dfrac{6}{5}$

Correct Answer : D

16. $\dfrac{6}{5}x = \dfrac{4}{9}$

$x = \dfrac{4}{9} \times \dfrac{5}{6}$

$x = \dfrac{20}{54} = \dfrac{10}{27}$

Correct Answer : C

17. $(1, 2)$ and $(-1, -2)$

$\text{Slope} = \dfrac{y_2 - y_1}{x_2 - x_1} = \dfrac{-2 - 2}{-1 - 1}$

$\text{Slope} = \dfrac{-4}{-2} = 2$

$y = mx + b$

$y = 2x + b, \;\; (1, 2)$

$2 = 2 + b$

$0 = b$

$y = 2x$

Correct Answer : B

18. $2k - 3 + 3k = 6(k - 4)$

$2k - 3 + 3k = 6k - 24$

$5k - 3 = 6k - 24$

$24 - 3 = k$

$21 = k$

Correct Answer : D

19. $2(x - 3) > 3(x - 6)$

$2x - 6 > 3x - 18$

$12 > x$

Correct Answer : A

20. $x - 4y = 3$

$\dfrac{3^x}{81^y} = \dfrac{3^x}{3^{4y}}$

$= 3^{x-4y}$

$= 3^3 = 27$

Correct Answer : D

1. Out of 200 students, 80 students favorite subject is Art. What percent of students favorite subject is Art?

   A) 30%
   B) 37.5%
   C) 40%
   D) 55%

2.
$$\left|\frac{x}{3} - 3\right| < 6$$
   What is a possible value of x in the above inequality?

   A) -9
   B) -10
   C) 27
   D) 25

3. Find the ratio of 1.5 to 2.5.

   A) 15 to 20
   B) 25 to 15
   C) 3 to 5
   D) 2 to 3

4. $\frac{2x + 1}{3x - 1} = \frac{6}{18}$ Find x.

   A) $\frac{4}{3}$
   B) $-\frac{4}{3}$
   C) $-\frac{3}{4}$
   D) $\frac{3}{4}$

5. Convert 105 kilograms to grams.(1kg =1000gr)

   A) 105,000
   B) 1050,000
   C) 105,000,000
   D) 155,000,000,000

6. If y varies inversely as x and x=10 when y=60, find y when x=20?

   A) 20
   B) 25
   C) 30
   D) 35

7. If $P(x+2) = x^2 + 3x + 1$ then find $P(-1)$?

A) -1
B) 0
C) 1
D) 2

8. In the polynomial below, a is the constant. If the polynomial is divisible by $P(x-2)$ then find the value of a=?

$$P(x) = 3x^3 + ax^2 - x + 2$$

A) -2
B) -4
C) -6
D) -8

9. What is the solution of the following equation?

$$\frac{3}{x-1} - \frac{2}{x+1} = \frac{6x}{x^2-1}$$

A) 1
B) 3
C) 5
D) 9

10. If $x = \dfrac{3^3}{\sqrt{81}}$, then find x.

A) 3
B) 9
C) 18
D) 27

11. Simplify the following equation.

$$\frac{x^4 - 16}{x^2 - 4} = ?$$

A) $\dfrac{x-4}{x+4}$

B) $\dfrac{x^2+4}{x^2-2}$

C) $x^2 - 4$

D) $x^2 + 4$

12. If $x\sqrt{0.64} = 1$ then find x = ?

A) 4

B) 5

C) $\dfrac{4}{5}$

D) $\dfrac{5}{4}$

13. If $x + y = 2$ and $x^2 - y^2 = 8$ then find $\frac{y}{x} = ?$

A) -1

B) -3

C) 1

D) $\frac{-1}{3}$

14. If $x = 1 + \sqrt{5}$ and $y = 1 - \sqrt{5}$ then $x \times y = ?$

A) -4

B) -5

C) $2\sqrt{5}$

D) $-4\sqrt{5}$

15. What is the mean of the following numbers?

1,17,24,36,28

A) 20

B) 21

C) 21.2

D) 21.5

16. Which of the following is equivalent to the complex number $\frac{3+i}{2-i}$?

A) 1-i

B) 1

C) i

D) 1+i

17.

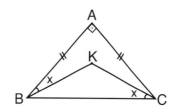

Find the angle of $m(\widehat{BKC}) = ?$

A) 100°

B) 115°

C) 135°

D) 120°

18. What is the area of the following square if the length of AC is $2\sqrt{2}$?

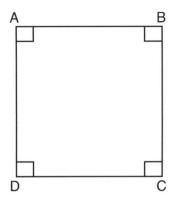

A) 2

B) 4

C) 8

D) 16

19. If the area of a circle is 16π, then find the circumference of the circle.

A) 4π

B) 8π

C) 10π

D) 12π

20. What is the radius of a circle with the equation $(x-4)^2 + (y-5)^2 = 81$?

A) 3

B) 6

C) 9

D) 12

Mixed Review
Test 10
Answer Key

1)	C
2)	D
3)	C
4)	B
5)	A
6)	C
7)	C
8)	C
9)	A
10)	A
11)	D
12)	D
13)	D
14)	A
15)	C
16)	D
17)	C
18)	B
19)	B
20)	C

1. $\dfrac{80}{200} = \dfrac{8}{20} = \dfrac{8 \times 5}{20 \times 5}$

$= \dfrac{40}{100} = 40\%$

Correct Answer : C

2. $\left| \dfrac{x}{3} - 3 \right| < 6$

$-6 < \dfrac{x}{3} - 3 < 6$

$-3 < \dfrac{x}{3} < 9$

$-9 < x < 27$

$x = -8, -7 \ldots\ldots 25, 26$

Correct Answer : D

3. Ratio of 1.5 to 2.5

15 to 25 = 3 to 5

Correct Answer : C

4. $\dfrac{2x + 1}{3x - 1} = \dfrac{6}{18}$

$\dfrac{2x + 1}{3x - 1} = \dfrac{1}{3}$

$3(2x + 1) = 3x - 1$

$6x + 3 = 3x - 1$

$3x = -4$

$x = \dfrac{-4}{3}$

Correct Answer : B

5. 105 kg = 105,000gr

Correct Answer : A

6. Inverse Variation

$y = \dfrac{k}{x}$

$60 = \dfrac{k}{10} \qquad k = 600$

$y = \dfrac{k}{x}, \quad y = \dfrac{600}{20} \qquad y = 30$

Correct Answer : C

7. $P(x + 2) = x^2 + 3x + 1$

$P(-3 + 2) = (-3)^2 + 3 \cdot (-3) + 1$

$P(-1) = 9 - 9 + 1$

$P(-1) = 1$

Correct Answer : C

8. $P(x) = 3x^3 + ax^2 - x + 2$

if the polynomial is the divisible by $P(x - 2)$

$x - 2 = 0, \quad x = 2$

$P(2) = 0$

$P(2) = 3(2)^3 + a \cdot (2)^2 - 2 + 2$

$P(2) = 3.8 + 4a - 2 + 2$

$P(2) = 24 + 4a$

$0 = 24 + 4a, \quad 4a = -24, \quad a = -6$

Correct Answer : C

9. $\dfrac{3}{x - 1} - \dfrac{2}{x + 1} = \dfrac{6x}{x^2 - 1}$

$3(x + 1) - 2(x - 1) = 6x$

$3x + 3 - 2x + 2 = 6x$

$x + 5 = 6x$

$5 = 5x$

$1 = x$

Correct Answer : A

10. $x = \dfrac{3^3}{\sqrt{81}}$

$x = \dfrac{27}{9} = 3$

Correct Answer : A

11. $\dfrac{x^4 - 16}{x^2 - 4} = \dfrac{(x^2 - 4)(x^2 + 4)}{x^2 - 4}$

Correct Answer : D

12. $x\sqrt{0.64} = 1$

$x\sqrt{\dfrac{64}{100}} = 1$

$x\dfrac{8}{10} = 1, \quad x = \dfrac{10}{8} = \dfrac{5}{4}$

Correct Answer : D

13. $x + y = 2$

$x^2 - y^2 = 8$

$(x - y)(x + y) = 8$

$(x - y) \cdot 2 = 8$

$x - y = 4, \quad x + y = 2$

$2x = 6, \quad x = 3, \quad y = -1$

$\dfrac{y}{x} = \dfrac{-1}{3}$

Correct Answer : D

14. $(1 + \sqrt{5})(1 - \sqrt{5})$

$= 1 - 5$

$= -4$

Correct Answer : A

15. mean $= \dfrac{1 + 17 + 24 + 36 + 28}{5}$

mean $= \dfrac{106}{5}$

mean $= 21.2$

Correct Answer : C

16. $i^2 = -1$

$\dfrac{3 + i}{2 - i}$

$= \dfrac{3 + i}{2 - i}\left(\dfrac{2 + i}{2 + i}\right)$

$= \dfrac{6 + 3i + 2i + i^2}{4 - i^2}$

$= \dfrac{6 + 5i - 1}{4 + 1}$

$= \dfrac{5 + 5i}{5} = 1 + i$

Correct Answer : D

17.

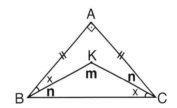

$2x + 2n + 90° = 180°$

$2x + 2n = 90°$

$x + n = 45°$

$m(K) + n + x = 180°$

$m(K) + 45° = 180°$

$m(K) = 180° - 45°$

$m(K) = 135°$

Correct Answer : C

18.

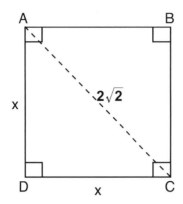

$x^2 + x^2 = (2\sqrt{2})^2$

$2x^2 = 8$

$x^2 = 4 ,\ x = 2$

Area $= x^2 = 4$

Correct Answer : B

19. Area of Circle $= \pi r^2$

$\pi r^2 = 16\pi$

$r^2 = 16 \quad r = 4$

$C = 2\pi r$

$= 2\pi.4 = 8\pi$

Correct Answer : B

20. $(8x - 4)^2 + (y - 5)^2 = 81$

$(x - h)^2 + (y - k)^2 = r^2$

$r^2 = 81$

$r = 9$

Correct Answer : C

Directions: For questions 1-20, solve each problem, choose the best answer from the choices provided, and fill in the corresponding bubble on your answer sheet.

For questions 36 - 38, solve the problem and enter your answer in the grid on the answer sheet.

Refer to the directions before question 36 for how to enter your answers in the grid. You may use any available space for scratch work.

Reference

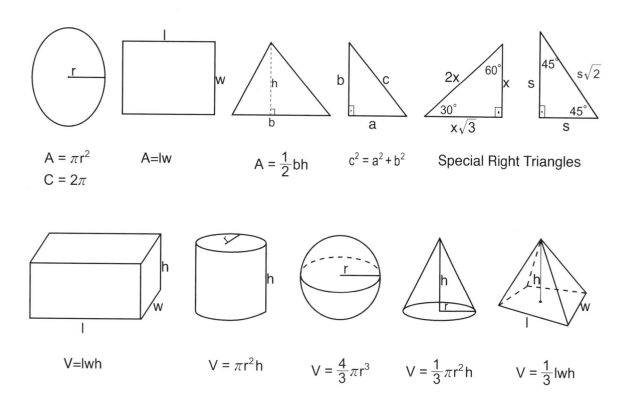

$A = \pi r^2$ $A = lw$ $A = \frac{1}{2}bh$ $c^2 = a^2 + b^2$ Special Right Triangles

$C = 2\pi$

$V = lwh$ $V = \pi r^2 h$ $V = \frac{4}{3}\pi r^3$ $V = \frac{1}{3}\pi r^2 h$ $V = \frac{1}{3}lwh$

The number of degrees of an arc in a circle is 360.

The number of radians of an arc in a circle is π.

The sum of the measures in degrees of the angles of a triangle is 180.

Practice Test

Part One

25 Minutes - 20 Questions
No Calculator Section

1. If the sum of three consecutive integers is 96, which of the following is the smallest one?

   A) 31
   B) 32
   C) 33
   D) 34

2. What is the solution to the equation below?

   $$4\left(x - \frac{1}{8}\right) = \frac{4}{6} + 3x$$

   A) $\frac{6}{7}$

   B) $\frac{7}{6}$

   C) 1

   D) $\frac{2}{3}$

3. What is the solution of the following equation?

   $$\frac{3}{x+1} - \frac{2}{x} = \frac{1}{x-1}$$

   A) $\frac{1}{2}$

   B) $-\frac{1}{2}$

   C) $\frac{1}{4}$

   D) 2

4. What is the value of k in the equation shown below?

   $$3k-5+4k=-4(k+4)$$

   A) 0
   B) 1
   C) -1
   D) 2

5. The total fare of four child movie tickets and two adult movie tickets cost $70. If each child's fare is one-third of each adult's ticket, what is the cost for one child ticket?

   A) $5
   B) $6
   C) $7
   D) $8

6. In the polynomial below, a is the constant. If the polynomial is divisible by P (x+2), then find the value of a.

   $$P(X) = 2x^3 + ax^2 - x + 2$$

   A) 2
   B) 3
   C) 5
   D) 7

7. $\dfrac{2x+4}{6} - \dfrac{x}{4} = \dfrac{3}{2}$ Find the value of x.

   A) 10
   B) 12
   C) 16
   D) 18

8. If $x > 0$ and $2(3x-6)^2 = 162$ then what is the value of x?

   A) 3
   B) 5
   C) 10
   D) 15

9. If y varies inversely as x and x=12 when y=60, find y when x=18.

   A) 20
   B) 30
   C) 40
   D) 50

10. $\sqrt[2]{x+32} - \sqrt[2]{x} = 4$, then x can be which of the following?

    A) 2
    B) -1
    C) 4
    D) 8

11. If A and B are real numbers, then what is A+B?

    $$\dfrac{2x+6}{x^2-1} = \dfrac{A}{x-1} + \dfrac{B}{x+1}$$

    A) 2
    B) 4
    C) -2
    D) -4

12. If $2x - 3y = 3$, then find $\dfrac{16^x}{64^y} = ?$

    A) 4
    B) 8
    C) 16
    D) 64

13. How many solutions does the system of equations shown below have?

$$2x=3y+6$$
$$4x-5y=20$$

A) Zero
B) 1
C) 2
D) Many / Infinity

14. If the following polynomial is divisible by P(x+1) then find the remainder.

$$x^{2015} + x^{2016} + x^{2017} + x^{2018}$$

A) 0
B) 1
C) -1
D) 2

15. Simplify $\sqrt{-5} + \sqrt{-20} + \sqrt{-125}$.

A) $-8i\sqrt{5}$
B) $8i\sqrt{5}$
C) $8i$
D) $-8i$

16. If $a = \sqrt{3} + 1$ and $b = \sqrt{3} - 1$, then find $\dfrac{a}{b} - \dfrac{b}{a} = ?$

A) 2
B) $\sqrt{3}$
C) $2\sqrt{3}$
D) $-2\sqrt{3}$

17. Which of the following equations passes through the coordinates (1,2) and (-3, -6)?

A) $y = 2x$
B) $y = 2x + 1$
C) $y = \dfrac{1}{2x} + 1$
D) $y = 2x + 2$

18. If $ab = \dfrac{1}{4}$, $bc = \dfrac{1}{3}$ and $ac = \dfrac{1}{12}$, then find $a \times b \times c = ?$

A) $\dfrac{1}{12}$
B) 12
C) -12
D) 3

19. At Star School, 180 out of 480 students favorite subject is science. What percent of students favorite subject is science?

A) 37%

B) 37.5%

C) 40%

D) 45%

20. If the equation $\dfrac{20x^2}{2x-1}$ is written in the form $K+\dfrac{5}{2x-1}$, which of the following gives K in terms of x?

A) 10x-5

B) 10x+5

C) 5x+10

D) 5x-10

Practice Test
Part One
Answer Key

1)	A
2)	B
3)	A
4)	C
5)	C
6)	B
7)	A
8)	B
9)	C
10)	C
11)	A
12)	D
13)	B
14)	A
15)	B
16)	C
17)	A
18)	A
19)	B
20)	B

Practice Test

Part One Solutions

1. $x + x + 1 + x + 2 = 96$

$3x + 3 = 96$

$3x = 93$

$x = 31$

Correct Answer : A

2. $4\left(x - \dfrac{1}{8}\right) = \dfrac{4}{6} + 3x$

$4x - \dfrac{1}{2} = \dfrac{2}{3} + 3x$

$4x - 3x = \dfrac{1}{2} + \dfrac{2}{3}$

$x = \dfrac{1}{2} + \dfrac{2}{3}$

$x = \dfrac{3}{6} + \dfrac{4}{6}$

$x = \dfrac{7}{6}$

Correct Answer : B

3. $\dfrac{3}{x+1} - \dfrac{2}{x} = \dfrac{1}{x-1}$

$3(x-1)x - 2(x-1).(x+1) = x(x+1)$

$3x^2 - 3x - 2(x^2 - 1) = x^2 + x$

$3x^2 - 3x - 2x^2 + 2 = x^2 + x$

$x^2 - 3x + 2 = x^2 + x$

$+2 = 4x$

$x = \dfrac{1}{2}$

Correct Answer : A

4. $3k - 5 + 4k = -4(k+4)$

$7k - 5 = -4k - 16$

$11k = -11$

$k = -1$

Correct Answer : C

5. $4c + 2a = \$70$

$c = \dfrac{a}{3}, \quad a = 3c$

$4c + 2(3c) = \$70$

$4c + 6c = \$70$

$10c = \$70$

$c = \$7$

Correct Answer : C

6. $p(x+2) = 0 \qquad x + 2 = 0, \ x = -2$

$p(-2) = 0$

$p(-2) = 2(-2)^3 + a(-2)^2 - (-2) + 2$

$p(-2) = 2(-8) + 4a + 2 + 2$

$0 = -16 + 4a + 4$

$0 = -12 + 4a$

$12 = 4a$

$3 = a$

Correct Answer : B

7. $\dfrac{2x+4}{6} - \dfrac{x}{4} = \dfrac{3}{2}$

$\dfrac{x+2}{3} - \dfrac{x}{4} = \dfrac{3}{2}$

$\dfrac{4(x+2)}{12} - \dfrac{3x}{12} = \dfrac{18}{12}$

$4x + 8 - 3x = 18$

$x + 8 = 18, \ x = 10$

Correct Answer : A

8. $2(3x-6)^2 = 162$

$\sqrt{(3x-6)^2} = \sqrt{81}$

$3x - 6 = 9$

$3x = 15$

$x = 5$

Correct Answer : B

9. $y = \dfrac{k}{x}$ (inverse variation)

$60 = \dfrac{k}{12}$, $\quad k = 60 \times 12 = 720$

$y = \dfrac{k}{x}$, $\quad y = \dfrac{720}{18} = 40$

Correct Answer : C

10. $\sqrt{x+32} + \sqrt{x} = 4$

if you use the elimination method

only Choice C can be the correct answer

if $x = 4$ $\quad \sqrt{4+32} - \sqrt{4} = 4$

$\sqrt{36} - \sqrt{4} = 4$

$6 - 2 = 4$

$4 = 4$

Correct Answer : C

11. $\dfrac{2x+6}{x^2-1} = \dfrac{A}{x-1} + \dfrac{B}{x+1}$

$2x + 6 = A(x+1) + B(x-1)$

$2x + 6 = Ax + A + Bx - B$

$2x + 6 = x(A+B) + A - B$

$2\cancel{x} = \cancel{x}(A+B)$

$\quad 2 = A + B$

$\quad 6 = A - B$

$+ \quad 8 = 2A$

$\quad 4 = A$

$\quad -2 = B$

$A + B = 4 - 2 = 2$

Correct Answer : A

12. $2x - 3y = 3$

$\dfrac{16^x}{64^y} = \dfrac{4^{2x}}{4^{3y}} = 4^{2x-3y}$

$= 4^3$

$= 64$

Correct Answer : D

13. $2x = 3y + 6$

$4x - 5y = 20$

$-2/ \quad 2x - 3y = 6$

$\quad 4x - 5y = 20$

$-4x + 6y = -12$

$\quad 4x - 5y = 20$

$+ \underline{\hspace{3cm}}$

$\quad\quad\quad y = 8$, $\quad x = 15$

The system has one solution

Correct Answer : B

14. $p(x+1) = 0$, $p(-1) = 0$

$= x^{2015} + x^{2016} + x^{2017} + x^{2018}$

$= (-1)^{2015} + (-1)^{2016} + (-1)^{2017} + (-1)^{2018}$

$= -1 + 1 - 1 + 1$

$= 0$

Correct Answer : A

15. $\sqrt{-5} + \sqrt{-20} + \sqrt{-125}$

$= \sqrt{5i^2} + \sqrt{20i^2} + \sqrt{125i^2}$

$= i\sqrt{5} + 2i\sqrt{5} + 5i\sqrt{5}$

$= 8i\sqrt{5}$

Correct Answer : B

16. $a = \sqrt{3} + 1$

$b = \sqrt{3} - 1$

$$\frac{\sqrt{3}+1}{\sqrt{3}-1} - \frac{\sqrt{3}-1}{\sqrt{3}+1}$$

$$= \frac{(\sqrt{3}+1).(\sqrt{3}+1) - (\sqrt{3}-1)(\sqrt{3}-1)}{(\sqrt{3}-1).(\sqrt{3}+1)}$$

$$= \frac{3 + 2\sqrt{3} + 1 - (3 - 2\sqrt{3} + 1)}{3 - 1}$$

$$= \frac{\cancel{3} + 2\sqrt{3} + \cancel{1} - \cancel{3} + 2\sqrt{3} - \cancel{1}}{2}$$

$$= \frac{4\sqrt{3}}{2} = 2\sqrt{3}$$

Correct Answer : C

17. $(1,2), (-3,-6)$

$\text{slope} = \frac{-6-2}{-3-1} = \frac{-8}{-4} = 2$

$y = mx + b$

$y = 2x + b, \quad (1,2)$

$2 = 2.1 + b$

$0 = b$

$y = 2x$

Correct Answer : A

18. $ab = \frac{1}{4}, bc = \frac{1}{3}, ac = \frac{1}{12}$

$a^2b^2c^2 = \frac{1}{4} \cdot \frac{1}{3} \cdot \frac{1}{12}$

$a^2b^2c^2 = \frac{1}{144}$

$abc = \frac{1}{12}$

Correct Answer : A

19. $\frac{180}{480} = \frac{18}{48} = \frac{3}{8} = \frac{3 \times 12.5}{8 \times 12.5}$

$\qquad = \frac{37.5}{100} = 37.5\%$

Correct Answer : B

20.

$$\begin{array}{r} 10x+5 \\ 2x-1 \overline{) 20x^2 } \\ \underline{-20x^2 \pm 10x} \\ 10x \\ \underline{10x \pm 5} \\ 5 \end{array}$$

$k + \frac{5}{2x-1} = 10x + 5 + \frac{5}{2x-1}$

$k = 10x + 5$

Correct Answer : B

55 Minutes - 38 Questions
Calculator Section

1. If x is a positive real number and $x - 2\sqrt{x} - 3 = 0$ then find $\dfrac{x}{x-1}$

   A) $\dfrac{1}{2}$

   B) $\dfrac{1}{4}$

   C) $\dfrac{9}{8}$

   D) $\dfrac{5}{3}$

2. If $2x^2 - 3x + 2 = 0$, then find $x^2 + \dfrac{1}{x^2} = ?$

   A) $\dfrac{1}{4}$

   B) 4

   C) 6

   D) 8

3. Simplify $\dfrac{x^2 - 6x - 16}{x^2 - 9x + 8} = ?$

   A) $x - 2$

   B) $\dfrac{x-2}{x+1}$

   C) $x - 1$

   D) $\dfrac{x+2}{x-1}$

4. At a Star dealership, a car sale price is $18,000 plus 7.5% sales tax. If the dealer applies a discount of 25% off from the sales price, find the price after including the discount and sales tax.

   A) $14,512.5

   B) $14,450

   C) $14,520

   D) $14,530

5. The average of five consecutive positive integers is 28. What is the greatest possible value of one of these integers?

   A) 24

   B) 25

   C) 26

   D) 30

6. $f(x) = \begin{cases} -2x + 5, & x < 0 \\ x^2 + 10, & x \geq 0 \end{cases}$

   From the above function find $f(2) + f(-3)$.

   A) 15

   B) 20

   C) 25

   D) -25

7. Which of the following graphs has no correlation?

A)

B)

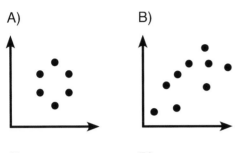

C)

D)

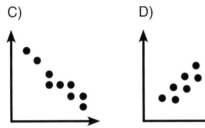

8. For the function below, m>0 is a constant and f(5)=110. What is the value of f(6)?

$$f(x) = mx^2 + 10$$

A) 124
B) 134
C) 144
D) 154

9. If $2^{2x-3} = 8^{x-6}$, what is the value of x?

A) 1 2
B) 15
C) 18
D) 21

10. If $f(x) = mx^2 - 6x - n + 6$ with a vertex point V(-3, 4), find m + n.

A) 10
B) 18
C) 20
D) 28

11. In the following figure O is the center of circle and radius is 4cm. Find the length of arc CD.

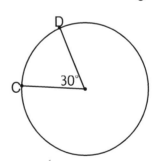

A) $\frac{2}{3}\pi$

B) $\frac{3}{2}\pi$

C) 3π

D) 2π

12. Which of the following complex numbers is equivalent to $(\frac{1+i}{1-i})^{2020}$?

    A) 1
    B) -1
    C) i
    D) -i

13. The area of the trapezoid is $A = \frac{(b_1 + b_2)h}{2}$. What is the height in terms of the base and area?

    A) $\frac{A}{b_1 + b_2}$
    B) $\frac{2A}{b_1 + b_2}$
    C) $\frac{b_1 + b_2}{A}$
    D) $A(b_1 + b_2)$

14. Simplify $\frac{x^2 - y^2}{x^2 - xy} \div \frac{x^2 + xy}{xy - x}$

    A) $x + 1$
    B) $y + 1$
    C) $\frac{x - y}{x}$
    D) $\frac{y - 1}{x}$

15. The table below shows the results of a survey on how students get to school. A circle graph is to be used to display the data. What percent of the graph represents Bus transportation?

Number of Students	Transportation
180	School Bus
60	Car
20	Walk
40	Bike

    A) 40%
    B) 45%
    C) 55%
    D) 60%

16. Use the graph to answer the question.

Students Favorite Sports

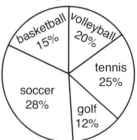

What percent of the students like Tennis?

    A) 5%
    B) 10%
    C) 15%
    D) 25%

17. Two classes took a science test. The first class had 20 students and their average test score was 90%. The second class had 24 students and their average score was 85%. If the teacher combined the test scores of both classes, what is the average of both classes together? Round your answer to the nearest percent.

A) 82%
B) 83%
C) 86%
D) 87%

18. In Mr. Tong's math team, students are trying to solve an easy test and a hard test. For each of the correct question in the easy test students will earn 10 points. For each of the hard test questions, students will earn 15 points. Jennifer solved a total of 20 questions and earned 275 points in all. How many easy questions did Jennifer solve?

A) 5
B) 6
C) 8
D) 10

19. Find the value of x in the diagram.

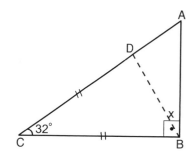

A) 13°
B) 16°
C) 36°
D) 38°

20. A dealership is selling a car for $18,000 plus 7.5% sales tax. If the dealers discount is 25% of the sales price, find the price after including the discount and sales tax.

A) $14,512.5
B) $14,450
C) $14,520
D) $14,530

21.
$$\left|\frac{2x}{3}-4\right| < 12$$

What is a possible value of x in the above inequality?

A) -12
B) -5
C) 24
D) 25

22.

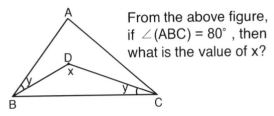

From the above figure, if $\angle(ABC) = 80°$, then what is the value of x?

A) 80°   B) 90°   C) 100°   D) 110°

23. Which of the following parabola functions could represent the graph in the picture?

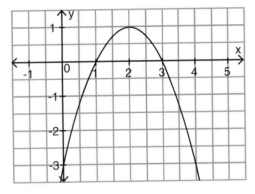

A) $f(x) = -x^2 + 4x + 3$

B) $f(x) = -x^2 - 4x + 3$

C) $f(x) = x^2 + 4x - 3$

D) $f(x) = -x^2 + 4x - 3$

24. If a is the average of 4k and 6, b is the average of 2k and 12, and c is the average of 6k and 18, what is the average of a, b, c in terms of k?

A) k+6

B) 2k+6

C) k+12

D) 2k+12

25.

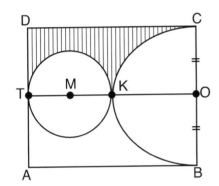

In the following figures, M and O are center of circles, ABCD is a square and AB=4 feet. What is the area of the shaded part?

A) $8 - \dfrac{3\pi}{2}$

B) $4 - \dfrac{3\pi}{2}$

C) $\dfrac{3\pi}{2} - 2$

D) $\dfrac{3\pi}{2}$

26. For what value of x is the equation
$x^2 - 3x - 5 = 0$ true?

A) $\dfrac{3 \pm \sqrt{29}}{2}$

B) $\dfrac{-1 \pm \sqrt{19}}{2}$

C) $\dfrac{-3 \pm \sqrt{26}}{4}$

D) $\dfrac{-3 \pm \sqrt{29}}{6}$

27. In the figure below, ABCD is a square and
$AE \perp EB$. EB=8, AE=6. What is the area of
the shaded part?

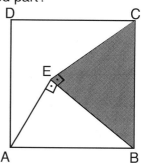

A) 16   B) 24   C) 32   D) 48

28. In the following figure O is the center of
circle, what is the measure of x?

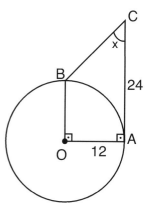

A) 15°   B) 25°   C) 30°   D) 45°

29. If the center of a circle is at (3,6), and the
radius of the circle is 4, what is the equation
of that circle?

A) $(x - 3)^2 + (y - 6)^2 = 4$

B) $(x - 3)^2 + (y - 6)^2 = 8$

C) $(x - 3)^2 + (y - 6)^2 = 16$

D) $(x - 6)^2 + (y - 3)^2 = 4$

30. If $g(x) = 2x - 3$, then find $g^{-1}(x)$?

A) $g^{-1}(x) = \dfrac{x + 2}{3}$

B) $g^{-1}(x) = \dfrac{x - 1}{3}$

C) $g^{-1}(x) = \dfrac{x + 1}{3}$

D) $g^{-1}(x) = \dfrac{x + 3}{2}$

31. Which of the following complex numbers are
equivalent to $\dfrac{a - bi}{a + bi}$?

A) $\dfrac{a^2 - 2abi + b^2}{a^{2+b^2}}$

B) $a^2 + b^2$

C) $\dfrac{a^2 - 2abi + b^2}{a^2 - b^2}$

D) $\dfrac{a^2 - 2abi - b^2}{a^2 + b^2}$

32. In the following cone shape the diameter is 18ft and height 12ft. Find the volume of cone. (Give your answer in terms of π)

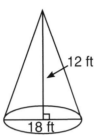

A) $150\pi\,\text{ft}^3$

B) $196\pi\,\text{ft}^3$

C) $324\pi\,\text{ft}^3$

D) $480\pi\,\text{ft}^3$

33. In the following cylinder shape if the volume of the cylinder is $72\pi\,\text{cm}^3$, then find the height of the cylinder.

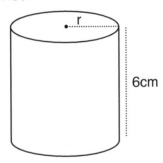

6cm

A) $\sqrt{3}\,\text{cm}$

B) $2\sqrt{3}\,\text{cm}$

C) $4\sqrt{3}\,\text{cm}$

D) 6cm

34. For the following right triangle, what is the cosine of angle C?

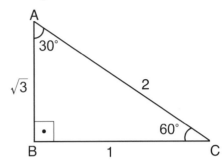

A) 1

B) $\dfrac{1}{2}$

C) $\sqrt{3}$

D) $2\sqrt{3}$

35. If $x^2 + 4x - 21 = (x + a)(x + b)$ for all values of x, what is one possible value of a + b?

A) -4

B) 4

C) 1

D) 5

Directions

For questions 36 - 38, solve the problem and enter your answer in the grid on the answer sheet as described below.

- Although not required, it is suggested that you write your answer in the boxes at the top of the columns to help you fill in the circles accurately. You will receive credit only if the circles are filled in correctly.

- Mark no more than one circle in any column.

- No question has a negative answer.

- Some problems may have more than one correct answer. In such cases, fill in only one answer on the grid.

- Mixed numbers such as $2\frac{1}{2}$ must be gridded as 2.5 or $\frac{5}{2}$. You cannot enter a mixed number because there is no circle that represents a space.

- Decimal answers: If you obtain a decimal answer with more digits than the grid can accommodate, it may be either rounded or truncated, but it must fill the entire grid.

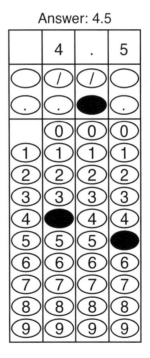

Answer: 303

Either Position is Correct

36. $6x - ay + 12 = 0$. If the slope of the equation is $\frac{1}{3}$, what is the value of $a = ?$

38. If 4 is one of the solutions of the equation $x^2 - 4ax - 12 = 0$, what is the value of a?

37. If $a - b = b - c = 6$ then find $a^2 + c^2 - 2b^2 = ?$

Practice Test
Part Two
Answer Key

1)	C	20)	A
2)	A	21)	B
3)	D	22)	C
4)	A	23)	D
5)	D	24)	B
6)	C	25)	A
7)	A	26)	A
8)	D	27)	B
9)	B	28)	D
10)	A	29)	C
11)	A	30)	D
12)	A	31)	D
13)	B	32)	C
14)	D	33)	B
15)	D	34)	B
16)	D	35)	A
17)	D	36)	18
18)	A	37)	72
19)	B	38)	0.25

1. $x - 2\sqrt{x} - 3 = 0$

   $x - 3 = (2\sqrt{x})^2$

   $(x - 3)^2 = (\sqrt{4x})^2$

   $(x - 3)^2 = 4x$

   $x^2 - 6x + 9 = 4x$

   $x^2 - 6x - 4x + 9 = 0$

   $x^2 - 10x + 9 = 0$

   $\wedge \qquad \wedge$

   x x   -9 -1

   $(x - 9) \cdot (x - 1) = 0$

   $x = 9$ or $x = 1$ (x can not be 1)

   $\dfrac{x}{x - 1} = \dfrac{9}{8}$

   Correct Answer : C

2. $2x^2 - 3x + 2 = 0$

   $\dfrac{2x^2}{2x} + \dfrac{2}{2x} = \dfrac{3x}{2x}$

   $x + \dfrac{1}{x} = \dfrac{3}{2}$

   $(x + \dfrac{1}{x})^2 = (\dfrac{3}{2})^2$

   $x^2 + \dfrac{1}{x^2} + 2 = \dfrac{9}{4}$

   $x^2 + \dfrac{1}{x^2} = \dfrac{9}{4} - 2 = \dfrac{1}{4}$

   Correct Answer : A

3. $\dfrac{x^2 - 6x - 16}{x^2 - 9x + 8}$

   $= \dfrac{(x - 8)(x + 2)}{(x - 8)(x - 1)} = \dfrac{x + 2}{x - 1}$

   Correct Answer : D

4. Discount 25%

   $\dfrac{25}{100} \times \$18,000 = \$4,500$

   New price = $\$18,000 - \$4,500$

   $\qquad\qquad = \$13,500$

   Sale Tax 7.5% = $\dfrac{7.5}{100} \times \$13,500$

   Sale Tax = $\$1,012.5$

   Final Price = $\$13,500 + \$1,012.5$

   $\qquad\qquad = \$14,512.5$

   Correct Answer : A

5. $\dfrac{x + x + 1 + x + 2 + x + 3 + x + 4}{5} = 28$

   $\dfrac{5x + 10}{5} = 28$

   $x + 2 = 28$

   $x = 26$

   greatest one = $x + 4$

   $= 26 + 4 = 30$

   Correct Answer : D

6. $F(2) = x^2 + 10 = 2^2 + 10 = 4 + 10 = 14$

   $F(-3) = -2x + 5 = -2(-3) + 5 = 6 + 5 = 11$

   $14 + 11 = 25$

   Correct Answer : C

7. No Correlation

   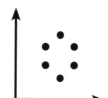

   Correct Answer : A

8. $F(x) = mx^2 + 10$

   $F(5) = 25m + 10$

   $110 = 25m + 10$

   $100 = 25m$

   $4 = m$

   $F(x) = 4x^2 + 10$

   $F(6) = 4 \times 6^2 + 10$

   $F(6) = 4 \times 36 + 10$

   $= 144 + 10$

   $= 154$

   Correct Answer : D

9. $2^{2x-3} = 8^{x-6}$

$2^{2x-3} = 2^{3x-18}$

$2x - 3 = 3x - 18$

$15 = x$

Correct Answer : B

10. $V(h,k) = (-3, 4)$

$4 = 9m + 18 - n + 6$

$-20 = 9m - n$

$x = \dfrac{-b}{2a}$, $-3 = \dfrac{-(-6)}{2m}$, $m = -1$

$-20 = 9(-1) - n$

$n = 11$

$m + n = 11 - 1 = 10$

Correct Answer : A

11. $ArcCD = \dfrac{2\pi r \, \alpha}{360}$

$= \dfrac{2.\pi.4.30}{360}$

$= \dfrac{2}{3}\pi$

Correct Answer : A

12. $\left(\dfrac{1+i}{1-i}\right)^{2020}$

$= \left(\dfrac{(1+i)(1+i)}{(1-i)1+i}\right)^{2020}$

$= \left(\dfrac{1+i+i+i^2}{1-i^2}\right)^{2020}$

$= \left(\dfrac{1+2i-1}{1+1}\right)^{2020} = \left(\dfrac{2i}{2}\right)^{2020}$

$= i^{2020}$

$= (i^2)^{1010} = (-1)^{1010} = 1$

Correct Answer : A

13. $A = \dfrac{(b_1 + b_2)h}{2}$

$2A = (b_1 + b_2)h$

$\dfrac{2A}{b_1 + b_2} = h$

Correct Answer : B

14. $\dfrac{x^2 - y^2}{x^2 - xy} \div \dfrac{x^2 + xy}{xy - x}$

$\dfrac{(x-y)(x+y)}{x(x-y)} \times \dfrac{x(y-1)}{x(x+y)}$

$= \dfrac{y-1}{x}$

Correct Answer : D

15. $\dfrac{Bus}{Total} = \dfrac{180}{300} = \dfrac{18}{30}$

$= \dfrac{3 \times 20}{5 \times 20} = \dfrac{60}{100}$

$= 60\%$

Correct Answer : D

16. From the graph 25% of students like tennis.

Correct Answer : D

17. $\dfrac{20 \times 90 + 85 \times 24}{44} = x$

$\dfrac{1800 + 2,040}{44} = x$

$x \approx 87\%$

Correct Answer : D

18. $e + h = 20$

$10e + 15h = 275$

$5e = 25$

$e = 5$

Correct Answer : A

19.

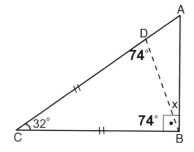

$$\frac{180 - 32}{2} = \frac{148}{2} = 74°$$

$$x + 74 = 90 \qquad x = 16$$

Correct Answer : B

20. Discount 25%

$$\frac{25}{100} \times \$18,000 = \$4,500$$

new price = $18,000 - $4,500

$$= \$13,500$$

Sale Tax 7.5% = $\frac{7.5}{100} \times \$13,500$

Sale Tax = $1,012.5

Final Price = $13,500 + $1,012.5

$$= \$14,512.5$$

Correct Answer : A

21. $\left| \frac{2x}{3} - 4 \right| < 12$

$$\frac{2x}{3} - 4 < 12$$

$$\text{or}$$

$$\frac{2x}{3} - 4 > -12$$

$$\frac{2x}{3} < 16 \text{ or } \frac{2x}{3} > -8$$

$$x < 24 \text{ or } x > -12$$

$$-12 < x < 24$$

Correct Answer : B

22.

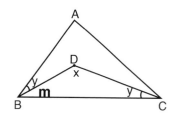

$$y + m = 80°$$

$$x + y + m = 180°$$

$$x + 80° = 180°$$

$$x = 100°$$

Correct Answer : C

23. From the graph the Vertex Point is $(2, 1)$.

$$V(x) = a(x - h)^2 + k$$

$$V(x) = a(x - 2)^2 + 1$$

From the graph you can use $(0, -3)$

$$-3 = a(a - 2)^2 + 1$$

$$-3 = 4a + 1$$

$$-4 = 4a, \quad a = -1$$

$$V(x) = -(x - 2)^2 + 1$$

$$V(x) = -(x^2 - 4x + 4) + 1$$

$$= -x^2 + 4x - 4 + 1$$

$$= -x^2 + 4x - 3$$

Correct Answer : D

24. $a = \frac{4k + 6}{2} = 2k + 3$

$$b = \frac{2k + 12}{2} = k + 6$$

$$c = \frac{6k + 18}{2} = 3k + 9$$

$$\frac{a + b + c}{3} = \frac{2k + 3 + k + 6 + 3k + 9}{3}$$

$$= \frac{6k + 18}{3} = 2k + 6$$

Correct Answer : B

25. $A(ABCD) = 4^2 = 16ft^2$

$A(DTOC) = 4 \times 2 = 8ft^2$

Area of small half circle $= \dfrac{\pi r^2}{2} = \dfrac{\pi}{2}$

Area of quarter of big circle $= \dfrac{\pi r^2}{4}$

$= \dfrac{\pi \cdot 2^2}{4} = \pi$

Shaded area $= 8 - (\dfrac{\pi}{2} + \pi) = 8 - \dfrac{3\pi}{2}$

Correct Answer : A

26. $x^2 - 3x - 5 = 0$

$x^2 - 3x = 5$

$(x - \dfrac{3}{2})^2 - \dfrac{9}{4} = 5$

$(x - \dfrac{3}{2})^2 = \dfrac{29}{4}$

$x - \dfrac{3}{2} = \mp\sqrt{\dfrac{29}{4}}$

$x = \mp\dfrac{\sqrt{29}}{2} + \dfrac{3}{2}$

$x = \dfrac{\mp\sqrt{29} + 3}{2}$

Correct Answer : A

27. Shaded area $= \dfrac{6 \times 8}{2} = 24$

Correct Answer : B

28.

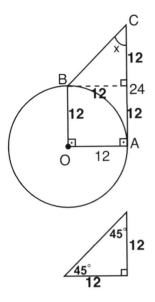

Correct Answer : D

29. $(x - h)^2 + (y - k)^2 = r^2$

$(x - 3)^2 + (y - 6)^2 = 16$

Correct Answer : C

30. $g(x) = 2x - 3$

$g^{-1}(x) = ?$

$y = 2x - 3$

$y + 3 = 2x$

$\dfrac{y + 3}{2} = x$

change x to y

$\dfrac{x + 3}{2} = y$ $\dfrac{x + 3}{2} = g^{-1}(x)$

Correct Answer : D

31. $\dfrac{a - bi}{a + bi} = \dfrac{(a - bi)(a - bi)}{(a + bi)(a - bi)}$

$= \dfrac{a^2 - abi - bai + b^2 i^2}{a^2 - b^2 i^2}$

$= \dfrac{a^2 - 2abi - b^2}{a^2 + b^2}$

Correct Answer : D

32. $V = \frac{1}{3}\pi r^2 h$

$V = \frac{1}{3}\pi . 81 . 12$

$V = 324\pi \text{ft}^3$

Correct Answer : C

33. Volume of cylinder $= \pi r^2 h$

$\pi r^2 . 6\text{cm} = 72\pi\text{cm}^3$

$r^2 . 6\text{cm} = 72\text{cm}^3$

$r^2 = \frac{72\text{cm}^3}{6\text{cm}}$, $r^2 = 12\text{cm}^2$

$r = 2\sqrt{3}\,\text{cm}$

Correct Answer : B

34. $\text{Cosine} C = \dfrac{\text{Adj}}{\text{Hypotenuse}}$

$= \dfrac{1}{2}$

Correct Answer : B

35. $x^2 + 4x - 21 = (x + a)(x + b)$

x   x   -3 +7

$(x - 3) . (x + 7) = (x + a)(x + b)$

$x = 3$ or $a = 3$ or $a = -7$

$x = -7$ $b = -7$ or $b = 3$

$a + b = -7 + 3 = -4$

Correct Answer : A

36. $6x - ay + 12 = 0$

Equation Slope $= \dfrac{6}{a}$

$\dfrac{6}{a} = \dfrac{1}{3}$, $a = 18$

Correct Answer : 18

37. $a - b = 6$

$\pm$ $\dfrac{b - c = 6}{a - c = 12}$

$a^2 - b^2 + c^2 - b^2$

$= (a - b) . (a + b) + (c - b) . (c + b)$

$= 6(a + b) - 6(b + c)$

$= 6a + 6b - 6b - 6c$

$= 6a - 6c$

$= 6(a - c)$

$= 6(12)$

$= 72$

Correct Answer : 72

38. $x^2 - 4ax - 12 = 0$

$16 - 4 \cdot 4a - 12 = 0$

$16 - 16a - 12 = 0$

$4 - 16a = 0$

$4 = 16a$

$\dfrac{1}{4} = a = 0.25$

Correct Answer : 0.25

47236555R00183

Made in the USA
Middletown, DE
05 June 2019